T0199834

Reinvention of Health Applications with IoT

Demystifying Technologies for Computational Excellence: Moving Towards Society 5.0
Series Editors: Vikram Bali and Vishal Bhatnagar

This series encompasses research work in the field of Data Science, Edge Computing, Deep Learning, Distributed Ledger Technology, Extended Reality, Quantum Computing, Artificial Intelligence, and various other related areas, such as natural-language processing and technologies, high-level computer vision, cognitive robotics, automated reasoning, multivalent systems, symbolic learning theories and practice, knowledge representation and the semantic web, intelligent tutoring systems, AI and education.

The prime reason for developing and growing out this new book series is to focus on the latest technological advancements – their impact on society, the challenges faced in implementation, and the drawbacks or reverse impact on society due to technological innovations. With these technological advancements, every individual has personalized access to all services and all devices connected with each other communicating amongst themselves, thanks to the technology for making our life simpler and easier. These aspects will help us to overcome the drawbacks of the existing systems and help in building new systems with the latest technologies that will help society in various ways, proving Society 5.0 as one of the biggest revolutions in this era.

Computing Technologies and Applications
Paving Path Towards Society 5.0
Edited by Latesh Malik, Sandhya Arora, Urmila Shrawankar, Maya Ingle, and Indu Bhagat

Reinvention of Health Applications with IoT
Challenges and Solutions
Edited by Dr. Ambikapathy, Ms. Shobana R., Dr. Logavani, and Dr. Dharmasa

Healthcare and Knowledge Management for Society 5.0
Trends, Issues, and Innovations
Edited by Vineet Kansal, Raju Ranjan, Sapna Sinha, Rajdev Tiwari, and Nilmini Wickramasinghe

For more information on this series, please visit: https://www.routledge.com/ Demystifying-Technologies-for-Computational-Excellence-Moving-Towards-Society-5.0/book-series/CRCDTCEMTS

Reinvention of Health Applications with IoT

Challenges and Solutions

Edited by

*Dr. Ambikapathy, Ms. Shobana R.,
Dr. Logavani, and Dr. Dharmasa*

CRC Press
Taylor & Francis Group
Boca Raton London New York

CRC Press is an imprint of the
Taylor & Francis Group, an **informa** business

First edition published 2022
by CRC Press
6000 Broken Sound Parkway NW, Suite 300, Boca Raton, FL 33487-2742

and by CRC Press
4 Park Square, Milton Park, Abingdon, Oxon, OX14 4RN

Library of Congress Cataloging-in-Publication Data

Names: Ambikapathy, editor.
Title: Reinvention of health applications with Iot : challenges and solutions / edited by
    Dr. Ambikapathy, Ms. Shobana R., Dr. Logavani, Dr. Dharmasa.
Description: First edition. I Boca Raton : CRC Press, 2022. I Series: Demystifying
    technologies for computational excellence I Includes bibliographical references
    and index.
Identifiers: LCCN 2021036964 (print) I LCCN 2021036965 (ebook) I
    ISBN 9780367763343 (hardback) I ISBN 9780367763374 (paperback) I
    ISBN 9781003166511 (ebook)
Subjects: LCSH: Medical informatics. I Medical care. I Internet of things.
Classification: LCC R858 .R45 2022 (print) I LCC R858 (ebook) I DDC 610.285–dc23
LC record available at https://lccn.loc.gov/2021036964
LC ebook record available at https://lccn.loc.gov/2021036965

ISBN: 978-0-367-76334-3 (hbk)
ISBN: 978-0-367-76337-4 (pbk)
ISBN: 978-1-003-16651-1 (ebk)

DOI: 10.1201/9781003166511

Typeset in Times
by KnowledgeWorks Global Ltd.

Contents

Preface

Internet of Things (IoT), as the name is coined, is a methodology of associating 'things' with the internet. Things here can be home appliances, sensors, or physical objects. IoT finds major application in the fields of health care, agriculture, retail, transportation, data analytics, and energy management, making the world smarter by reinvention of infrastructures and services for quality living. When discussing IoT concepts with students and research scholars, we found they were facing several challenges in understanding broad perspectives on the topic. This led us to write this book, to explain IoT using simple and understandable language. This book provides a brief description on various applications of IoT, its challenges and proposed solutions, helping readers learn about IoT technology from its rudimentary to dominating applications.

About the Editors

Dr. Ambikapathy holds a PhD and has 17 years' teaching experience. Currently, she is working as Head of the Department of Electrical and Electronics Engineering and Head of IPR Cell at Galgotias College of Engineering and Technology. She has authored nine engineering books, filed eight patents, and published 30 research papers in various reputed international journals (Scopus and SCI) and conferences. She is involved in various funded projects from government organizations such as the Ministry of Micro, Small and Medium Enterprises (MSME) and the Dr. A.P.J. Abdul Kalam Technical University in Lucknow, India. She has received various awards, including the Women's Research Award International from the Organization of Scientific's Research and Development, the International Award for Women Leadership from the World Federation Science and Technology and Research Foundation of India, and the Dedicated Services Award from the Rotary Club Delhi South End. She is a reviewer for many reputed international journals. She also delivers expert lectures on various topics such as awareness on intellectual property rights, motivational ways to inspire students, and optimization of micro grids. While head of the department, she made MOUs with different industries through which she has organized many events. She has also filed patents through collaborative research.

Ms. Shobana R. is currently working as Assistant Professor in the Department of Electrical and Electronics Engineering in Galgotias College of Engineering and Technology (GCET), Greater Noida, India. She has more than five years' experience in teaching both undergraduate and postgraduate students. She is an active member of IEEE and a student counsellor for IEEE women in engineering (WIE) at GCET. Her fields of interest include the areas of soft computing, AI, and system identification. She has published many papers in Scopus and international conferences and has written a few book chapters on machine learning.

Dr. Logavani is Assistant Professor with the Government College of Engineering (GCE), Salem, Tamil Nadu since 2013 and has 14 years' academic experience. She completed a doctoral degree in the area of power system economic scheduling. She has published articles in reputed journals and conferences. She is an active member of IEEE and a student counsellor of IEEE's student chapter of GCE. She has been actively involved in various academic and administrative works in her career. Her areas of expertise includes power electronics, renewable energy, and embedded control.

Dr. Dharmasa is an IEEE Senior Member and works as a Program Manager MSc EE in the Electrical and Computer Engineering Department at the National University in Oman. He has published 30 papers in international conferences and journals. He is associated with the international journals *Be Press Canada*, *Bulgarian Academy*, *EU IET UK*, and *IEEE USA*. His areas of research interest include strategic evaluation of performance of wireless network for multimedia traffic; power system analysis and HV; power system protection; reliability; renewable energy; engineering industrial practice; and counselling on science and engineering education and library information. In 2013, he won the Outstanding IEEE Branch Counselor and Advisor Award from the US IEEE president, and in 2015, he received the Outstanding Recruitment Officer Award from IEEE US. He received a meritorious research grant from AICTE and CSIR New Delhi and the Power Research Development Corporation (PRDC), Bengaluru, and the Youngest-Professor Award from SNIST-Deemed University, Hyderabad. In 2017, he became an IJEE Associate Member Japan and delivered expert talks at various universities and ministries in India, Saudi Arabia, Bahrain, UAE, Eritrea, and Oman. In 2019, Dr. Dharmasa received a 10-year contributor award from the IEEE Oman Section.

1 Deep Machine Learning for Sensing, Analysis, and Interpretation in IoT Healthcare

S.O. Owoeye, K.I. Adenuga,
O.J. Odeyemi, and C.B. Emele

CONTENTS

1.1   INTRODUCTION

The world has witnessed a giant leap in science and technology over the past few decades. Smart technology is now the order of the day, from smart devices, smart appliances, and smart vehicles to even smart houses—all made possible with the introduction of Internet of Things (IoT). The idea of networking smart devices came to light in 1982 when a Coca-Cola vending machine was modified to report its inventory over the internet [1]. The term "Internet of Things" was first mentioned in the early 1990s by Kevin Ashton [2].

IoT is used to describe a system of interrelated computing devices, mechanical and digital machines, objects, animals, or people provided with unique identifiers (UIDs) and has the ability to transfer data over a network without requiring human-to-human or human-to-computer interaction [3]. This definition is continuously changing with introduction of new technology such as deep machine learning, embedded systems, and robotics. An increasing number of industries are automating their operations through IoT to ensure higher efficiency and increasing their business worth. As IoT applications continue to increase, there arises a need for more secured systems to ensure that consumers' privacy is protected; such concerns can be addressed by ensuring that IoT-based devices meet an acceptable standard before they are rolled out to consumers for use. One such standard is that companies should adopt a 'defence in depth' approach to IoT development and encrypt data at each stage [4].

1.2   HOW IoT WORKS

An IoT system consists of processors that collect data from the environment, this is the first stage of communication, and the data collected are then transferred to an IoT gateway or hub that collates the incoming data. After collation, data is transferred to a back-end user interface system, a smart phone, or human–machine interface (HMI) where it is accurately analysed. Accurate analysis is essential for a functional IoT system. This analysis could be done with artificial intelligence (AI), machine learning, deep learning, neural networks and reinforcement learning, the result from the analysis will then prompts the system to take a specific action. Figure 1.1 shows how the IoT system works [3].

FIGURE 1.1   How the IoT system works [3].

Every IoT system needs four major components to function effectively: sensors, connectivity, data processing, and a user interface.

1.2.1 SENSORS

A sensor is an input device that collects data from its immediate environment by detecting or sensing changes. Sensors are used in our everyday life, from simple light sensors that sense ultraviolet (UV) rays to soil sensors that sense the soil's relative PH.

1.2.2 CONNECTIVITY

The data received by the sensor is transmitted to the cloud or any other gateway, through a source of network connectivity, which could either be cellular, satellite, Wi-Fi, Bluetooth, or any other means of data transmission. The choice of connectivity varies across different smart devices, but it performs a particular function, which is the transmission of data from an input source to an IoT gateway.

1.2.3 DATA PROCESSING

The collected data is now in the cloud. At this stage, a processing algorithm is needed to analyse the data accurately. AI and machine learning then come into play. An AI could be deployed to perform statistical and numerical analysis of the data.

1.2.4 User Interface

Early computer users could only communicate and perform tasks from the computer's terminal. However, this is not the case anymore. A user interface is needed to ensure the end-user understands the received information.

1.3 APPLICATIONS OF IoT

IoT has found diverse applications in our daily lives, as millions of smart devices are connected over the internet through which they continually transmit and receive data, thereby expanding the potential applications of IoT. Some of the areas where IoT can be applied are discussed in subsequent sections [5].

1.3.1 Consumer Applications

An increasing amount of IoT devices are created for consumer use, a typical example is in home automation. One in ten homes is now either fully or partially automated with IoT-based lighting systems, camera systems, heating and air conditioning, and security systems. IoT devices are also used to assist people with disabilities. We have smart wheelchairs that perform autonomous operations for the physically challenged and hearing aids for hearing-impaired people.

1.3.2 Commercial Applications

In the commercial sector, IoT systems can assist in integrating communications, control, and information processing across various transportation systems. Smart traffic communication is now achievable with the help of IoT, self-driving cars, and many other systems.

1.3.3 Industrial Applications

IoT can be deployed for industrial usage in the manufacturing industries, especially in the oil and gas sector, where large amounts of raw data are generated, stored, and sent by the drilling gear for cloud storage and analysis [6]. In industries, IoT significantly improves the maintenance process, overall safety, and efficiency. The agriculture industry also makes use of IoT, such as in helping farmers make decisions on when to irrigate farmland or harvest a particular crop.

1.3.4 Infrastructure Applications

Infrastructure application of IoT includes monitoring and controlling the operations of rural and urban infrastructures like roads, bridges, rail tracks and on- and off-shore wind farms [7]. This helps increase workers safety by ensuring that risky structural conditions are monitored remotely through IoT and not physical.

1.4 IoT FOR HEALTHCARE

One of the popular and most important uses of IoT is in the healthcare sector. IoT for healthcare is generally called the Internet of Medical Things (IoMT), which describes the application of IoT for medical purposes, such as data collection, analysis, and research in relation to health and remote health monitoring, or 'Smart Healthcare'. Smart healthcare is a digitized healthcare system that uses IoT-based systems to collect and analyse medical data. IoT has several uses in the healthcare sector, which are discussed in next section.

1.4.1 MEDICAL DIAGNOSIS

By using body sensors and contact lenses, IoT devices can be used to track particular body metrics and make inductive deductions off the result to diagnose conditions like malaria, diabetes, and COVID-19. For instance, common symptoms of COVID-19 include fever and chest pain, to deduce whether a patient has the disease, a temperature sensor could be placed at a strategic part of the body. If there is an abnormal rise in the body temperature, it is possible to make a deduction, and a person could be quarantined until further accurate testing methods are employed. Also, in medical diagnosis, using deep machine learning algorithms, a system can be trained to analyse abnormal patterns to predict cancer at an early stage.

1.4.2 ROBOTIC SURGERIES

The healthcare sector is becoming increasingly overwhelmed, hence, there is need for faster and more effective medical tools. IoT-based robotic devices can be used in healthcare to perform more precise surgical operations on patients. This would come in very handy in remote and dangerous locations, such as war front or rural areas, where it is difficult to send human doctors.

1.4.3 RECUPERATION

After performing major surgical operations, patients need several days under constant monitoring to make a full recovery. With the use of IoT, health monitoring can be done from remote locations. A sensor can be placed on the patient's body to track essential metrics and alert medical staff if any complication arises. This would help decongest hospitals, allowing doctors to have time for other emergencies.

1.4.4 MONITORING AND DESTROYING PATHOGENS

Toxic pathogens are everywhere—on surfaces and in the air. Despite best practices by hospitals to decontaminate facilities to stop the spread, pathogens continue to exist in the facilities. However, several IoT-based technologies are now being developed to kill pathogens without the need for chemical agents. Among the emerging technologies are those using high-powered UV LED technology and fluorescent UV that has been around for many years, but legacy systems are not particularly durable, and performance degrades over time. Combined with robotics and other permanent infrastructure, UV destruction of pathogens using LEDs is an emerging field—especially as the costs and performance of the technology continue to improve. IoT fits into the picture as the deployment and tracking of usage for such systems rolls into facility infrastructure and processes [8].

1.4.5 Hospital Operations Management

Medical equipment in hospitals needs to consistently be in good condition. However, with the increase in the number of patients at hospitals, proper monitoring of the condition of these types of equipment is becoming increasingly difficult while still attending to patients. IoT can be used to monitor the current condition of equipment, making it easier for hospital workers to know which equipment is defective and when to replace it [23].

1.5 OVERVIEW OF DEEP MACHINE LEARNING

Deep machine learning is a branch of AI that involves multiple layers of connected networks, consisting of numbers of neurons to extract features from input data and make predictions off such features; it is also called deep structured learning or simply deep learning. Deep learning was developed to solve the flaws associated with machine learning, such as performance lags. As the amount of data increases, machine learning could struggle to process the amount of soft data such as images, video files, audio files, and structured text. In the name 'deep machine learning,' the word 'deep' comes from the fact that deep learning networks use multiple hidden interconnected layers between the input and the output. This new technology has proved to be very useful in healthcare. The Massachusetts Institute of Technology (MIT) used deep learning algorithms to predict breast cancer up to five years in advance [9]. Classic machine learning algorithms would require scientists to manually define rules and logic for detecting cancer, which takes a lot of time and expertise. However, with deep learning, scientists could feed 90,000 full-resolution mammogram scans from 60,000 patients and let the AI find common patterns between patients who had breast cancer and those who do not. Figure 1.2 shows why deep learning is so useful nowadays [10].

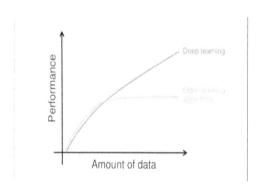

FIGURE 1.2   Why deep learning? [10]

The image above shows the advantage of deep learning when compared to older learning algorithms. Older learning algorithms lack scalability, as more data is fed into the system, overall performance decreases while error increases. This, however, is not the case with deep learning models. As the quantity of data fed into the system increases, the performance also increases. This scalability feature of deep learning machines causes more accurate models to be developed.

The history of deep learning dates back to the 1960s. In 1967, Ivakhnenko and Lapa published the first all-purpose working algorithms for deep, supervised, feed-forward and multilayer perceptions [11]. However, the term deep learning was introduced in 1986 by computer scientist, Rina Dechter [12]. Consequently, deep learning became widespread and more algorithms were developed.

The deep learning sphere witnessed a revolution in 2012 when a team led by George E. Dahl used multitasked deep neural networks (DNNs) to predict the biomolecular target of a drug [13]. In visual recognition from images or objects, significant progress was made around 2012 when graphics processing units (GPUs), capable of fast implementation of convolutional neural networks (CNNs) were created. This led to the development of computer vision systems with superhuman performance in recognizing patterns from visual images.

1.6 APPROACHES TO DEEP LEARNING

Every deep learning task can be grouped under one of these three types of learning: supervised learning, semisupervised learning, or unsupervised learning.

1.6.1 SUPERVISED LEARNING

Supervised learning, also known as supervised machine learning, is the task that involves using labelled datasets to train systems to either classify data or accurately predict algorithms. This is the most common type of machine learning.

Every supervised learning model needs training data and a corresponding label (Figure 1.3). This training data is fed into the system where feature engineering is applied to extract necessary features before being fed into the machine-learning algorithm alongside the label. Weights are adjusted to ensure that the model is fitted correctly, and then predictions are generated. Supervised learning algorithms are classified into regression and classification.

1.6.1.1 Regression

Regression is used to make predictions for continuous data. It does this by trying to understand the mathematical relationship between dependent and independent variables. An example is trying to predict the expected population of a hospital using information such as the number of staff. Some popular regression techniques are linear and logistic regression.

1.6.1.2 Classification

Classification is used to make predictions for discrete data. In other words, we are trying to map a target data to its corresponding label. An example is in image recognition for making predictions off handwritten digits.

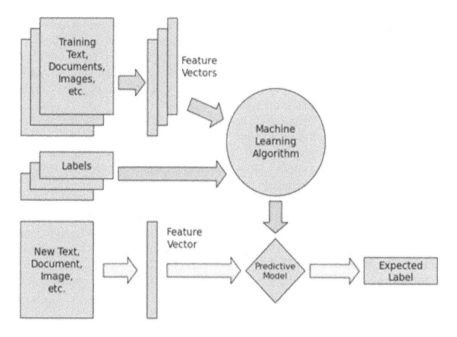

FIGURE 1.3   Supervised learning [14].

1.6.2   UNSUPERVISED LEARNING

Unsupervised learning also referred to as unsupervised machine learning uses machine learning algorithms to analyse datasets without pre-existing labels. Outputs are predicted by clustering sets of data based on the relationships between variables.

Figure 1.4 shows the difference between supervised and unsupervised learning is the absence of labels to feed into the system. It is mostly used in situations requiring some form of exploratory analysis. The main methods used in unsupervised learning techniques are clustering, association, and dimensionality reduction.

1.6.2.1   Clustering

Clustering involves grouping observations based on the similarity between them. Unlike classification problems where we know the data labels, here, we do not know what will be formed after clustering.

1.6.2.2   Association

Like clustering, association is also used to find the relationship between variables in a given dataset. It allows the establishment of associations among data objects in a large database.

1.6.2.3   Dimensionality Reduction

When dealing with complex datasets, it is always a great idea to perform some sort of dimensionality reduction. This reduces the number of inputs to a set size while not

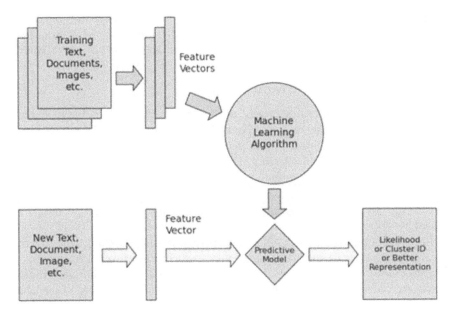

FIGURE 1.4 Unsupervised learning [14].

compromising the integrity of the dataset. It helps to avoid errors such as over fitting and makes it easier to visualize a dataset.

1.6.3 SEMISUPERVISED LEARNING

From the name, in semisupervised learning, a small portion of the data is labelled while a larger portion is unlabelled. Essentially, it is more or less a combination of both supervised and unsupervised machine learning. Figure 1.5 shows semisupervised learning.

1.7 DEEP MACHINE LEARNING NEURAL NETWORK ARCHITECTURES

Dr. Robert Hecht-Nielsen, the inventor of the neuro-computer, defined the neural network as a computing system that consists of a number of simple but highly interconnected processing elements that can process information using their dynamic

FIGURE 1.5 Semisupervised learning [15].

state response to external inputs [16]. Some examples of popular deep learning archi-tecture are artificial neural networks (ANNs), DNNs, generative adversarial net-works (GANs), recurrent neural networks (RNNs), and deep belief networks (DBNs).

1.7.1 ARTIFICIAL NEURAL NETWORKS

ANNs, simply called neural networks, are systems built to mimic the biological functioning of the human brain. The human brain is composed of 86 billion nerve cells called neurons [16] that are connected by axons, which act as synapses to carry out specific functions when activated. Through this looping process, a neuron can send messages to other neurons in the unit. Figure 1.6 gives the design of biological neural circuit.

Like the biological neural circuit, an ANN is composed of multiple nodes, con-nected by links and capable of interacting with each other.

Each link is a weight, and the ANN learns by continuously adjusting these weights according to a learning rule metric, until the error value is just small enough. Such systems learn to perform the task by analysing various examples. In image recog-nition, the system can learn to identify images of an animal according to the label name, such that, when the label is absent, the system will be able to make predictive inferences off the animal image.

Figure 1.7 shows a simple ANN model. It has three input neurons and produces two output neurons. As in every deep learning model, there are multiple hidden lay-ers that have a particular task to perform. There are two types of ANN: Feedforward ANN and feedback ANN.

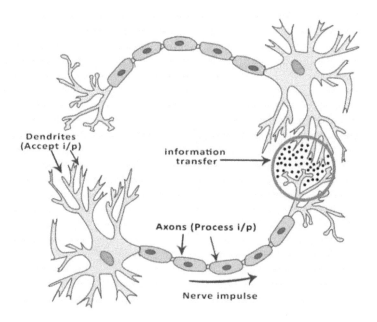

FIGURE 1.6   Biological neural circuit [16].

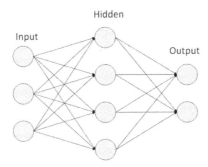

FIGURE 1.7 One-layer artificial neural network [16].

In a feedforward ANN, the flow of information is in one direction only, and there is no feedback. The loop ends when a transmitting unit successfully sends information to a receiving unit. Conversely, the feedback ANN makes use of feedback loops.

1.7.2 Deep Neural Networks

A DNN is a complex form of the ANN. It is simply an ANN with multiple hidden layers.

Figure 1.8 shows a DNN model. The major difference between the DNN and ANN is the number of hidden layers. The DNN and ANN both consist of the same components: neurons, synapses, weights, biases, and functions. DNNs are capable of modelling complex nonlinear relationships by dedicating each hidden layer to perform a specific operation. For example, in an image recognition program, the first hidden layer can be used to train the system on face features. The second hidden layer can be used to analyse other things like background, colour, etc.

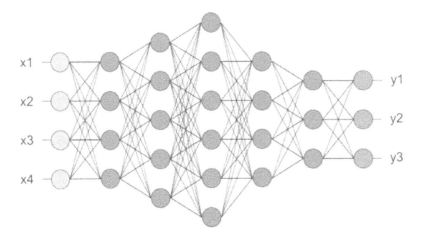

FIGURE 1.8 Deep neural network with five hidden layers.

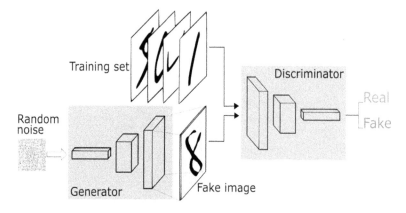

FIGURE 1.9   Generative adversarial networks [17].

1.7.3   GENERATIVE ADVERSARIAL NETWORKS

Generative adversarial networks (GANs) are DNNs that use two networks called the Generator, which generates new data instances, while the other, and the Discriminator, evaluates them for authenticity. These networks are sited against each other, and they are in a constant battle until some form of equilibrium is reached. Equilibrium is achieved when the Discriminator can no longer tell real images from fake ones created by the Generator (Figure 1.9).

1.7.4   RECURRENT NEURAL NETWORKS

Recurrent neural networks (RNNs) are DNNs that allow data to flow in any direction. RNNs are different from the other neural networks because of the presence of memory. This memory allows for RNNs to be ideal in neutral language processing (NLP) to predict a sequence of information or in time series problems (Figure 1.10).

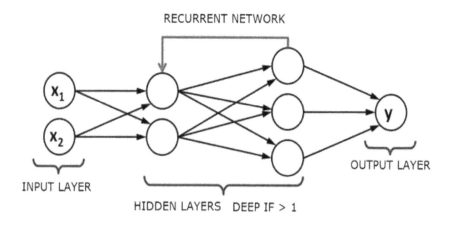

FIGURE 1.10   Depiction of recurrent neural network [18].

1.7.5 DEEP BELIEF NETWORKS

In deep learning, a deep belief network (DBN) is a type of DNN composed of several layers of hidden units with interconnections between the layers, but not within units of each layer [19]. A DBN can be visualized as a stack of restricted Boltzmann networks (RBM) where the hidden layer of one RBM is the visible layer of the RBM above it. DBNs have the ability to reconstruct their inputs then use them as feature detectors during training.

1.8 APPLICATION OF DEEP LEARNING IN IoT HEALTHCARE

Deep machine learning has limitless functionalities in the field of healthcare. If utilized efficiently, healthcare systems would be systematically upgraded to accommodate an increasing number of patients while also ensuring a higher standard of treatments. The application of deep learning in IoT healthcare is made in three stages: sensing, analysis, and data interpretation. At first, input data is generated by sensors and taken as healthcare dataset. Based on various metrics, important features are extracted from the input data in a process known as feature selection, and then any of the numerous deep learning algorithms can be performed on the feature-selected data. We will be looking at specific instances where deep learning is applied in IoT healthcare.

1.8.1 CLASSIFYING IMAGE DATA FOR DISEASE DETECTION (MALARIA)

It is estimated that more than half a million people die from malaria every year, while more than 500 million people contract the disease annually [20]. To curb these spiralling numbers, deep learning can be utilized for early detection as well as prediction of future hotspots of the disease. This first step to doing this is data collection. Malaria screeners are employed to take images of segmented cells from thin blood smears. Samples of a malaria-infected cell and an uninfected cell are shown in Figures 1.11 and 1.12. It is observed that the parasitized cell shows a painted spot across the surface.

The task here is to classify these cells through a process that is capable of distinguishing between infected and uninfected cells. A number of deep learning

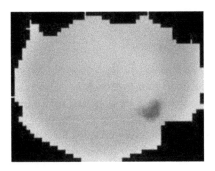

FIGURE 1.11 A parasitised cell [21].

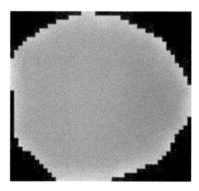

FIGURE 1.12   An uninfected cell [21].

algorithms can be applied, but CNNs provide the best result in dealing with image data. The model is built by layering multiple convolutional layers on top of each other. The model can then be trained and evaluated. A well-trained model should guarantee accuracy of more than 80% to avoid false positive and false negative errors as much as possible.

1.8.2   PREDICTING EPIDEMIC OUTBREAKS

Healthcare organizations, in general, make use of deep learning to monitor as well as predict possible outbreaks all over the world. Data could be collected via satellites, social media, or even from real-time updates. Several deep learning models have already been deployed to successfully predict the growth rate and locate hotspots of the current COVID-19 outbreak, some of which have shown accuracy values above 90%. This would be useful in third-world countries that do not have access to proper health systems. One of the deep learning algorithms commonly used for this prediction is the ANN based on incremental learning techniques. This model is useful, as the predicted data showed only a slight dip when compared to the actual occurrence. ProMED, as shown in Figure 1.13, did something similar by developing a web-based program that allows health organizations to monitor and predict disease outbreaks in real-time.

1.8.3   PATTERN IMAGING ANALYTICS

Imaging analytics is very important in today's health organizations. Radiologists can make use of deep learning algorithms to recognize changes in the scan, and this helps them to detect and diagnose health conditions at a very early stage. One such break-through was recorded at the Indiana University-Purdue University Indianapolis; an algorithm that can correctly predict relapse rates for acute myelogenous leukaemia (AML) with an accuracy of around 90–100% remission rates was developed. This was done by making use of bone marrow and medical history from AML patients, along with information from healthy individuals [23].

ProMED-mail
About ProMED-mail»

| Latest | Search | Plants | Hot Topics | Errata |

Latest Posts on ProMED-mail

16 Dec 2014 Avian influenza (106): Italy (VN) poultry, HPAI H5N8, OIE
15 Dec 2014 Equine herpesvirus, equine - Egypt: (QH) 1st rep. OIE
15 Dec 2014 Ebola virus disease - ex Africa (52): WHO, Sierra Leone,
   Nigeria, Rwanda aid
15 Dec 2014 Congenital malformations, ovine - Israel: Shuni virus susp, RFI
15 Dec 2014 Human enterovirus D68 - North America (20): update
15 Dec 2014 Influenza (42): USA, more early signs predict severe influenza
   season
15 Dec 2014 Lumpy skin disease, bovine - Cyprus (04): (Northern Cyprus)
   control policy
15 Dec 2014 Dengue/DHF update (61): Americas, Asia, Pacific, Europe
15 Dec 2014 Chikungunya (77): French Polynesia
15 Dec 2014 Crimean-Congo hemorrhagic fever - Pakistan (14): (PB)
15 Dec 2014 Hantavirus update - Americas (50): Argentina (BA)
15 Dec 2014 Rocky mountain spotted fever - Brazil (08): (SP) fatalities
14 Dec 2014 Hepatitis B & C - Australia: (AC)
14 Dec 2014 Ebola virus disease - ex Africa (51): Cuba, safe suits, iced
   underwear, susp.

FIGURE 1.13 ProMed-mail web interface [22].

REFERENCES

[1] V. Pandey, V. Kushwaha, A. Rukhsar, and S. Shinde, "A survey of Internet of Things and its applications," International Journal of Advanced Research in Computer and Communication Engineering, Vol. 6, Issue 3, March 2017.

[2] K. Ashton, "That 'Internet of Things' thing," RFiD Journal, Vol. 22, 97–114, June 2009.

[3] M. Rouse, "Internet of things (IoT)," Techtarget, 2019. [Online]. Available: https://internetofthingsagenda.techtarget.com/definition/Internet-of-Things-IoT. [Accessed 19 December 2020].

[4] I. Brown, "Regulation and the Internet of Things," Oxford Internet Institute, 2015.

[5] S. Vongsingthong and S. Smanchat, "Internet of Things: A review of applications and technologies," Suranaree Journal of Science and Technology, Vol. 21, 359–374, 2014.

[6] A. Gilchrist, *Industry 4.0 – The Industrial Internet of Things*. Apress Media, 2016.

[7] J. Gubbi, R. Buyya, S. Marusic, and M. Palaniswami, "Internet of Things (IoT): A vision, architectural elements, and future directions," Future Generation Computer System, Vol. 29, Issue 7, 1645–1660, February 2013.

[8] M. Maiman, "IoT technology for healthcare in 2020," Techtarget, 2020. [Online]. Available: https://internetofthingsagenda.techtarget.com/blog/IoT-Agenda/IoT- technology-for-healthcare-in-2020. [Accessed 19 December 2020].

[9] J. Ma, R. Sheridan, P. Liaw, A. Dahl, and V. Svetnik, "Deep neural nets as a method for quantitative structure-activity relationships." Journal of Chemical Information and Modelling, Vol. 55, 263–274, 2015.

[10] H. Zheng, J. Fu, T. Mei, J. Luo, "Learning multi-attention convolutional neural network for fine-grained image recognition," In Proceedings of the IEEE international conference on computer vision, 2017, pp 5209–5217.

[11] A.G. Ivakhnenko and V.G. Lapa, *Cybernetics and Forecasting Techniques*. American Elsevier Publishing Co, 1968

[12] R. Dechter, "Learning while searching in constraint-satisfaction problems," Cognitive Systems Laboratory, 2012.

[13] Data Science Association, "Multi-task Neural Networks for QSAR Predictions," Data Science Association, 14 June 2017. [Online]. Available: http://www.datascienceassn.org/content/multi-task-neural-networks-qsar-predictions. [Accessed 19 December 2020].

[14] A. Kumar, "Introduction to Machine Learning," All Programming Tutorials, 25 May 2018. [Online]. Available: https://www.allprogrammingtutorials.com/tutorials/introduction-to-machine-learning.php. [Accessed 19 December 2020].

[15] C. Dossman, "AI Scholar—A Holistic Approach to Semi-Supervised Learning," Medium, 16 May 2019. [Online]. Available: https://medium.com/ai³-theory-practice-business/ai-scholar-a-holistic-approach-to-semi-supervised-learning-51d82a2ee759. [Accessed 19 December 2020].

[16] K.N. Vinay and S.M. Kusuma, "Home automation using Internet of Thing," International Research Journal of Engineering and Technology (IRJET), Vol. 02, Issue 03, June 2015.

[17] R. Gandhi, "Generative Adversarial Networks—Explained," Towards Data Science, 10 May 2018. [Online]. Available: https://towardsdatascience.com/generative-adversarial-networks-explained-34472718707a. [Accessed 19 December 2020].

[18] H. Luo, J. Wang, C. Yan, M. Li, and Y. Pan, "A novel drug repositioning approach based on collaborative metric learning," IEEE/ACM Transactions on Computational Biology and Bioinformatics, Vol. 56, 2019.

[19] G. Hinton, "Deep belief networks," Scholarpedia, Vol. 4, Issue 5, 5947, 2009.

[20] Centers for Disease Control and Prevention, "Malaria – Malaria's Impact Worldwide," U.S. Department of Health & Human Services, August 2016. [Online]. Available: https://www.cdc.gov/malaria/malaria_worldwide/impact.html. [Accessed 21 December 2020].

[21] Q. Quan, J. Wang, and L. Liu, "An effective convolutional neural network for classifying red blood cells in malaria diseases," Interdisciplinary Computer Life Science, Vol. 12, 217–225, 2020.

[22] P. Kathuria, "12+ Machine Learning Applications Enhancing Healthcare Sector 2020," upGrad blog, 17 August 2019. [Online]. Available: https://www.upgrad.com/blog/machine-learning-applications-in-healthcare/. [Accessed 21 December 2020].

[23] B. Rajwa, K. Wallace, A. Griffiths, and M. Dundar, "Automated assessment of disease progression in acute myeloid leukemia by probabilistic analysis of flow cytometry data," IEEE Transactions on Biomedical Engineering, Vol. 64, Issue 5, 1089–1098, May 2017.

2 IoT-Based Personalized Health and Fitness Monitoring System
The Next Big Thing

Pushpendu Rakshit, Pramod Kumar Srivastava, and Omkar Chavan

CONTENTS

2.1   INTRODUCTION

The Internet of Things is an environmental system that includes a smart device that works on sensors, processing technologies, and networks with a purpose of connecting and data exchange on these devices via the internet (Figure 2.1). IoT devices make life easier, as they can be controlled on single programmed device. It is energy saving, less time consuming, and the technology makes use of artificial intelligence (AI) that offers security and ease of use. A smart home or automated place can be entirely controlled on smart phone applications. IoT devices use wireless sensor network (WSN) that connect each device on internet; the integrated systems help smooth functioning and can all be controlled together at the same time. Today, various countries are focusing on smart cities. An advanced city can feature enhanced infrastructural models, public security models, transportation, and an optimized

DOI: 10.1201/9781003166511-2

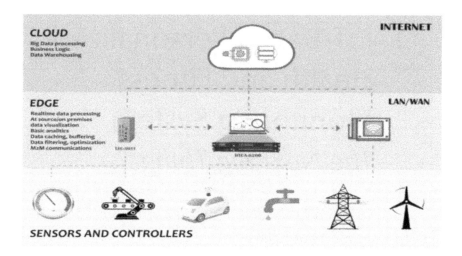

FIGURE 2.1   Sensors and controllers.

analytical system for crime detection, etc. With the help of IoT, various systems have been deployed on a broad scale around the city. Industry is developing at rapid pace and IoT is extensively used in various sectors. IoT acts as a catalyst for the industry and helps industries grow beyond their set boundaries. The main purpose of IoT with respect to industry is the smooth and rapid functioning of supply chain and internal processes. IoT plays an important role for the supply chain industry. An IoT feature called a radio frequency identification (RFID) chip helps to keep track of goods and is one method of automatic identification and data capture. IoT devices are an integral part of the supply chain process, which is an essential part of industry; IoT plays an important role in every step of the industrial process.

2.2   INDUSTRY 4.0

Industry 4.0 is a study model that describes the latest development and changes in industry over a period of time. In today's world, industries are developing with the help of technologies to increase their efficiency and productivity. The aim of Industry 4.0 is to improve manufacturing, logistics, and industrial units; increase productivity, making it consumer-centric; increase automation and optimization; and to help businesses search new opportunities and models that will help them grow. The concept of a smart factory is a part of Industry 4.0, where a computer can connect to another computer via the internet and can make an ultimate decision on the development of an industrial process with the help of AI—without any human involvement. IoT helps to increase the efficiency of Industry 4.0, and as a result, companies receive more accurate market data, manufacturing units become more productive, and waste of resources is reduced. IoT cyber systems coordinate with each other and communicate with humans and participants across the entire organization in synchronic time. This helps a smart factory to create a virtual copy of processes and make decentralized decisions. Smart sensors and other smart devices under IoT not only drive the forces of innovation in Industry 4.0 but also majorly contribute to smart production, automated homes, smart factories, high-tech smart cities, and smart mobility. The use of IoT in manufacturing helps to upgrade manufacturing process, logistics, business processes, business operations, and helps in digital transformation. An increase in efficiency and productivity helps businesses to achieve internal goals in early stages and provides a pathway for higher goals. The real-time consumer data provided by sensors and smart devices helps business to track the tastes and habits of consumers and helps to identify consumer insights and product development. As a result, an increase in the quality of supply chain and production gives business a competitive advantage with increase in satisfaction of customers' expectations. Hence, we can conclude that the concept of Industry 4.0 helps business and industry to have better outcomes and sustainability with the help of automation and enhancement of process created by smart devices and other instruments of IoT. Smart devices are those devices equipped with computing and communication capabilities that can constantly connect to a network.

IoT exist to aid communication among internet-working devices and applications, supporting physical entities interconnected over cyberspace. IoT begins with entities denoted as distinct interactive digital devices. RFID is an example of such system [1]. Digital wearables/Things are tagged with the help sensors in these gadgets for their proof of identity and tracking them in future, controlled and supervised by means of distant computers/digital devices allied over the internet. IoT links the environment, individuals, devices, and logistical shackles into single assembly line, thus snowballing agility, protection, and cost-efficiency in pharmaceutical processes [2]. The usage of IoT and sensors could help avoid critical situations by minimizing production downtime and ensure workplace safekeeping. Additionally, the assimilated data could generate a complete scenario of device consumption. In combination with artificial intelligence and predictive analytics, the industry paves the way for predictive conservation of equipment [3]. These tools also help to predict business growth and success. Realizing the potentials of gear shifts of technologies resulted in a market differentiator for industries contending in this 'new normal' atmosphere amid the corona virus pandemic. IoT-based devices are expected to increase in India from 60 million in the year 2016 to 1.9 billion by the year 2020, but there may be an impact due to pandemic crisis. Digitally connected smart phones and machine-to-machine (M2M) devices are also anticipated to grow to 112 million by the year 2022. In Asia, the demand for such devices would surpass 35 billion, making Asia the largest market. As per the reports of McKinsey digital 2019, about 127 new digital devices connect to internet by every second. As per I-Scoop, about 8.87% of global pharmaceutical companies in 2019 adopted IoT healthcare technologies [4]. Also, Forbes approximates 646 million IoT sensor-based digital devices would be implemented in hospitals, clinics, and medical offices amid the corona crisis by 2020 following social distancing. According to Grand View Research, the expansion of the global IoT healthcare market would be $534.3 billion by the year 2025. According to Forbes, even annual spending on IoT security would increase by $631 million by the year 2021. This chapter attempts to correlate the boosting of IoT and sensors in the pharmaceutical sector—requiring configuration of personalization scopes, potential opportunities, understandings future growth and culmination of technology—with the medicinal industries principles [5]. As per Collins dictionary, 'hyperconnectivity' means the use of various system(s) and digital device(s) to ensure one is constantly connected to social network(s) and sources of information [6].

According to a McKinsey analysis report, the use of smart technology under Industry 4.0 has been beneficial in various ways such as:

a. It helped to reduce maintaining cost by 10%–15% and also resulted in reduction of machine downtime by 30%–50%. Therefore, the lifespan of industrial equipment has increased.
b. It also helped increasing the productivity by 45%–55% due to an increase in digital performance management, remote monitoring and control, and technology collaboration.
c. The use of a smart tracking system and cloud data computing resulted in 85%+ accuracy due to a data-driven design module and data-driven demand-supply.
d. The improved logistic 4.0 model helped reduce cost of supplies by 20% to 50%. As a result, Industry 4.0 helps reduce costs to and increase profit for the company.

An article on sourcetoday.com, 'How IoT will Impact Different Industries' is a detailed explanation of automation in different sectors of industry. The detailed information focuses on impacts of IoT on agriculture, energy, and supply chain. An article on I-Scoop.eu entitled 'Business Guide to Industrial IoT' describes the stages of Industrial IoT across major industries. It also focuses on the concept of Industry 4.0 and describes it in detail [7]. A study on wipro.com 'What can IoT do for Healthcare?' describes the transformation of the healthcare industry. IoT has completely changed the way of doing business/s and automation would help to increase efficiency in the healthcare industry. A research paper by Kosacka-Olejnik and Pitakaso entitled, "Industry 4.0: State of the Art and Research Implications" is a detailed analysis of Industry 4.0.

2.3 RESEARCH METHODOLOGY

A review of literature draws attention to the need of further explorative research. Mentioning the major aims, this chapter used qualitative methods on secondary sources to proceed with development of a prototype. The analysis helps to build a model based on the review of literature from existing work from multiple sources and researchers. This study would differ from past studies as the technology for business keeps getting upgraded with recent trends in technologies. The prototype demonstrated includes both the aspects from IoT assimilation to implementation projecting correlations between Industry 4.0 and Pharma 4.0.

2.4 OBJECTIVES

1. To explore the best technology adoption practices by Indian pharma industries.
2. To understand the scope of IoT implementation to smart Pharma 4.0 in India.
3. To design a smart pharma operational prototype grounded in IoT and sensors.

2.5 IoT: A GAME CHANGER IN PHARMA

The internet is a massive comprehensive worldwide network of linked servers, consoles, mainframes, tablets, fablets, and smart cellular devices, which is governed by protocol/s for most of the connected devices. It empowers distribution and reception of all communications with reliable data having interconnectivity with distant servers, clouds, and vivid analytics platforms [8]. IoT denotes a network of hardware or physical things (objects) sending, receiving, or dispersing information using cyberspace or other communication technologies. These network(s) further allow monitoring, synchronizing, and governing actions across the internet/alternative network(s).

From the technological point of view, the internet is an assemblage of entities or things entrenched with hardware/electronics, software, sensors, and connectivity, holding great worth in its ability to swap data with the manufacturer, operator, and/or customers with other connected devices [9]. Thus, these all can be incorporated with Indian pharma to make it into smart pharma. Devices/gadgets are exceptionally distinguishable over its embedded technological platforms with probabilities to interpret within the prevailing infrastructures.

2.6 ADVANTAGES OF INTERNET OF THINGS (IoT) AND INDUSTRY 4.0

- IoT is an integral system that helps two devices to connect with the help of the internet. It is commonly knowns as machine-to-machine communication. As a result, we get more transparency, fewer inefficiencies, and greater quality.
- The functionality of each smart device increases the efficiency of utilization of resources, and can also monitor natural resources. IoT smart devices interact and communicate with each other via the internet and complete tasks on behalf of humans, resulting in minimizing human interference and errors in process.
- The primary aim of IoT is the increased speed of functions and processes. As smart devices use AI, they create a process chain that saves time and resources.
- Due to use of cloud computing, the data under IoT is secured and more accurate without errors. This enhanced data collection helps to derive more accurate results and makes work easier for managerial decisions.
- Since physical objects are controlled digitally, centralized with wireless infrastructure, there is a high scale of automation and better control on processes.
- Manufacturing or industrial unit technologies are able to communicate results faster and with greater efficiency without human intervention.
- IoT smart devices and smart processes provide accurate help so the exact quantity of resources can be determined at the optimal rate and time. As a result, we can monitor the expiration of raw materials and can improve the quality and safety of products.
- The integrated system of all devices helps and allows each to be controlled via one click or through a single application (app).

- This technology has a great impact on industry. With automation in industrial units, we can diagnose and monitor every machine at any point in time. We can keep track of toxic gas emissions, for example, allowing for quality control that can avoid harm to workers and help maintain a pollution-free environment.
- IoT smart devices and sensors are highly used in medical industries. These devices can help monitor heart rate, pulse, blood pressure, etc., and also help to diagnose major issues or anomalies. These smart devices are sold individually also and can be purchased at any medical shop or in hospitals. They are helpful to senior citizens and people with disabilities. For instance, diabetes meters (glucometers) help patients check their blood sugar levels and blood pressure instruments help to monitor blood pressure, pulse, and heart beats. Also, during the COVID-19 pandemic, infrared forehead thermometers were commonly used at railway stations, shops, airport, and other public places to check individual body temperatures in an attempt to helps identify COVID-19 patients.
- The main aim of the Industry 4.0 concept is to enable individuals to derive more efficiency with less input of resources.
- Industry 4.0 is cost effective, allocates quality resources, is less time consuming, and is efficient during processes.
- Industry 4.0 introduces smart factories with highly automated production-line processes, less downtime, and enhanced machine monitoring.
- Industry 4.0 is based on overall equipment effectiveness (OEE) that includes three main factors: availability, performance, and quality.
- Industry 4.0 also offers agility and flexibility in factories. It is easy to set production targets with higher efficiency and it's easier to introduce new products to the production line. This creates new opportunities for business to penetrate market with new products in less time.
- According to industrial regulations, pharmaceutical and medical devices must not have a manual process during manufacturing. With the help of automated compliance by technologies, one can keep a track of entire process, data logging, quality inspections, etc.
- Industry 4.0 also provides improved customer service and enhanced customer satisfaction. With the help of an automated tracking system, we can trace the capabilities and can quickly solve problems. Also, there will be fewer issues with product availability, product quality, and will offer more products for customer choice. As a result, there will be an increase in sales and profitability.
- Industry 4.0 primarily focus on reducing cost by better utilization of resources, fewer quality issues, faster production, and low operating costs.
- With effective production-line and quality control, the technology helps to create innovative opportunities. With the help of OEE, we can optimize the supply chain or production lines, develop new products, change processes in business models, and renovate the existing techniques, etc. This will help obtain high returns on investment in business.

2.7   NEEDS IN HEALTH MANAGEMENT

IoT devices help monitor each vertical of the healthcare sector. It improves the interaction between doctor and patient. Monitoring the patient's health remotely prevents readmission of the patient to the hospital, helps reduce healthcare costs, and improves treatment quality. IoT has transformed the entire healthcare industry with connectivity across regions allowing people to interact and deliver healthcare solutions. The application model benefits patients, hospitals and clinics, physicians, doctors, families, and insurance companies. IoT devices like fitness wearables, glucometers, infrared forehead thermometers, blood pressure monitors, and heart rate monitors help patients keep track of their own health [10]. Many people have changed their way of living, especially senior citizens, by constantly tracking their health conditions. These devices track the daily activities of an individual and an alert mechanism sends a report to family members and healthcare providers. Apart from tracking individual health, these smart devices of IoT are useful at various places in hospitals. This includes sensors that track the real-time location of medical equipment such as monitor equipment, nebulizers, wheelchairs, defibrillators, etc. Also, the hospital staff smart badge helps track staff location in real time. IoT provides hygiene monitoring devices that help prevent patient infections. It also helps in asset management, especially regarding medicines. The inventory control feature alerts staff to the shortage of medicines in the hospital. Other devices help monitor and remotely control hospital security, fire safety, temperature control, etc.

IoT has a four-step model in redefining the healthcare sector (Figure 2.2):

1. Implementation of interconnected smart devices that collect data. These devices include sensors, monitors, camera systems, actuators, etc.
2. Data collected from the devices are in analogue form and need to be converted into digital form for data processing.
3. After the data is digitized, arranged, and pre-processed, it is moved to the cloud or data centre.
4. In the final step, the data is analysed with advanced analytical tools that help to draw actionable insights for effective decision making.

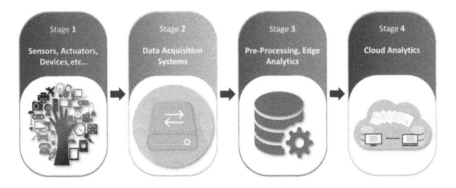

FIGURE 2.2 The prototype on an IoT-based personalized health monitoring system. (Provided by author.)

This enables hospitals to monitor patients in real time, and results in cutting down unnecessary costs for doctors as well as patients. It helps doctors and physicians to keep complete transparency in decision making based on evidence. Due to real-time monitoring of patients, it is easier to diagnose early stages or even prevent disease, improving proactive treatment [11]. It is easy to manage medical instruments and keep track of required quantities of medicine with the help of these devices. The data generated from devices helps in effective decision-making as well as in smooth functioning of operations, reduced errors, and waste.

The following five entities could be considered the five levels behind an IoT Pharma system:

1. A *device platform* consisting of device hardware and software uses a microcontroller (or system-on-chip [SoC]/custom chip) and software for the device API and web applications would prove helpful for smart pharma.
2. *Connecting and networking* (connective protocols and circuits) enables networking of devices and physical objects (called wearable things) and enables the internet connectivity to remote services.
3. *Server and web programming* enable web applications and web services of pharma.
4. *Cloud platforms* enable storage, computing prototype, and product development platforms related to smart pharma.
5. *Online transaction* processing online analytics, data analytics, predictive analytics, and knowledge discovery, enabling a wider application of an IoT system.

2.8 IMPACT OF INTERNET OF THINGS (IoT) ON FITNESS INDUSTRIES

IoT has completely changed the way of business and the business (industrial) model. Industry 4.0 is the fourth revolutionary stage in the industrial revolution. IoT forms an integral part of Industry 4.0. With the automation due to smart devices and smart equipment, IoT has increased the potentiality of the industry and manufacturing sector [12]. IoT is one of the main forces that includes data collections and analytics, enhanced automation, and optimization of workflows and processes. Devices are programmed and IoT enables them to follow entire processes without any error or human interference. IoT has completely transformed the supply chain and production line in Industry 4.0. Supply chain is an important stage for industries and IoT helps to enhance supply chain management more effectively [13]. An RFID microchip is based on scanning technology. It is a kind of bar code that allows individuals to track products or services in real time, allowing industries more quality control and transparency of the supply chain in various ways. IoT has majorly contributed to manufacturing processes and improved the connectivity of logistics. Smart supply chain management, commonly known as logistics 4.0, is data- and IoT-intensive and is based on semiautonomous decisions. IoT enables smart factories, smart manufacturing units, and smart logistics to form Industry 4.0. As smart devices are used at every stage, it is easy to keep track of a process from beginning to end delivery. IoT has completely transformed the industrial unit and in upcoming phases, there will be more advancements in the industrial sector.

2.9   MAJOR COMPONENTS OF IoT SYSTEMS INTEGRATED WITH SMART PHARMA

- *Physical objects* with embedded software into hardware.
- *Hardware* consisting of a microcontroller, firmware, sensors, control units, actuators, and communication modules.
- *Communication modules* feature software consisting of device application programs and device interfaces and communication over the network and communication circuit/port(s) and middleware for creating communication stacks using protocols such as 6LoWPAN, CoAP, LWM2M, IPv4 (internet of protocol version 4), IPv6 (internet of protocol version 6), and others.
- *Software,* which forms action messages, information, and commands that the devices receive and then output to the actuators. This enables actions such as glowing LEDs, robotic hand movements etc.

2.10   PLATFORMS AND INTEGRATION TOOLS

- *ThingsSpeak* is an open data platform with an open application program interface. It consists of APIs that enable real-time data collection, geolocation data, and data processing and visualization.
- *Nimbits* is a cloud platform that ropes numerous programming/coding languages, including Arduino, Java script, HTML or the Nimbits.io.Java library. The data can be time/geo stamped.
- The *IoT Toolkit* offers smart objects API, HTTP to CoAP semantic mapping, and the diversified tools for assimilating various IoT-connected sensor networks and protocols.

2.11   FRAME WORK DESIGNING

Figure 2.3 shows the conceptually designed interworking of connected devices, consisting of a physical object, a controller, sensor, and actuators, and the internet to form a connection to a web service and mobile service provider. Generally, IoT consists of internet-connected devices and physical objects, where a number of objects can gather the data at remote locations. This further helps in creating communication with units with acquiring, analysing, and storing the data. An all-purpose framework entails the devices interacting with data from various sources to a database, then to a data centre of an enterprise cloud server [14]. The IoT framework used in a number of applications, as well as in enterprise and business processes, is, in general, more complex than the one represented by the above-mentioned framework. Internet of Things-Pharma Manufacturing (IoT-PM) paraphernalia would radically have an impact on the upkeep and nursing procedures of pharma and healthcare engineering plants/businesses, resulting in massive energy savings each year [15]. Advancements

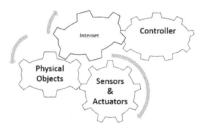

FIGURE 2.3 IoT conceptual framework. (Provided by author.)

in sensor technology, cyberspace, cloud computing, mobile computing, machine learning, augmented reality, virtual reality, machine learning, and big data technologies have led to reasonably priced sensors and digitally connected devices, massively snowballing IoT-PM and additional technological variations in smart pharma for better future growths.

2.12 IMPLICATIONS

Pharmaceutical companies in India must look forward to strategies that spur the adoption of the latest trends in technology, follow the best branding practices such as targeting the audience, create brand image, build trust, and spread the word about the usage of Industry 4.0. Pharmaceutical branding is a vital way to generate awareness of the benefits and potential of certain drugs. IoT technologies are in their budding phases of growth in the pharma and healthcare sectors, and its influence on the worldwide healthcare industry is undisputable. Businesses who would espouse these trends would gain the benefit of IoT, however, designing low-energy, low-cost IoT networks and solutions are still in the primary phases. Thus, this chapter sketched the role of IoT and smart sensors in the pharma manufacturing sector to make smarter for future discoveries and clinical trials. Pharma's mounting attention in IoT is motivated by increasing demand and pioneering healthcare businesses that are generating a market demand to boost modern pharma and healthcare needs. Users are progressively consuming smartphones, digitally allied cellular sensing systems, and digital wearable devices.

2.13 CONCLUSION

The Indian pharma marketplace, laterally with the marketplaces of China, Brazil and Russia, could be at the forefront in development within these marketplaces. The Indian market has diverse features, positioning it as an exclusive business podium. Initially, branded generics control manufacturing up to 70%–80% of the retail marketplace. Next, local companies have relished a leading place determined by formulation development competences and initial investments. Thus, prices are low, determined by strong competition. While India ranks tenth globally in terms of value, it is ranked third in volume. IoT characterizes an absolutely digitally allied life and all our health data would be obtained from our activities with wearable devices, a rich source of information for science and medicine. Nano sensors could possibly screen the way we eat, our sleeping patterns, blood sugar count, blood pressure, calories burnt, steps we've walked, type of cavities, or the bacterial contamination we have in our mouth/body. These would help to not only alert us as patients at the initial stage, but would also help to diagnose an ailment at very early stages. These advents of digital disruption and interconnectivity would benefit from a reinvention of features in the healthcare science sector. The concept of telemedicine and online distribution channels are well accepted in the industry today. Smart devices also invite the need for smart pharma. Modern interconnected technologies are providing great help to users to avail medicinal and healthcare support at their doorstep. Even medical consultations and counselling are possible due to advent of technology at a very reasonable cost. All these are a gift of IoT and allied sensor technologies to human kind.

REFERENCES

[1] Ariane P. Industry 4.0 in the Medical Technology and Pharmaceutical Industry Sectors. BIOPRO Baden Wurttemberg GmbH, 2016.

[2] Adoption of Internet of Things in pharma manufacturing [Internet]. 2017. [cited 12 May 2019].

[3] Automation, IoT and the future of smarter research environments [Internet]. Pharma IQ News 2018. [cited 26 May 2019].

[4] Burmeister C., Lüttgens D., Piller F.T. Business model innovation for Industrie 4.0: Why the "Industrial Internet" mandates a new perspective on innovation. Die Unternehmung 2016, 70, 124–152.

[5] Dimiter V. Medical Internet of Things and big data in healthcare. Healthcare Informatics Research 2016 Jul, 22(3), 156–163.

[6] Improving efficiency in pharma manufacturing through IoT technologies [Internet]. SpendEdge 2018. [cited 15 April 2019]

[7] Internet of Things in Clinical Trials [Internet]. JLI Social Media 2018. [cited 24 May 2019].

[8] Lee, J.; Kao, H.-A.; Yang, S. Service innovation and smart analytics for industry 4.0 and big data environment. Procedia CIRP 2014, 16, 3–8.

[9] Markarian J. The Internet of Things for pharmaceutical manufacturing. Pharmaceutical Technology 2016, 40(9), 54–58.

[10] Taylor D. Pharmaceutical manufacturing is labelled a success with newly integrated plant operations [Internet]. decisyon 2019. [cited 18 May 2019].

[11] Rayes A., Salam S. Internet of Things—From Hype to Reality. Springer International Publishing, 2017

[12] Sridhar A., Varia H. IoT could make a difference in pharmaceutical manufacturing and supply chains [Internet]. Aranca 2017. [cited 5 June 2019].

[13] Staines R. Healthcare AI market worth $10bn plus by 2024 – report [Internet]. Pharmaphorum, 2018. [cited 26 April 2019].

[14] Steven M.N., Gail F.D. Animal research, the 3Rs, and the "Internet of Things": Opportunities and oversight in international pharmaceutical development. ILAR Journal 2017, 57(2), 246–253.

[15] Wolf C., Floyd S.W. Strategic planning research: Toward a theory-driven agenda. Journal of Management 2017, 43, 1754–1788.

3 A Novel LC-DEH Algorithm to Enhance Efficiency and Security for Reliable Data Transmission in Blockchain with IoT-Based Healthcare Systems

G. Uganya, Radhika Baskar, M. Balasaraswathi,
N. Vijayaraj, and D. Rajalakshmi

CONTENTS

DOI: 10.1201/9781003166511-3

3.1 INTRODUCTION

In this chapter, we focus mainly on healthcare applications that use the Internet of Things (IoT). IoT plays a major role in remote healthcare monitoring systems. Gathering information related to a patient or user's health is made easy by use of IoT. It not only helps to improve the patient health, but it also improves the productivity of the healthcare industry. IoT-based healthcare applications have the benefits of better treatment with reduced cost and accurate data collection. Still, there are many issues and challenges in IoT-based medical applications. Therefore, blockchain-based IoT applications are chosen to enhance security and efficiency [1]. Blockchain can be used in IoT applications of the transport industry, smart homes, supply chain management, distributive economy, medical care, agriculture, and waste management. Within the transport industry, it can be used in effective traffic management and vehicle control to prevent accidents. The blockchain-based smart home can be used to improve efficiency and security. Blockchain-based smart medical care can be used in patient data security and secure communication by tracking and monitoring patient health information using wearable devices and monitoring equipment. IoT devices continue gathering medical data through the internet that can be stored in the cloud. IoT used in blockchain-based applications in medical field has the benefits of end-to-end communication, continuous recording and monitoring, data tracking, and data analysis. IoT-based grid applications have many issues and challenges including interoperability, slow adoption of new technologies, easy hijacking of devices, security, and privacy issues. A blockchain-based smart grid system enhances the security and privacy policies due to its decentralized and distributed architecture.

The cryptography hash algorithm is the main function used to improve security by changing the input value to hash value. The output hash value is called a compressed function and that should be less than the input message. The compressed value ranges from 160 to 512 bits. The increased hash value prevents the data from vulnerable attacks. It can be divided into MD5, SHA224, SHA256, SHA384, SHA512, SHA3-224, SHA3-256, SHA3-384, and SHA3-512. These hash algorithms are used to improve security by encrypting the message input. The hash algorithm can be obtained by the private key, public key, message, and address value. The sender uses the private key to transfer the message and the receiver uses the public key to receive the message. But still, it requires an efficient hash algorithm to enhance the security and accuracy for reliable data transmission. For that reason, we proposed lightweight cryptography and a double encryption hash algorithm (LC-DEHA) to protect the secret key and public key. The double encryption hash algorithm provides a large hash value to prevent hash-value hacking. It can improve security efficiently by preventing the hijacking of data and information. This algorithm is used to prevent the misuse of medical information and provide greater security. It provides greater security compared to the hash algorithm with single encryption.

The major contribution of the chapter is summarized here:

- A general overview of IoT, and security challenges, blockchain technology including architecture, types, and its issues.
- Review of blockchain technology with IoT applications, and its challenges.
- A classification of different cryptography hash algorithm used in block-chain with IoT applications.
- A detailed explanation of LC-DEHA with results.
- Performance analysis of hash output, efficiency, and time allocation for various cryptography algorithm with LC-DEHA.

The rest of the chapter is organized as follows: Section 3.2 discusses the overview of IoT and its security issues, blockchain technology including definition, structure, types, and its applications with IoT. Different types of hash algorithms are discussed in Section 3.3. Section 3.4 explains the related works on various cryptography hash algorithms. In Section 3.5, the proposed method of LC-DEHA and its results are discussed. Finally, Section 3.6 concludes the chapter.

3.2 OVERVIEW

3.2.1 DEFINITION OF IoT

IoT is the latest developing technology that encompasses the huge number of electronic devices that are not connected but communicate with each other through the internet. It also improves the power and processing of data to real-time applications. Mainly, IoT devices can collect information from the physical world and this collected information will be stored in the cloud. Some examples of IoT devices are smart home appliances, smart wearables, sensors, radio-frequency identification (RFID) tags, etc. It has a huge number of devices that collect and transmit information to the cloud environment through any kind of communication or connectivity. After reaching the cloud, the information is processed by software. The main purpose of IoT is to improve the communication between the users and the production of real-time application data to get a desired output. It offers new opportunities for leading business, skills to calculate the data, enhancement of monitoring, services, and products, and enhances process control. Figure 3.1 shows the architecture of the Internet of Things. It will be considered in three layers: The physical layer, network layer, and application layer.

In the physical layer, the sensors and actuators are used to gather the information continuously from the environment. The collected information is transferred to the network layer through the gateway. Here, the data is translated into usable information. In the application layer, the data is processed and stored in the cloud. Gateways or routers are used as an intermediator to transfer the information from one layer to another. The application layer is responsible for filtering the massive data from sensors and pre-processing the data. It implements data encryption and decryption techniques to prevent the system from security attacks. The rapid growth of IoT applications leads to security vulnerabilities. So, blockchain with IoT-based medical applications will be chosen to enhance security.

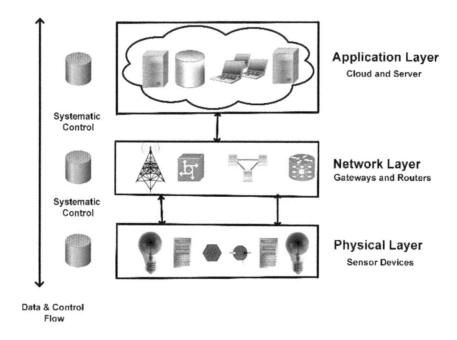

FIGURE 3.1   Architecture of Internet of Things.

3.2.2   Security Issues in IoT Architecture

IoT architecture can be classified into the physical layer, network layer, and application layer. This chapter focuses mainly on the IoT-based smart healthcare system. The physical layer consists of sensing devices to gather the information including heartbeat, blood pressure, and oxygen levels from the physical user. This layer is connected to the cloud in the application layer through the network layer. The application layer consists of cloud and mobile devices to store the information. It also carries the instructions from the application layer to the physical layer.

The application layer has three major security issues. These are productive computing, encryption of cloud information, and protection of user's information. The mobile device will be connected to the cloud by using authentication technology. If it does not use a proper authentication mechanism, it will be vulnerable to a malicious attack. The application layer needs a proper authentication security mechanism based on its number of devices in the application layer. In the network layer, the applications are connected to the physical layer through a network including gateway, router, mobile, and wireless network. The network layer adopts a regular communication protocol due to the rapid development of the 5G network. The IoT physical layer is linked with the cloud through the network. For example, collected health data is continuously gathered from a wearable IoT device and transferred to the cloud over the wireless network. This layer faces two major possible security attacks. Many devices use unauthorized access and services, leading to security vulnerabilities including denial of service (DoS) attacks. Many IoT devices are connected through Zigbee and Wi-Fi networks for short-distance communication, but are vulnerable to security threats due to the lack of an encryption scheme for communication messages.

Despite the many security mechanisms like authentication, encryption, trust management, and software-defined networks, IoT-based applications still have many issues and challenges due to its scalability, heterogeneous devices, and centralized architecture. Security solutions are needed for decentralized IoT applications. From this point of view, we will choose blockchain-based IoT applications to enhance security, and efficiency with less time.

3.2.3 Definition of Blockchain

Blockchain technology is a decentralized architecture that is used to store transactional records in digital form. These digital forms of transactional records are called blocks. These blocks are linked in chain format, hence the name blockchain technology. Every data transaction is verified by the digital signature of the user. The verification of a transaction is used to protect the information from data alteration by an attacker.

Figure 3.2 shows the architecture of blockchain technology. In the first step, the user requests a data transaction. In the second step, the transaction is created in the block. Then the block is broadcasted to all nodes in the peer-to-peer network for validation. Now all nodes present in the network are going to verify the digital signature to add the block in the chain. After verification, the block is added to the chain. Finally, the verified transaction is executed securely. It can

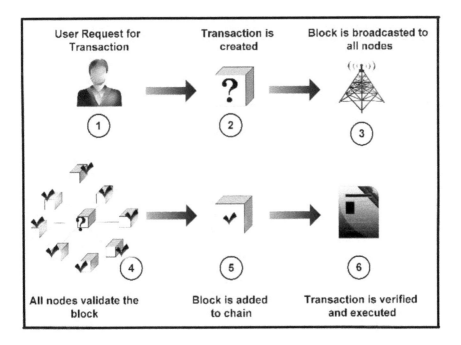

FIGURE 3.2 Architecture of blockchain technology.

FIGURE 3.3   Example of block in blockchain technology.

be used in many applications including business industry, production, and supply chain, etc. This technology is highly secure due to its digital signature feature. Because every node validates the digital signature during the transaction, it leads to a fraud-free transaction and protects the data from an attacker. It can also be used in secure data transmission due to its decentralized architecture and its greater automation ability.

Figure 3.3 shows the example of a block in blockchain technology. The block is divided into header and body. The header consists of a timestamp, hash of the previous block, Merkle root of the node, nonce, and version. Merkle root is kept in block body, which contains the Merkle tree hash value. In this root, all the transactions are converted into a single line of text by using the hash value. The nonce represents the number used once, which is permitted to operate the random value of the block.

The block is classified into main branches of blocks, side branches of blocks, and orphan blocks. In main branch blocks, the transactions are tentatively established. Missed transactions in the main branch are called side branches. Orphan blocks are not directly connected with the main branch. It improves security and efficiency due to its special features, which include tamper proof and immutable data, decentralization, and distributed records. Figure 3.4 shows the special features of blockchain technology.

3.2.4   THREE CATEGORIES IN BLOCKCHAIN TECHNOLOGY

Blockchain technology is categorized into private, public, and consortium blockchains based on selected applications. Table 3.1 shows the comparison of three types of blockchain architecture. In public blockchain architecture, anyone can participate and access the data. This type of architecture is decentralized and permissionless architecture. A consensus algorithm is applied to all miners in the public blockchain network. It has drawbacks of low efficiency and less security. In private blockchain architecture, the participant node needs permission to access the data. It has high efficiency and tamper proof data. It is developed within the

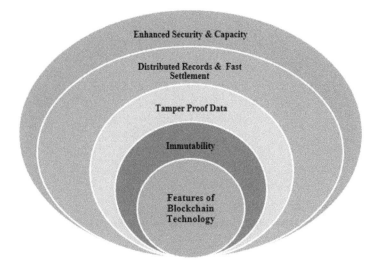

FIGURE 3.4   Special features of blockchain technology (demoblockchain.org).

organization and centralized architecture. The consortium blockchain is developed either in public or restricted architectures with partial decentralized architecture. In this type, the consensus algorithm is applied to selected nodes that have tamper-proof data and high efficiency.

Figure 3.5 shows the number of hits of blockchain category web searches in the United States from 2019 to 2020. From this figure, we understand that private blockchain is developed more in the world compared with public and consortium

TABLE 3.1

Comparison of Blockchain Architecture Types

Types of Blockchain Architecture	Private Blockchain	Public Blockchain	Consortium Blockchain
Authorization for reading	Controlled	Public	Public/Controlled
Immutability	Tampered and collusion attacks	Difficult to tamper	Tampered and collusion attacks
Efficiency	Good	Poor	Good
Decentralization	No	Yes	Partial
Consensus algorithm	Need permission	Permissionless	Need permission
Resolve of consensus	Within the group	All miner nodes	Within selected nodes
Approval time	Command of milliseconds	Command of minutes	Command of milliseconds
Energy consumption	Low	High	Low
Secrecy	Trusted	Anonymous	Trusted
Proof of work	Light	Costly	Light

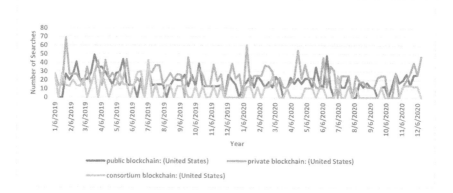

FIGURE 3.5 Number of hits of blockchain category web searches in the United States from 2019 to 2020. (Google Trends.)

blockchain. But private blockchain is established within organizations and industry, i.e. smart homes, smart industries, and smart educational institutions. Smart healthcare and transportation are used by public blockchain architecture due to its large area decentralized structure. In some applications like energy trading and the finance and insurance industries, companies use public blockchain architecture although it has many challenges due to its scalability issue.

This chapter will focus on the development of a public blockchain network because it can be used to enhance security in large-scale area as well as needs development to improve efficiency with less time consumption. Mainly, it can be used in secure communication and transferring information in IoT-based applications due to its special characteristics.

3.2.5 BLOCKCHAIN WITH IoT APPLICATIONS

Blockchain technology can be used in IoT applications of the transport industry, smart homes, supply chain management, distributive economy, medical care, agriculture, and waste management. Figure 3.6 shows the blockchain with IoT applications.

3.2.5.1 Transport Industry

Vehicular communication systems are the main network in intelligent transportation systems. IoT can be used in secure and efficient traffic management including automatic vehicle charging, recognition of license plates, and vehicle navigation systems. These applications can be classified into automobile to automobile and automobile to structure. There are still many security and key management issues in transport communication systems [2]. It has features of more movement, huge capacity, and heterogeneity of devices compared with the traditional transport network. In addition, the various kinds of devices all with different central authorities create many research challenges in intelligent transport systems [3]. In this issue, blockchain technology can be used to remove the central authority.

FIGURE 3.6   Blockchain with IoT applications.

3.2.5.2   Supply Chain Management

Blockchain technology is mainly used in supply chain management due to its scalability, flexibility, and transparency [4]. It provided three major areas including perceptibility, optimization, and request. It can be used in the logistics and processing of products by transferring and securely tracking things without a third party [5]. Table 3.2 shows the scope of article implementation of blockchain-based IoT applications. Blockchain-based supply chain management has benefits of better customer satisfaction and healthier relationships between product supplier and manufacturer, high efficiency, enhanced risk, and cash flow. But it needs more concentration on customer service, risk, and planning management of industry service.

3.2.5.3   Smart Home

IoT-based smart home applications are implemented in highly scalable areas by using blockchain technology to improve security and efficiency because it has special characteristics including immutable and tamper-proof records. Dorri et al. proposed lightweight IoT architecture with a blockchain network to examine smart home applications and supply chain management [6]. This method is used to improve security and privacy by using overlap and cloud networks. Conoscenti et al. proposed distributed blockchain network to enhance security and privacy in smart homes and cities [7]. Lombardi et al. proposed a less expensive yet trustworthy blockchain model for decentralized home applications [8]. This method is also applied to store the energy of in-home applications. Blockchain-based smart homes have challenges including scalability, more energy consumption, and irreversibility of process. This chapter will concentrate more on these issues.

3.2.5.4   Smart City

IoT devices like sensors, actuators, and lights are used to gather and investigate data continuously. These data are used to improve the architecture, public conveniences, and facilities in the smart city. But an IoT-based smart city has many issues due to its centralized architecture and scalability. The integration of IoT with blockchain

TABLE 3.2

The Scope of Article Implementation of Blockchain-Based IoT Applications

Author and Ref. No	Year	Smart Home	Smart City	Smart Grid	Supply Chain Management	Smart Medical Care	Smart Industry
Herbert et al. [9]	2015	×	✓	×	×	×	×
Sun et al. [10]	2016	×	✓	×	×	×	×
Bahga et al. [11]	2016	×	✓	×	✓	×	✓
Biswas et al. [12]	2016	×	✓	×	✓	×	×
Dorri et al. [6]	2016	✓	×	×	✓	×	×
Hardjono et al. [21]	2016	×	✓	×	×	×	✓
Conoscenti et al. [7]	2017	✓	✓	×	×	×	×
Sikorski et al. [22]	2017	×	×	×	×	×	✓
Ghuli et al. [13]	2017	×	✓	×	×	×	×
Prabhu et al. [23]	2017	×	×	×	✓	×	×
Shafagh et al. [24]	2017	×	×	×	✓	×	×
Korpela et al. [25]	2017	×	×	×	✓	×	✓
Lombardi et al. [8]	2018	✓	✓	✓	×	×	×
Xu et al. [26]	2018	×	×	×	✓	×	×
Davidsen et al. [27]	2018	×	×	×	✓	×	✓
Chakraborty et al. [28]	2018	×	×	×	✓	×	×
Singh et al. [29]	2019	✓	×	×	×	×	×
Chen et al. [30]	2019	×	✓	×	×	✓	×
Xu et al. [20]	2019	×	×	×	×	✓	×
Ajao et al. [31]	2019	×	×	×	×	×	✓
Singh et al. [32]	2020	×	✓	×	×	×	×
Lee et al. [33]	2020	✓	×	×	×	×	×
Guo et al. [15]	2020	×	✓	✓	×	×	×
Cheng et al. [34]	2020	×	×	×	✓	✓	×
Tamilarasi et al. [35]	2020	×	×	×	×	✓	×

technology provides a new set of services and facilities to achieve a smart city. It is used to develop digital ledgers from trillions of computers. Because it has special characteristics like transparency, immutability, and secure digital uniqueness. Herbert et al. proposed the decentralized peer-to-peer network to validate software licenses and copyright [9]. The transaction of the message consists of input, signature, and output. J. Sun et al. proposed a blockchain-based smart city system to develop the framework using the dimensions like a human being, technology, and organization [10]. Bahga et al. proposed blockchain technology for the industrial IoT. It provides machine-to-machine communication without a third party and distributed and secured ledger and assets [11]. Similarly, Biswas et al. discussed the secure smart framework to integrate blockchain technology with smart IoT devices. It can be implemented mainly to secure the communication from attacks [12]. Ghuli et al. proposed a method to transfer the rights from one user to another without an intermediator for financial and nonfinancial services [13]. Blockchain-based smart city systems have many research issues and challenges including secure communication, privacy, storage, efficiency, throughput, and cost.

3.2.5.5 Smart Grid

An IoT-based smart grid has characteristics including collecting and monitoring the information, restoring and managing the energy, reduction, and conservation of electricity [14]. It can be used in measuring smart meter parameters, power consumption, charging vehicles, and managing power. But due to its centralized architecture, it has many issues and challenges including interoperability, slow adoption of new technologies, easy hijacking of devices, security, and privacy issues. So, the blockchain-based smart grid system can enhance security and privacy policies due to its decentralized and distributed architecture. Guo et al. proposed blockchain technology for electric transactions. This technology is used to design smart contracts for the secure and reliable transaction of electricity [15]. Tan et al. proposed an energy scheduling system for preserving privacy using blockchain with smart contracts. It is mainly designed to trading and scheduling the power with transparency, but has scalability issues [16]. Li et al. proposed a blockchain-based energy trading system for smart microgrid systems. It is mainly designed to reduce the delay time for transaction confirmation using a credit-based payment system [17]. Similarly, Zheng et al. discussed a power trading system using consortium-based blockchain technology; however, it is not practically implemented due to its energy consumption [18]. The blockchain-based smart grid needs more concentration on issues and challenges including power consumption and electricity trading.

3.2.5.6 Smart Medical Care

IoT-based medical care is used in tracking and monitoring patient health information using wearable devices and monitoring equipment. The IoT devices are used to used continually gather medical data through the internet that can be stored on the cloud. It has the benefits of end-to-end communication, continuous recording and monitoring, data tracking, and data analysis. Figure 3.7 shows use of IoT in medical care. However, it has research challenges including security, privacy, integration of multiple devices and protocols, data overload, and accuracy [19].

IoT in Medical Care		
Benefits	**Applications**	**Challenges**
1) Monitoring and Reporting	1) Small Sensors	1) Data Security & Privacy
2) End to End Communication	2) Hearables	2) Integration of Multiple Devices
3) Data Collection	3) Computer Vision Technology	3) Integration of Multiple Protocols
4) Continuous Tracking	4) Moodables	4) Data Overload
5) Remote Medical Assistance	5) Healthcare Charting	5) Accuracy & Cost

FIGURE 3.7 IoT in medical care applications.

These issues and challenges are overcome by using blockchain technology due to its special characteristics. It can be used in large scale applications to transfer the data securely and managing the medical supply chain. Xu et al. proposed a block-chain-based healthcare system on a huge scale. In this method, the medical data cannot be deleted due to its features including accountability, and revocability [20]. Tamilarasi et al. proposed a lightweight encryption-based swarm optimization tech-nique for healthcare applications.

This method is mainly used to encrypt healthcare data [35]. Gul et al. proposed a blockchain-based healthcare system that is beneficial for customers [36]. Rouhani et al. proposed a patient medical care data approach in the hyperledger platform to overcome the restrictions in public and private blockchain [37]. Lee et al. proposed a blockchain-based fingernail analysis method. In this work, a microscopy sensor is used to capture the nail image for analysing the human physiological nature. The neural network is used for analysing the feature extraction. Blockchain technology is used for providing secure communication [38]. This chapter will concentrate on IoT with blockchain technology challenges like scalability, operation speed, lack of knowledge and standards, consensus mechanism, privacy identity, energy consump-tion, irreversibility, and resiliency.

3.3   CRYPTOGRAPHY HASH ALGORITHM

The cryptography hash algorithm is a mathematical function used to convert the variable size input value into a fixed-size output value. The output is called a hash value or message digest. The output hash value should be less than the input mes-sage, so it is known as a compressed function. The generated hash value should be 160–512 bits. It is a quicker process compared to the symmetric encryption algorithm. It is difficult to find an input value from output due to its irreversible property. It also has a collision-resistant property and it denotes that the hash func-tion produces a collision-free output hash value. Cryptography hash algorithm can be divided into Message Digest 5 (MD5), SHA224, SHA256, SHA384, SHA512, SHA3-224, SHA3-256, SHA3-384, SHA3-512.

Message Digest 5: MD5 is one of the cryptography hash algorithms that produce the 128-bit output hash. It can be expressed as a 32-digit hexadecimal number to secure the files. It has four rounds and 64 steps to produce the hash value. It provides secure communication due to its irreversible property. It is impossible to make the two messages with the same hash value. In this function, every step result will be added to the previous step. The secure hash algorithm is classified into three families.

SHA224: SHA224 is a kind of 224-bit one-way hash function. It is designed by the US National Security Agency (NSA). This method works on the SHA256 algo-rithm, in which it instead uses a different initial value that is truncated to 224 bits. It provides 112 bits of security, which usually accepts the length of three DES (Data Encryption Standard). Secure hash algorithm (SHA) uses a message schedule of 64 words (each 32-bit) and eight working variables (each 32-bit), which are collectively called H, and produces a hash value of eight 32-bit words. SHA224 produces a 224-bit (28-byte) hash value, considered as a hexadecimal number, 56 digits long. When we have to select a 112-bit of security, then SHA224 is quite appropriate for that.

SHA256: The SHA-2 family consists of six hash functions with digest lengths of 224, 256, 384, or 512 bits. SHA256 is one of the strongest hash functions. SHA generates an almost unique 256-bit signature for a text. It is widely used in some of the most popular authentication and encryption protocols, which include SSL, TLS, SSH, and PGP. It is a cryptographic keyless hash function with a 256-bit digest length. It is used for secure password hashing. The SHA256 algorithm works based on the Merkle-Damgård construction method. A message is processed by blocks of 512 that are 16×32 bits, in which each block requires 64 rounds. SHA256 is less complex to code than SHA-1. The SHA256-bit key acts as a good partner function for AES (Advanced Encryption Standard). One of the most popular cryptocurrencies, Bitcoin, uses SHA256 for transaction verification.

SHA384: SHA384 is a kind of 384-bit hash function of cryptographic algorithm SHA-2. It is designed by the NSA. This method works based on the SHA512 algorithm, in which it instead uses a different initial value and is truncated to 384 bits. SHA384 can be considered a truncated version of SHA512. For example, if you need the hash to generate both a 256-bit HMAC (Hash based Message Authentication Code) key and a 128-bit encryption key, SHA384 is a preferred choice.

SHA512: SHA512 is a hash function of the cryptographic algorithm of SHA-2. It is very similar to SHA256, except it uses blocks of 1024 bits and can also get an input of maximum string length 2^{128} bits, which are quite larger. In SHA512, the message is broken into 1024-bit chunk. The initial hash values and round constants are made up of 64 bits. There are about 80 rounds. The word size used for calculation is 64 bits long. It generates an almost unique 512-bit signature for a text.

SHA3-224: SHA-3 is the latest SHA released by the National Institute of Standards and Technology (NIST). The main purpose of SHA-3 is that it can be substituted directly for SHA-2 in the case of present applications and also to improve the robustness of NIST. For SHA3-224, the output size d is 224. Its capacity is 448. The rate of SHA3-224 is equal to block size i.e., 1600-c, which is exactly 1152. A single instance of SHA3-224 function processes input messages at 303.58 MHz.

SHA3-256: SHA3-256 has lower performances than the SHA2-256. This was partially due to political reasons in the SHA-3 design process. It has a 256-bit key size and uses a sponge structure with the Keccak permutation. A single instance of an SHA3-256 function processes input messages at 306.65 MHz. The output size and security strengths in bits for collision are higher than SHA3-224 because the size of the bit is increased.

SHA3-384: An SHA3-384 hash object does not instantiate directly. It uses a new function, logically joining all the arguments into a single string and returning the digest encoded as a binary string. A single instance of an SHA3-384 function processes messages at 310.75 MHz. The operations done for are AND, XOR, and NOT. The capacity of SHA3-384 against length extension attack is 768 and the security in bits against collision attack is 192.

SHA3-512: In SHA3-512 of digest (), it returns the binary digest of the message that has been hashed so far. A single instance of an SHA3-512 function processes input messages at 316.25 MHz. The capacity of SHA3-512 against length extension attack is 1,024 and the security in bits against collision attack is 256. The operations done for SHA3-512 are the same as that of SHA3-384 i.e., AND, XOR, and NOT. The block size of it is 576 bits.

3.4 RELATED WORKS

Blockchain-based IoT applications need cryptography algorithms to improve efficiency and security. IoT applications use the encryption algorithm for changing the data from understandable form to unreadable form. Then it uses a decryption algorithm to change this unreadable form data back to its original form. But blockchain technology uses the hash algorithm, which is a one-way function. It converts the variable amount of input to the fixed size of output, called a hash value. The output value is less than the input value. Ebrahim et al. discussed the different lightweight cryptography algorithms and their limitations [39]. Lim et al. proposed a Crypton algorithm for RFID and sensor devices with a key size of 64,126 and 128 bits. It can be used to secure the differential cryptanalysis techniques from vulnerable attacks. But it has a limitation of efficiency in software systems [40]. Panarello et al. discussed the literature review on the blockchain with IoT applications [41].

Lefebvre et al. proposed a robust soft hash algorithm for digital image signature. In this paper, they have implemented a one-way function for images. By using random transform and principal component analysis, they have extracted the characteristics of robustness against the geometrical transformation of rotating and scaling and image processing attacks, which are compressing, filtering, blurring, and so on [42]. Pittalia discussed the detailed survey on hash algorithms in cryptography. In this paper, Pittalia discusses the importance of hash functions, described various popular hash functions, and comparative analysis of various hash algorithms, which are SHA1, MD5, and so on [43]. Divya et al. proposed a hybrid cryptography algorithm for cloud computing security. In this paper, they have discussed the designing of a new security method by using a hybrid cryptosystem for data security in the cloud. This method provided high security on data transmission over the internet [44]. Ajao et al. proposed a cryptography hash algorithm-based blockchain technology for managing decentralized ledger databases in the oil and gas industry. This paper proposes an improved method for the securing and monitoring of petroleum product distribution records using blockchain technology. This method helped to secure the transaction and to protect records from tampering, fraudulent activity, and corruption [45].

Alotaibi et al. proposed secured mobile authentication using a combination of hash, cryptography, and steganography. In this paper, they have discussed the security authentication system, which is implemented by combining hash, cryptography, and steganography mechanisms that provided enhanced mobile security [46]. Kale et al. discussed a survey on different types of hash algorithms. This paper gives knowledge of various kinds of hash functions and discusses appropriate hash functions for particular problems [47]. Kheshaifaty et al. proposed a method to prevent multiple accessing attacks using the captcha crypto hash function. In this paper, they discussed implementation of the captcha crypto hash function, which has an effective improvement in securing data of about 30% over the old system. Mainly, they have used a multi-layer combination, which is the more secure and authentic system [48]. Liu et al. proposed a keyed hash function constructed using the hyperchaotic Lorenz system, which serves as an absorption function to absorb input message by using multiparameters time-varying perturbations. The proposed method can be used in information integrity, identification, and figure signature [49].

Zaru et al. did a general survey on cryptography. This paper discussed how cryptography is used to achieve some of the goals like confidentiality, data integrity, authentication, etc. They concluded that Kerberos is far better than PGP because it is scalable and its scope could be very large [50]. Rajasekar et al. proposed a multifactor signcryption scheme for secure authentication that is achieved by the combination of hyperelliptic curve cryptography and bio-hash function. The proposed method uses multiple-factor authentication to make more secure personal data. They have used signcryption which is a lightweight cryptography method to minimize biometric recognition error, dictionary attack, DoS attack, impersonation attack, and so on [51]. Jyothi et al. analysed cryptography encryption of network security. In this work, they have done a detailed survey to find the best way to secure data. At last, on comparing all the techniques, they found cryptography helps in safeguarding the confidential personal information [52].

Debnath et al. discussed a general review on a journey of secured hash algorithms. In this work, they have discussed the data encryption method and their upgradation. They have highlighted to use of modern standard SHA-3 instead of SHA-1 and SHA-2 [53]. Gnatyuk et al. proposed a secure hash function communication system. In this work, they discussed their new hash function implementation based on SHA-2. This resulted in increasing the word size and increasing the message digest. It also reduced the number of rounds in compression function, which will increase the speed of data processing [54]. Harer proposed decentralized business modelling and instance tracking with the help of a blockchain. In this paper, the author implemented a hierarchical versioning and modelling approach to create and manage public and private models of transactions. The combination of current model versioning and blockchain technology resulted in enterprise models of decentralized network peers and also instant process tracking with metadata [55].

Agrawal et al. proposed a blockchain-based secured traceability system for the textile and clothing supply chain. In this paper, they discussed the implementation of traceability in the supply chain and its necessities. They also enlisted the advantages of blockchain technology for the implementation of traceability [56]—mainly the cryptography algorithm that can secure the key pair and message effectively. However, it requires a more secure hash algorithm to protect the key pair including a private key and public key and a message with address hash. The proposed algorithm LC-DEHA will be discussed in the next section.

3.5 PROPOSED METHOD

3.5.1 LC-DEHA

Lightweight cryptography double encryption hash algorithm (LC-DEHA) is proposed to improve security by preventing attackers from identifying the key pair and message. Figure 3.8 shows the flowchart of the proposed method. Cryptography hash algorithm is important in blockchain technology to produce the immutable hash

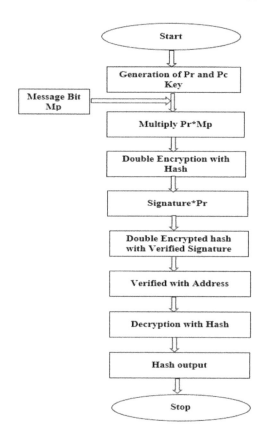

FIGURE 3.8   Flowchart of LC-DEHA.

output. Mainly message digest and secure hash algorithm hash functions are used in blockchain technology.

The proposed algorithm can be combined with a cryptography hash algorithm to improve the security in key pair and message data. A hash function has components including private key, public key, address hash, and message data. The private key and public key are generated for the sender and receiver, respectively. The private key will be multiplied with message data. Then the multiplied data are double-encrypted with the hash value. The private key is multiplied with a digital signature for verification. The encrypted hash value with the digital signature is transferred to the receiver side where the signature with public key hash value will be verified with the public key for transferring the message. The digital signature is validated for decrypting the message. Figure 3.9 shows the generated hash output for various cryptography hash algorithm. These hash values are irreversible to avoid attacks.

3.5.2   RESULTS AND DISCUSSIONS

This section discusses the results and their performance in terms of efficiency, hash output, and time allocation. Figure 3.10 shows the health data used for our proposed method.

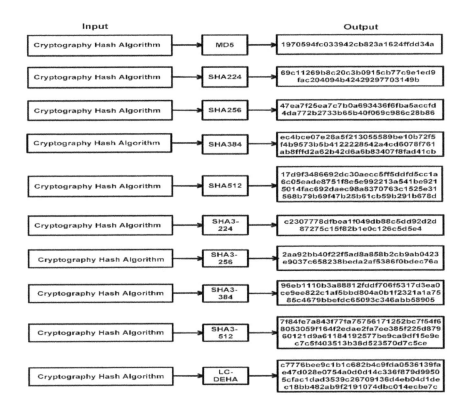

FIGURE 3.9 Generated hash output for cryptography hash algorithm.

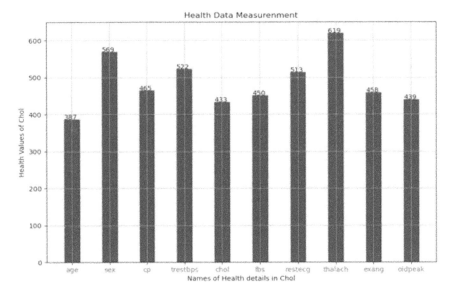

FIGURE 3.10 Health data.

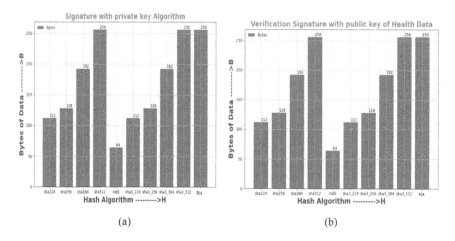

(a)   (b)

FIGURE 3.11   Verified signature hash output (a) private key (b) public key.

Figure 3.11 shows the verified signature hash output for the private key and public key. The private key is used for sending the message with a digital signature in the sender node. The public key is used for receiving the message by validating the private key with a signature. In our work, double encryption is proposed with a cryptography hash algorithm. MD5 produces the hash value of 64 bytes by double encryption. Similarly, SHA224 and SHA3-224 produce the 112 bytes of the hash value. SHA256 and its third generation generated the 128-byte hash value, which is mainly used in blockchain technology. SHA384, SHA512, and its third-generation family generated 256 bytes hash values using a double-encryption cryptography algorithm. Also, this work is implemented in the RS algorithm. Figure 3.12 shows the verified digital signature of address hash and decoding hash. Figure 3.12(a) denotes the hash value of the health data address with a verified digital signature. Figure 3.12(b) denotes the decoding output hash value with a validated signature. From this hash

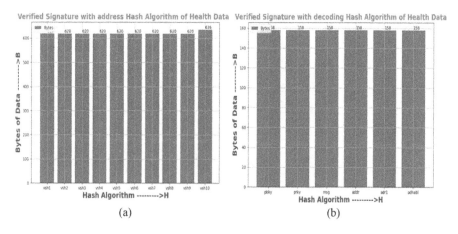

(a)   (b)

FIGURE 3.12   Verified digital signature (a) address hash (b) decoding hash.

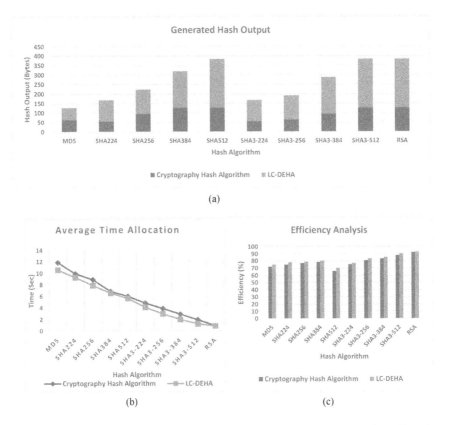

FIGURE 3.13 Performance analysis (a) generated hash output, (b) average time allocation and (c) efficiency signature.

output, it produces large and irreversible output and it cannot be identified by anyone without authority.

3.5.3 PERFORMANCE COMPARISON

The hash output can be a fixed size variable and produced from variable-size input values. The hash value is generated by multiplying the private key and message. It can be written by,

$$H_f\left(P_r * M_p\right) = H_O \tag{3.1}$$

where H_f = hash function; P_r = private key; and M_p = message bytes.

Figure 3.13 shows the performance comparison of produced hash output, time allocation, and efficiency for the cryptography hash algorithm and lightweight cryptography double encryption hash algorithm. Time allocation is defined as the amount of time to generate the hash value for the key pair, message, and address. An efficiency denotes the quality of the hash output, which cannot be identifiable by a third party without authorization. It can be analysed with hash functions including SHA224, SHA256, SHA384, SHA512, MD5, SHA3-224, SHA3-256, SHA3-384, SHA3-512, and RSA (Rivest–Shamir–Adleman). From this analysis, LC-DEHA produces the large bytes hash value to improve the security and enhance efficiency with reduced time allocation compared to the cryptography hash algorithm.

3.6 CONCLUSION

An IoT-based smart healthcare system uses emerging technology to continuously monitor patient health data. But it has limitations due to its centralized architecture and scalability issues. Blockchain-based healthcare systems can be used to monitor and protect health data because it has the special characteristics of immutable records, transparency maximized storage, and decentralized architecture. First, this chapter discusses the general overview of IoT and its security issues, blockchain technology, and its applications including smart home, smart medical care, smart grid, transport industry, and supply chain management. In blockchain technology, the cryptography hash algorithm can be used to enhance security by converting the input message into an unchangeable hash value. This work concentrates on hash algorithms including message digest, secure hash algorithm, and RSA algorithm. This algorithm is used a single encryption scheme to convert the key pair and message into unchangeable hash output. However, it still requires an efficient algorithm to improve the security in the hash algorithm. This work introduces the LC-DEHA to prevent the hijacking of the password/key pair and message. The performance of the proposed algorithm can be compared with various cryptography hash algorithms in terms of hash output, efficiency, and time allocation. From this analysis, the proposed method produces large hash output to improve security and efficiency with less time allocation.

REFERENCES

[1] Uganya, G., Radhika and Vijayaraj, N., 2020. A survey on internet of things: Applications, recent issues, attacks, and security mechanisms. *Journal of Circuits, Systems and Computers*, 30(5), p. 2130006.
[2] Lin, J., Yu, W., Zhang, N., Yang, X., Zhang, H. and Zhao, W., 2017. A survey on internet of things: Architecture, enabling technologies, security and privacy, and applications. *IEEE Internet of Things Journal*, 4(5), pp. 1125–1142.
[3] Ekedebe, N., Lu, C. and Yu, W., 2015, June. Towards experimental evaluation of intelligent transportation system safety and traffic efficiency. In 2015 IEEE International Conference on Communications (ICC) (pp. 3757–3762). *IEEE*.
[4] Kshetri, N., 2018. 1 Blockchain's roles in meeting key supply chain management objectives. *International Journal of Information Management*, 39, pp. 80–89.
[5] Tan, A.W.K., Zhao, Y. and Halliday, T., 2018. A blockchain model for less container load operations in China. *International Journal of Information Systems and Supply Chain Management (IJISSCM)*, 11(2), pp. 39–53.
[6] Dorri, A., Kanhere, S.S. and Jurdak, R., 2016. Blockchain in internet of things: challenges and solutions. arXiv preprint arXiv:1608.05187.
[7] Conoscenti, M., Vetro, A. and De Martin, J.C., 2017, May. Peer to Peer for Privacy and Decentralization in the Internet of Things. In 2017 IEEE/ACM 39th International Conference on Software Engineering Companion (ICSE-C) (pp. 288–290). IEEE.

[8] Lombardi, F., Aniello, L., De Angelis, S., Margheri, A. and Sassone, V., 2018. A blockchain-based infrastructure for reliable and cost-effective IoT-aided smart grids. In Living in the Internet of Things: Cybersecurity of the IoT-2018 (pp. 42–46).

[9] Herbert, J. and Litchfield, A., 2015, January. A novel method for decentralized peer-to-peer software license validation using cryptocurrency blockchain technology. In Proceedings of the 38th Australasian Computer Science Conference (ACSC 2015) (Vol. 27, p. 30).

[10] Sun, J., Yan, J. and Zhang, K.Z., 2016. Blockchain-based sharing services: What blockchain technology can contribute to smart cities. *Financial Innovation*, 2(1), pp. 1–9.

[11] Bahga, A. and Madisetti, V.K., 2016. Blockchain platform for industrial internet of things. *Journal of Software Engineering and Applications*, 9(10), pp. 533–546.

[12] Biswas, K. and Muthukkumarasamy, V., 2016, December. Securing smart cities using blockchain technology. In 2016 IEEE 18th International Conference on High Performance Computing and Communications; IEEE 14th International Conference on Smart City; IEEE 2nd International Conference on Data Science and Systems (HPCC/SmartCity/DSS) (pp. 1392–1393). IEEE.

[13] Ghuli, P., Kumar, U.P. and Shettar, R., 2017. A review on blockchain application for decentralized decision of ownership of IoT devices. *Advances in Computational Sciences and Technology*, 10(8), pp. 2449–2456.

[14] Shankar, A., Sivakumar, N.R., Sivaram, M., Ambikapathy, A., Nguyen, T.K. and Dhasarathan, V., 2021. Increasing fault tolerance ability and network lifetime with clustered pollination in wireless sensor networks. *Journal of Ambient Intelligence and Humanized Computing*, 12(2), pp. 2285–2298.

[15] Guo, J., Ding, X. and Wu, W., 2020. A blockchain-enabled ecosystem for distributed electricity trading in smart city. *IEEE Internet of Things Journal*, 8(3), pp. 2040–2050.

[16] Tan, S., Wang, X. and Jiang, C., 2019. Privacy-preserving energy scheduling for ESCOs based on energy blockchain network. *Energies*, 12(8), p. 1530.

[17] Li, Z., Kang, J., Yu, R., Ye, D., Deng, Q. and Zhang, Y., 2017. Consortium blockchain for secure energy trading in industrial internet of things. *IEEE Transactions on Industrial Informatics*, 14(8), pp. 3690–3700.

[18] Zheng, D., Deng, K., Zhang, Y., Zhao, J., Zheng, X. and Ma, X., 2018, November. Smart Grid Power Trading Based on Consortium Blockchain in Internet of Things. In International Conference on Algorithms and Architectures for Parallel Processing (pp. 453–459). Springer, Cham.

[19] Venkatachalam, K., Devipriya, A., Maniraj, J., Sivaram, M., Ambikapathy, A. and Iraj, S.A., 2020. A novel method of motor imagery classification using EEG signal. *Artificial Intelligence in Medicine*, 103, p. 101787.

[20] Xu, J., Xue, K., Li, S., Tian, H., Hong, J., Hong, P. and Yu, N., 2019. Healthchain: A blockchain-based privacy preserving scheme for large-scale health data. *IEEE Internet of Things Journal*, 6(5), pp. 8770–8781.

[21] Hardjono, T. and Smith, N., 2016, May. Cloud-based commissioning of constrained devices using permissioned blockchains. In Proceedings of the 2nd ACM International Workshop on IoT Privacy, Trust, and Security (pp. 29–36).

[22] Sikorski, J.J., Haughton, J. and Kraft, M., 2017. Blockchain technology in the chemical industry: Machine-to-machine electricity market. *Applied Energy*, 195, pp. 234–246.

[23] Prabhu, K. and Prabhu, K., 2017. Converging blockchain technology with the internet of things. *International Journal of Educational Research*, 3(2), pp. 122–123.

[24] Shafagh, H., Burkhalter, L., Hithnawi, A. and Duquennoy, S., 2017, November. Towards blockchain-based auditable storage and sharing of iot data. In Proceedings of the 2017 on Cloud Computing Security Workshop (pp. 45–50).

[25] Korpela, K., Hallikas, J. and Dahlberg, T., 2017, January. Digital supply chain transformation toward blockchain integration. In Proceedings of the 50th Hawaii International Conference on System Sciences.

[26] Xu, Q., Aung, K.M.M., Zhu, Y. and Yong, K.L., 2018. A blockchain-based storage system for data analytics in the internet of things. In New Advances in the Internet of Things (pp. 119–138). Springer, Cham.

[27] Davidsen, M., Gajek, S., Kruse, M. and Thomsen, S., 2018. Empowering the economy of things.

[28] Chakraborty, R.B., Pandey, M. and Rautaray, S.S., 2018. Managing computation load on a blockchain-based multi-layered internet-of-things network. *Procedia Computer Science*, 132, pp. 469–476.

[29] Singh, S., Ra, I.H., Meng, W., Kaur, M. and Cho, G.H., 2019. SH-BlockCC: A secure and efficient Internet of things smart home architecture based on cloud computing and blockchain technology. *International Journal of Distributed Sensor Networks*, 15(4), p. 1550147719844159.

[30] Chen, Y., Ding, S., Xu, Z., Zheng, H. and Yang, S., 2019. Blockchain-based medical records secure storage and medical service framework. *Journal of Medical Systems*, 43(1), p. 5.

[31] Ajao, L.A., Agajo, J., Adedokun, E.A. and Karngong, L., 2019. Crypto hash algorithm-based blockchain technology for managing decentralized ledger database in oil and gas industry. *J Multidisciplinary Scientific Journal*, 2(3), pp. 300–325.

[32] Singh, S., Sharma, P.K., Yoon, B., Shojafar, M., Cho, G.H. and Ra, I.H., 2020. Convergence of blockchain and artificial intelligence in IoT network for the sustainable smart city. *Sustainable Cities and Society*, 63, p. 102364.

[33] Lee, Y., Rathore, S., Park, J.H. and Park, J.H., 2020. A blockchain-based smart home gateway architecture for preventing data forgery. *Human-centric Computing and Information Sciences*, 10(1), pp. 1–14.

[34] Cheng, X., Chen, F., Xie, D., Sun, H. and Huang, C., 2020. Design of a secure medical data sharing scheme based on blockchain. *Journal of Medical Systems*, 44(2), p. 52.

[35] Tamilarasi, K. and Jawahar, A., 2020. Medical data security for healthcare applications using hybrid lightweight encryption and swarm optimization algorithm. *Wireless Personal Communications*, pp. 1–22.

[36] Gul, M.J., Subramanian, B., Paul, A. and Kim, J., 2020. Blockchain for public health care in smart society. *Microprocessors and Microsystems*, p. 103524.

[37] Rouhani, S., Butterworth, L., Simmons, A.D., Humphery, D.G. and Deters, R., 2018, July. MediChain TM: a secure decentralized medical data asset management system. In 2018 IEEE International Conference on Internet of Things (iThings) and IEEE Green Computing and Communications (GreenCom) and IEEE Cyber, Physical and Social Computing (CPSCom) and IEEE Smart Data (SmartData) (pp. 1533–1538). IEEE.

[38] Lee, S.H. and Yang, C.S., 2018. Fingernail analysis management system using microscopy sensor and blockchain technology. *International Journal of Distributed Sensor Networks*, 14(3), p. 1550147718767044.

[39] Ebrahim, M., Khan, S. and Khalid, U.B., 2014. Symmetric algorithm survey: a comparative analysis. arXiv preprint arXiv:1405.0398.

[40] Lim, C.H. and Korkishko, T., 2005, August. mCrypton–a lightweight block cipher for security of low-cost RFID tags and sensors. In International Workshop on Information Security Applications (pp. 243–258). Springer, Berlin, Heidelberg.

[41] Panarello, A., Tapas, N., Merlino, G., Longo, F. and Puliafito, A., 2018. Blockchain and IoT integration: A systematic survey. *Sensors*, 18(8), p. 2575.

[42] Lefebvre, F., Czyz, J. and Macq, B., 2003, September. A robust soft hash algorithm for digital image signature. In Proceedings 2003 International Conference on Image Processing (Cat. No. 03CH37429) (Vol. 2, pp. II–495). IEEE.

[43] Pittalia, P.P., 2019. A comparative study of hash algorithms in cryptography. *International Journal of Computer Science and Mobile Computing*, 8(6), pp. 147–152.

[44] Timothy, D.P. and Santra, A.K., 2017, August. A hybrid cryptography algorithm for cloud computing security. In 2017 International Conference on Microelectronic Devices, Circuits and Systems (ICMDCS) (pp. 1–5). IEEE.

[45] Ajao, L.A., Agajo, J., Adedokun, E.A. and Karngong, L., 2019. Crypto hash algorithm-based blockchain technology for managing decentralized ledger database in oil and gas industry. *Multidisciplinary Scientific Journal*, 2(3), pp. 300–325.

[46] Alotaibi, M., Al-hendi, D., Alroithy, B., AlGhamdi, M. and Gutub, A., 2019. Secure mobile computing authentication utilizing hash, cryptography and steganography combination. *Journal of Information Security and Cybercrimes Research (JISCR)*, 2(1).

[47] Kale, A.M. and Dhamdhere, S., 2018. Survey paper on different type of hashing algorithm. *International Journal of Advance Scientific Research Algorithm*, 3(2).

[48] Kheshaifaty, N. and Gutub, A., 2020. Preventing multiple accessing attacks via efficient integration of captcha crypto hash functions. *IJCSNS*, 20(9), pp. 16–28.

[49] Liu, H., Kadir, A. and Liu, J., 2019. Keyed hash function using hyper chaotic system with time-varying parameters perturbation. *IEEE Access*, 7, pp. 37211–37219.

[50] Zaru, Z.A. and Khan, M., 2018. General summary of cryptography. *Journal of Engineering Research and Application,* 8(2), pp. 68–71.

[51] Rajasekar, V., Premalatha, J. and Sathya, K., 2020. Multi-factor signcryption scheme for secure authentication using hyper elliptic curve cryptography and bio-hash function. *Bulletin of the Polish Academy of Sciences Technical Sciences*, 68(4), pp. 923–935.

[52] Jyothi, V.E., Prasad, B.D.C.N. and Mojjada, R.K., 2020, December. Analysis of Cryptography Encryption for Network Security. In IOP Conference Series: Materials Science and Engineering (Vol. 981, No. 2, p. 022028). IOP Publishing.

[53] Debnath, S., Chattopadhyay, A. and Dutta, S., 2017, November. Brief review on journey of secured hash algorithms. In 2017 4th International Conference on Opto-Electronics and Applied Optics (Optronix) (pp. 1–5). IEEE.

[54] Gnatyuk, S., Kinzeryavyy, V., Kyrychenko, K., Yubuzova, K., Aleksander, M. and Odarchenko, R., 2018, October. Secure hash function constructing for future communication systems and networks. In International Conference of Artificial Intelligence, Medical Engineering, Education (pp. 561–569). Springer, Cham.

[55] Harer, F., 2018. Decentralized business process modeling and instance tracking secured by a blockchain.

[56] Agrawal, T.K., Sharma, A. and Kumar, V., 2018. Blockchain-based secured traceability system for textile and clothing supply chain. In Artificial intelligence for fashion industry in the big data era (pp. 197–208). Springer, Singapore.

4 Introduction to Blockchain Technology and Its Role in the Healthcare Sector

Sumit Koul and Tulasi Krishna

CONTENTS

4.1 INTRODUCTION

Blockchain is an unchangeable and transparent digital asset using cryptographic hashing and decentralization. Blockchain technology can be understood through the example of a Google Doc. After the creation of a Google Doc, it can be shared with a group of people, distributed rather than being copied and moved, thus creating a decentralized distribution chain where everyone can use the document at once. All changes are recorded in real time, thus enabling transparent modifications so that no one would have to wait for another party. Parties access the document whenever they wish. Blockchain technology helps in risk reduction, protects from fraud, and provides transparency in a scalable way for numerous uses. The example of a Google Doc is less complicated than blockchain, but the analogy is appropriate as it exemplifies three critical concepts of the technology given in Figure 4.1.

DOI: 10.1201/9781003166511-4

55

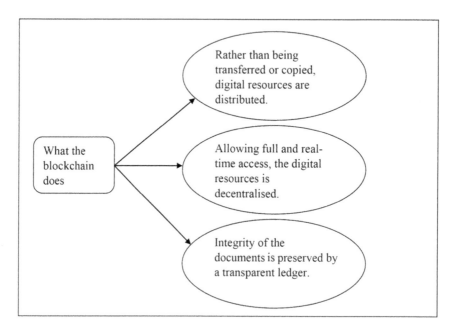

FIGURE 4.1   Role of blockchain.

Blockchain was initially created for the cryptocurrency Bitcoin to be operated on as a ledger system, providing enough transparency. With time, however, it has been adopted in numerous areas such as in Ethereum blockchain due to security and transparency it provides. Vitalik Buterin, a Russian-Canadian developer, published a white paper in late 2013, proposing a platform integrating computer code in blockchain functionality, giving birth to Ethereum, a platform on which developers can create programs to communicate on the blockchain. Tokens represent any type of digital asset, can execute functionality as per programming instructions, and can track ownership; tokens can be created by Ethereum programmers. Tokens can be concert tickets, contracts, music files, or even patient medical records. This has widened scope of blockchain to infuse further sectors such as government, media, as well as identity security. Many corporations are presently developing and researching products as well as ecosystems that work completely on this burgeoning technology. As applied in the Ethereum blockchain, smart contracts are enrichments to blockchain technology and provide code directly to control connections or redistributions of the assets, like crypto-tokens or pieces of data, between multiple parties, as per predefined rules between the involved parties. Ethereum blockchain can store data objects and enable expansion of applications to interact with blockchains and can be applied, in the healthcare domain, to improve care coordination.

Healthcare technology should communicate securely, provide effective care delivery, and exchange data appropriately, for instance, through access to electronic health records (EHRs). However, healthcare researchers face delayed communications, fragmented data, and different workflow tools. Providers face reluctance to exchange data because of possible liability and financial penalties associated with data sharing and perceived notions that it harms patient information security guidelines. Moreover, mismatched, and vendor-specific health systems make it difficult to coordinate and ensure patient-centric care due to communication gaps. Another problem pertains to the shortage of safe connections to autonomous health systems for creating reachable networks while maintaining privacy. Basic interoperability for data exchange between systems is provided by standards such as Health Level 7 (HL7) and Fast Healthcare Interoperability Resources (FHIR), however, this is restricted to applied standards and, in addition, requires data mapping among maximum possible systems. These systems are extremely difficult to maintain because a change in interface by one party further requires other parties to adapt as well. There are some limitations to attaining healthcare system interoperability including incompatible software and the insufficient access to data outside the healthcare environment, such as clinic databases protected by a firewall. The cure to such problems is the employment of blockchain technology, which gives transactions via decentralization with pseudo-anonymity. However, deploying blockchain technology involves certain complexities.

Blockchain has been coined by many researchers including Ahram et al. (2017) using bitcoin the new technology that was introduced is the blockchain technology. It offers a secure way for transactions. Blockchain is introduced to several fields such as smart contract, health care, supply chain etc. The security of data and the currency is a challenge to the blockchain. With the help of application programming interface (API), the data can be protected. Casino et al. (2019) has provided an organized analysis of all applications based on the technologies like blockchain in numerous domains aiming to investigate the current state of blockchain automation with its implementations. Further highlights of some descriptions of blockchain automation can modernize the daily routines of various businesses. For this purpose, Casino analysed a large number of research papers from reputed journals during the previous decade and numerous reports from grey literature in this literature review.

This chapter presents a comprehensive study and classification of all the applications based on blockchain technology across numerous fields such as healthcare, business, supply chain, data management, and privacy based on an organized and planned content analysis, further highlighting the main path as well as ongoing research in arising areas. In addition, this chapter highlights the limitations of technology across various industries and sectors identified in the literature. Based on the outcome, this chapter points to the research gap and further explorable possibilities of the technology, both from the practitioner and academic point of view.

Efanov and Roschin (2018) studied that blockchain technology is a highly innovative technology and its application is wide spread. Bitcoin, the first cryptocurrency, was based on blockchain automation. Blockchain can be described as public ledger. The data are saved in blocks that register bitcoin transactions. Blockchain has the property of decentralization. Blockchain has developed in stages: Digitization of currency is known as blockchain 1.0, blockchain 2.0 is based on digitization of the financial system, and blockchain 3.0 was in field of digital society. The security of data was one of the main issues faced by blockchain and it can be resolved by cryptographic hash. Maesa and Mori (2020) discuss the application of blockchain 3.0.

Blockchain is a technology which is emerging in almost every field of industry today. The term distributed ledger is also known as decentralized ledger. Assuming the trust among the participants, the facts as well as figures are accessible to many participants and also administered by them. Blockchain is one of the technologies used for implementing a decentralized ledger. The data are entered in blocks, which have a header and body to enter the data. The data is tamper-proof and cryptographic hash are used for securing the data. Blockchain transfers the values between various parties in moves called transactions. The main issue discussed here about blockchain is its scalability and efficiency. The properties of blockchain discussed here are atomicity, synchronicity, availability, immutability, and immortality. The blockchain can be used in the sectors of supply chain management, decentralized notary, electoral voting, health care, identity management systems, access control systems, etc. Numerous applications of Blockchain 3.0 show that this technology is still on trend after a few years from its birth and indicates that there is potential of it progressing in the coming years.

Mohsin et al. (2019) empathizes that security of the data is one of the important aspects to consider while transferring data. For decades, the security of data was a hurdle before the developments in technology. Most people think that if data is saved with password, then the data is authenticated. These passwords can be cracked and the data can be leaked. The best technology to secure data is the use of encryption. Using digital rights management, commercial domains and digital content can be protected. The popular blockchain platforms are Bitcoin (BTC), Ethereum, Monero, ICON, Steem, etc. Blockchain technology offers efficiency, security, resilience, transparency, and security. In researching this chapter, it was found that information in the form of publications or the percentage of IEEE publications associated with blockchain research increased each year since 2013. The proposed model delivers a complete investigation of the present work, which further provides the importance and significance of blockchain as well as its nomenclature in various related fields. The study also investigated the application and various functions to facilitate the usage of blockchain. Viriyasitavat and Hoonsopon (2019) have shown blockchain is one of the technologies that is changing the industry. The rise of blockchain applications is widespread in fields like medicine, insurance, Internet of Things (IoT), etc.

The invention of blockchain has made many changes in the fields of business. The main element in blockchain technology is its agreement for sharing information, replication, and transactions among the users and it is widely used in business process management. Blockchain is decentralized, resistant to tampering, and is unchangeable. Digital signatures and cryptographic hash are used to secure data. Consensus is an agreement among the groups of nodes on the integrity of the information. Properties of consensus are safety, liveness, fault tolerance etc. After that, we suggest a design including key technologies based on the features, and further the guidelines regarding the innovation of various businesses processes in the era of blockchain. The basic elements of this design for overcoming time inconsistency is the use of practical Byzantine fault tolerance (PBFT) by way of smart contracts as well as the bias arising about nodes to perform consensus, thus making the consensus more flexible and reliable at the same time, that responds to the user needs in the field of business process interoperation in a better way. Koul (2021) has explained characteristics of the machine learning as well as deep learning in the field of agriculture and considered its different methods. Yaga et al. (2018) emphasizes that blockchain is one of the new emerging technologies in the hub of technology. Big data can be stored in blockchain, making it tamper-resistant and decentralized. In blockchain, data is entered in blocks and can be transferred to the other organizations without delay. The technology of Bitcoin widely spread in 2009. The data entered in blocks are in a encrypted manner. Hashing is the method of applying cryptographic hash function of data. Data are entered in a digital ledger and it is saved in blocks with each block having a block data as well as a block header. These blocks are chained together, hence the term blockchain. Once the data is entered, it cannot be altered. There are many applications in many fields, such as healthcare and finance, where future blockchain technology has widespread application to all field of industry. Yang (2019) has explained the blockchain concept and its importance in various fields. The main concerns are safety, application of blockchain, and IoT with regard to blockchain's use in business and its possible real-world challenges. A rapid increase in its research makes it more valuable compared to existing technologies such as machine learning, deep learning, big data etc.

Blockchain is a peer-to-peer (P2P) data prototype where the information is stored in blocks in a chronological manner. Blockchain began its development with cryptocurrency and now uses Ethereum blockchain with smart contracts; in the future, blockchain can be utilized in the research ecosystem for the next stage of blockchain advancement. Blockchain consists of six layers: data, network, consensus, contract, service, and applications. The characteristics of blockchain discussed here are decentralization, security, transparency, traceability, immutable, anonymity, and authentication. Blockchain-based platforms include Ethereum and Hyperledger. The security of data in blockchain can be ensured through a P2P network, asymmetric encryption, a distributed ledger, or smart contracts. Blockchain technology is used in fields of finance, health care, and in 5G networks. The challenges in this field are technical challenges, in consensus mechanisms, its scalability, capacity, chain structures etc. Zheng et al. (2017) emphasize that innovation in blockchain has brought many changes in almost every industry. Blockchain can be considered a digital ledger that helps feed and secure data in a safe manner. Security and scalability are chief concerns and are easily tackled with the help of blockchain automations. Since the Bitcoin block size was limited to one megabyte, every 10 minutes, the block is mined and it restricted to seven transactions. Here the authors speak about blockchain automations. A user earns two types of keys, a private key and a public key. The main distinctiveness of blockchain is its decentralization, anonymity, tenacity, and controllability. The blockchain can be categorized into three types: private blockchain, public blockchain, and consortium blockchain. Sectors like finance, health care, and IoT used blockchain to enhance their working capabilities with minimum losses as well as to procure data.

4.2 COMPONENTS OF BLOCKCHAIN

Blockchain is based on three chief concepts: blocks, nodes, and miners. Figure 4.2 shows blockchain components.

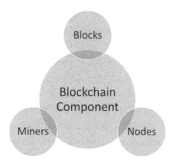

FIGURE 4.2   Components of blockchain.

4.2.1   BLOCKS

Each chain comprises several blocks, with each block having three basic elements. First, every block contains information. Second, creation of the block allows the generation of a nonce as well as a block header hash. A nonce is a whole number that is 32 bits. Third, a nonce is linked with hash, also a whole number, which is 256 bits and must be enormously small. On the formation of foremost block of the chain, cryptographic hash is obtained by the nonce. Once the data is assigned to the block, it is attached with hash and the nonce continuously unless and until it is extracted.

4.2.2   NODES

Decentralization is an important concept of blockchain technology. The chain cannot be owned by an individual computer or an organization, rather it is a distributed ledger connected to the chain via nodes. Nodes are electronic devices responsible for the functioning of the network to newly mined blocks that are updated and verified by the chain while maintaining their own copies of the blockchains. The ledger allows easy checking and viewing of every action because every participant is provided with a number showing transactions, namely, the unique identification number. The integrity of blockchain and trust can be maintained by exposing public information via a system of checks and balances. Hence, blockchains ensure scalability of trust through technology.

4.2.3   MINERS

Mining is a procedure by which novel blocks are formed to make a chain. Mining a block of chain is a tedious process, particularly for huge chains, because blocks not only have their own hash and nonce, but also because each block denotes hash of the preceding block. Special software is, therefore, preferred to solve highly the complex problem of finding a nonce for generating an accepted hash. Before finding the correct nonce–hash combination, about 4 billion potential combinations must be mined since hash is 256 bits and nonce is just 32 bits. This nonce is then called the "golden nonce" and once it is found, the block could be added to chain. If the change is desired on any block of the chain, then not only the desired block, but all succeeding blocks must be re-mined. Thus, blockchain technology is extremely difficult to be manipulated, requiring a lot of time and computing power. Upon successful mining of a block, all nodes accept the change.

4.3 BACKGROUND OF BLOCKCHAIN

Though it is a new technology, blockchain already claims a great history. The timeline of some significant and noteworthy events in this technology's development are given in Table 4.1.

TABLE 4.1

Historical Timeline of Blockchain Technology

2008	Satoshi Nakamoto works on purely electronic online currency systems, with popular names such as Bitcoin. He has given the concept of Bitcoin (BTC) for individuals.
2009	First BTC transaction between Nakamoto and Hal Finney (a computer scientist).
2010	A programmer named as Laszlo Hanycez in Florida successfully purchased two pizzas from Papa John's with help of Bitcoin. He transferred 10,000 bitcoins, valued at about 60 USD at that time, but 80 million USD today. It is assumed that BTC market cap exceeds $1 million.
2011	One bitcoin is equal to 1 USD, thereby creating the cryptocurrency parity with USD. An initiative was taken by many organizations such as Wikileaks to collect bitcoin as aid.
2012	Famous television shows such as 'The Good Wife' mention blockchain and cryptocurrency, adding technology into pop culture. Vitalik Buterin, an early Bitcoin developer, launched Bitcoin Magazine.
2013	The Bitcoin market cap exceeded 1 billion USD officially. For the first time, BTC has achieved 100 USD per bitcoin value. Initially, BTC has a main role in blockchain, but other potential uses like smart contracts, patient records, etc., are shown in a whitepaper by Vitalik Buterin about the Ethereum Project.
2014	Companies such as The D Las Vegas hotel, Zynga, and Overstock.com, all start to consider BTC as a method of payment. A great achievement by Vitalik Buterin is the Ethereum Project generating more than 18 million USD in bitcoin. By doing this, there are lots of chances for blockchain to introduce new concepts with enhancements. R3, with more than 200 blockchain businesses, is designed to devise novel ways in which blockchain can be applied in technology. In addition, PayPal shows interest in BTC.
2015	More than one lakh vendors accept the concept of bitcoin. Blockchain theme is analysed by share traders in private cooperation like San Francisco, National Association of Securities Dealers Automated Quotations (NASDAQ) companies, etc.
2016	IBM declares a blockchain plan for cloud-based solutions. Japan's government approves the authenticity of blockchain and cryptocurrencies.
2017	Bitcoin attains high worth at 1,000 USD per bitcoin for the first time. A 150 million USD mark is reached for the cryptocurrency market. Jamie Dimon, the CEO of JPMorgan Chase, says that blockchain can give better answers to the queries in future, thus providing the ledger system with an assurance from the Wall Street. Bitcoin reaches 19,783.21 USD per bitcoin for first time. Arab countries like Dubai make a commitment to use blockchain by 2020 in their administration.
2018	A social media sites like Facebook show interest in blockchain and also introduce its own cryptocurrency. A banking platform is developed by IBM based on blockchain along with Barclays and Citibank.

4.4   BLOCKCHAIN IN HEALTH CARE

Blockchain is a system for the storage and sharing of information that is secured due to its transparency. Each block in the chain is both its own dependent link in the collective chain as well as independent unit consisting of its own information, and this forms a network controlled by members who share and store the information, instead of third party. Blockchain technology has a lot of uses in the health care sector, including enhancing capabilities in various subsectors such as the use of wearable health devices and tracking gadgets keeping health information up-to-date, and storing and backing up data digitally. Blockchain research in health care is at the moment is inadequate. However, blockchain is on the brink of enhancing the healthcare sector with the of decentralization which makes it easy to understand. It also accounts to safety of patient records and it will change the hierarchy of healthcare. This means a novel structure is constructed for patients in which they can care themselves. Two major issues, namely, data ownership and its security, need to be addressed in health care today. There is a deficiency of secured structure for sensitive medical data, leading to possible data-breaches, which have severe consequences. The Office for Civil Rights (OCR) of the US Department of Health and Human Services recorded a lot of information breaches that led to exposure about 13 million healthcare records in 2018. Moreover, the Ponemon Institute steered a study on behalf of IBM Security, revealing that the total mean cost of such data exceeded 7.91 million USD in the United States, where the health sector topped the per capita cost (Ponemon Institute, [Cost of Data Breach Study, 2018]). Another issue is the notion that patients have complete ownership of their medical information, with this notion increasing relative to the increase of personalized wearables and medicines. Both issues have led to noteworthy moral consequences that need to be studied. Technology like blockchain is the perfect way of providing the answer. Blockchain technology provides a system that is protected by many layers and cannot be hacked easily. Moreover, each layer has its own system to access data. This suggests that to record data, the blockchain provides an everlasting solution, attach free and verified systems which provides the authenticity to users. Blockchain is a mechanism in which transactions are recorded in a decentralized mechanism of ledgers. A block, which is immutable, is connected to another block to form a group that is concurrent with cryptographic hashes. For example, if a person wishes a transaction there remains the security of the passwords and also makes the data confidential. This confidentiality remains restricted to the user and is used for the users interest. These personal password keys are obtained by linear arithmetical function, typically elliptic curve multiplication. Then, the transaction is broadcasted to P2P system of miners and nodes, which is a group of transactions to form a block. A miner is always a full node, but a node is not always a miner. Each miner then competes to solve an acknowledged hash-output of the transactions encoded in the block.

There is a need of blockchain in healthcare. The lack of a central administrator is the biggest reason that makes the blockchain technology revolutionary. This is because of the tangibility of the database that consists of bits and bytes. When the database contents are stored in the system's physical memory, its data can become corrupted by anyone who has access to the system. The requirement of a central administrator is removed using cryptography with blockchain technology. Moreover, the users have control over their transactions and data. As healthcare involves sensitive patient data and requires quick accessibility of such information, these records can be streamlined by blockchain and sharing can be securely enabled. This technology offers data privacy, security, and scalability in one place. The blockchain concept in health care seems to be an evolutionary journey, implementing the technology in steps. Disparately, blockchain technology is an emerging technology which can improve the healthcare sector and can shows significance results. There are many subsectors in health care needing to be enhanced. From these subsectors, some of the beneficial points are outlined in next sections.

4.4.1   RECORDS OF INDIVIDUALS OR GROUPS OF PATIENTS

Accessing of longitudinal patient records that require compilation of medical data including disease registries, lab outcomes, and treatments can be done with the help of blockchain, including wearable and ambulatory data that assist providers to better deliver care and maintenance.

4.4.2   MASTER PATIENT INDICES

Often, information can be duplicated or mismatched in health care. For every field, different EHRs have different schemata, leading to different ways to enter and manipulate data. By using the blockchain technology the preservation of data is specific. For every individual the information pertaining to that individual cannot be mismatched with the data related to other party. The user can easily specify about the required data and that can be attained by its specific address.

4.4.3   ADJUDICATING CLAIMS

As blockchain technology works on exchange-based validation, it can automatically verify the claims where there is agreement between the network and the original request for data. Additionally, as there is no central authority, fewer errors are estimated.

4.4.4   MANAGEMENT OF SUPPLY CHAIN

Contracts based on blockchain technology can help the management to synchronize the supply – and demand cycles throughout whole period of days or months or years without any major interruption. Transaction through blockchain technology benefits the healthcare organizations to get better outcome with a minimum loss as well as reduced the delays.

4.4.5   INTEROPERABILITY

Blockchain technology is becoming more reliable with the concept of interoperability. EHR interoperability can easily manage with blockchain technology. The processing of the storing the data is reliable. The costs and burden linked with data reconciliation can be eliminated by the sharing of the blockchain network with authorized providers in a standardized and a secure way.

Apart from these, blockchain can transform the management of revenue cycles, drug supply, and clinical trials. The way ahead for blockchain's use in health care relies on the willingness of healthcare establishments to create the needed technical infrastructure. This technology is expensive and there are concerns related to its integration with present technology and speculation about its social adoption.

Blockchain has revolutionized health care over the last year along with significant investments. Blockchain seems to transform the big-data world. Abu-elezz et al. (2019) discuss some of the advantages and disadvantages of blockchain applications to the healthcare sector. Abu-elezz et al. has discussed the use of blockchain in healthcare sector and also has focused on how the blockchain technology is applicable in protecting the information regarding medical field (patients' data). It is a developed data structure where the data are stored in blocks. Every block contains four elements, namely, hash of the current block, data, timestamp, and former block. Numerous types of blockchain technology are present now. Abu-elezz et al. has considered study in blockchain technology form 2017 onwards and studied the existing literature form various journals such as IEEE, Springer, PubMed and Science Direct. The collected data is processed for filtering for which there are three phases: identification, screening, and eligibility. Next come data extraction and synthesis. As a result, 84 studies were found and of those only 70 were found to be unique; the others were removed. After another selection procedure, 37 studies were considered for this research. From these studies the benefits of blockchain technology were found to be security and authorization, personalized health care, assistance in monitoring patient status, aid in tracking and transmission of patient health data, and management of medical insurance, clinical trials opportunities, and pharmaceutical supply chain etc. Along with these benefits there are some threats to using the technology including issues of authorization, security, high energy consumption, scalability, slow processing speed, and insufficient technical skills.

Alkhushyni et al. (2019) emphasized that the healthcare industry is significantly affected by the world becoming more digitized, where one can record and save all the data in computers or mobile devices. The issue of recording healthcare data can be resolved by introducing blockchain technology. Authors discussed the usability of technology software for electronic healthcare records. It was not possible to assure the safety of data in the current state as healthcare records are not connected. Many patients are not willing to provide all their personal details to researchers. The transferring of health data from one healthcare institution to another is typically achieved through fax or postal mail. If patients were stored in blockchain, it will help healthcare institutions to receive patient data quickly and securely through a blockchain private key. The institutions' EHR have to provide privacy policies to assure the safety and security of patient information. To do this, first the healthcare organization must store information on blockchain, then the transaction is completed and uniquely identified and is now ready for the institution to directly make queries to the blockchain. Finally, the patient can specifically authorize any individual to access their medical information.

Badr et al. (2018) has considered blockchain as one of most emerging techniques in many fields. Blockchain resolves the issues of security. In this paper, the author presents the idea of pseudonym-based encryption with different authorities (PBE-DA), which ensures the validity of EHRs. PBE-DA helps to create a virtual identity for patients that helps to hide the actual identity from the cloud database. The PBE-DA has a high degree of efficiency and security for EHR systems. Security of IoT devices is a challenge for cybersecurity. The blockchain like Hyperledger fabric provides strong agreement. Badr et al. studied different technologies that help blockchain to be more efficient. Three tiers of architecture based on blockchain are considered as well as investigated. The first layer connects the patient with the IoT device through the gateway. The second layer is the ledger that shares the information between the providers of the EHRs. In the last layer, the conformity concerns are defined among different EHR contributor.

Chen et al. (2019) has considered leakage of data from EHRs as a major problem. Blockchain helps to store the data in blocks using cryptography algorithms to ensure data security. Different medical organizations can access the EHRs stored on the blockchain and the data is encrypted and entered in a cloud server. The searchable symmetric encryption (SSE) scheme is a noninteractive scheme that scans potential encrypted files and compares the keywords to determine whether they exist in the scanned files. This scheme is based on a single keyword system. SSE can detect malicious behavior of outside servers. In this paper, Chen et al. discuss smart contracts in Ethereum, which is a computer-based program that enforces the negotiation of a contract by digitally facilitating the transaction without the help of third parties. The transactions can be tracked and they are irreversible. It provides security to the contract law and cost of transactions can be reduced. In Ethereum, the smart contracts can be accessed via a small calculation on blockchain or the distributed ledger. The first implementation in blockchain has introduced which is known as Ethereum. Ethereum blockchain has built-in turing complete virtual machine set up. Using ethereum blockchain, a block can be created or deleted for the system. This reflects that the analysis of security and data becomes feasible and effective. This reflects that the analysis of security and data becomes feasible and effective. EMR systems are based on blockchain technology. EMRs are secure, accessible as well as controlled by the patient. Within the system, the patient can record data and send to it to a healthcare provider within seconds regardless of distance. The mobile application introduced in this study is called Healthcare Data Gateway and it uses a simplified technique called Indicator-centric Schema to collect and organize the data and secure the data from the third party entity. Blockchain in the field of health care helps to feed and transfer the information securely and easily.

Dagher et al. (2018) discuss blockchain in the field of healthcare as a great advancement that helps to digitally record patient data and can transfer the data to other healthcare providers in a secure manner. Anciles is a database framework with the ability to interact with the third parties in a secure manner. Like EHRs, Anciles also stores in hashes and sends the link of query in hypertext transfer protocol secure (https). Anciles focuses more on the ownership rights of the patients. Finally, the blockchain automation works on a consensus algorithm and it increases the rationale as soon as nodes are added to the system. Wood, G. (2014a, 2014b) limitations of EHR are, first, the collusion of 51% of mining nodes that results in rewriting the structure. Secondly, unauthorised persons can access the secure system. Lastly, storing of large data may contain higher cost because of distributed system in blockchain. The software used by Ancile is made up of the Database Manager, Cipher Manager and Ethereum-Go Client. Ancile can solve some of the limitations of EHR but it is not a permanent solution.

Ekblaw et al. (2016) discuss a blockchain automation that can be applied to EHRs. They have addressed four core issues related to MedRec, such as disintegration; slow access of data based on medical and patient agency; interoperability; and how the quality of data and research in medical is enhanced. In the MedRec block, data ownership and viewership permissions are sent between the P2P network and the member's of private network. Smart contracts on Ethereum help in the patient-provider relationship, which gives permission to access the data. By using cryptographic hashes, the data security is ensured. Here, providers can add relevant data for patients and the patient can transfer the data to providers. Hasselgren et al. (2020) using bitcoin, the blockchain technology was introduced. Impact of blockchain in the field of healthcare is increasing rapidly. Block chain feeds the data in block and it is linked with the previous and future blocks and the data are entered in a cryptographic manner in order to secure the data. Blockchain is decentralized and persistent. Blockchain is of three types, namely, public, private, and consortium. Ethereum supports smart contracts. Smart contracts reduce the third party influence which makes the data more secure and efficient. In healthcare sector the blockchain get used with EHR, clinical trial system and PHR. Hyperledger fabric and Ethereum are the mostly used platforms in blockchain. The access of data, data integrity, provenance and interoperability are issues that have to be improved in the field of blockchain.

According to Heston (2017), Estonia was one of the first countries to identify the potential of blockchain technology. Blockchain can control financial transactions securely. Along with Guardtime, a data security company, Estonia secured the healthcare records of 1 million citizens. The introduction of blockchain in healthcare helps to reduce the cost of medical expenses and better insurance claim coordination took place. The project in Estonia was a success because of the ability of keeping the medical records secure without affecting the security the data was able to share with the other medical providers and companies for insurance. As technology grows, so too does the use of blockchain technology. In 2009, Bitcoin began with a single bitcoin and now grew to more than 4,331 coins by 2017.

Hussein et al. (2018) discuss how the data stored in EHR may affect security because the data stored in cloud storage completely safeguarded. Here, the system prefers to use a modified cryptography hash generator to guarantee the safety. The modified cryptography uses discrete wavelet transform to create a new sequence of data. Discreet wavelet transform (DWT) use a genetic algorithm (GA) to minimize the time of transition node whenever data request is chosen and which is reliable as well. WT helps to attain accurate time information about the frequency. The cryptography hash rationale is characterized as deterministic and changeable with rapid calculations. The proposed system in this paper contains six parts: network node, cryptographic hash generator, request for queuing, operations based on GA technology, database and the blockchain structure. The proposed system has more security and it can resist various attacks compared to other systems. This proposed system has more scalability, immunity, security and robustness.

Liu et al. (2019) consider how the healthcare field is becoming more digitized every day and EHR has become one of the most needed tools in the medical field. EHR feeds data and helps to transfer the data to other medical organization. The blockchain-based EHR is more secure and it is decentralized. The existing schemes in blockchain technology have some drawbacks, including the schemes giving framework only and not returning the implementation details and the high cost of computation. In this paper, the authors briefly discuss the blockchain and some techniques related to it. Blockchain is one of the advanced technologies that helps to save large amount of data in a secure manner. Blockchain has three types: public, consortium, and private. Some features of blockchain are decentralization, resistance against feed tampering, openness, autonomy, and anonymity. In the medical field, the basic requirements for sharing data are security and privacy protection, data access, patient control, and unified standard. Delegated Proof of Stake is a consensus mechanism to make sure that all the legitimate nodes have the same global ledger. Proxy re-encryption guarantees the safety of the facts as well as figures. The proposed system by Liu et al. discussed that the patients who are having same symptoms of diseases can contact to discuss about their disease. Moreover, it satisfies many of the requirements that the patient needs with minimum cost of communication.

Omar et al. (2019) found that in the medical field, data are now stored in EHR, which saves data in the cloud. But saving data in the cloud is not secure as there can be cyberattacks at any time. The chief aim is to discuss a client-friendly cloud-based system that is more secure and integrative. Pseudonymity of data can be achieved using cryptography. Pseudonymity means any input cannot recognize any kind of party in the defined set-up since the client is protected by the robust key. The system uses elliptic curve cryptography and this process follows as first the operator sends a request to the system with a defined user name and password. After these are entered into the system, the information will be stored in a private accessible unit (PAU), which is sent by the operator. Next, the blockchain receives a unique identification number from the PAU and returns the same unique identification number to access in future. This unique identification number helps in finding the particular block in which information will be received. The operator then receives that unique identification number from PAU, which is obtained through blockchain. Now the operator has to sign in to send the data and acceptor has to do the same process for collecting the information. Finally, the acceptor gets the information through the PAU.

Zubaydi et al. (2019) emphasizes that blockchain is the process of feeding data in ledger in a digital manner. All the transactions in blockchain are recorded and approved because transaction is valid whenever an authorised person is agreeing to give consensus to the end-user. The Ethereum blockchain supports transaction of various applications. The medical-related applications are mostly based on the Ethereum platform. The data recorded in EHRs can be transferred securely and it helps to transfer and manage data to the peers without a central authority. Blockchain works along with concepts of smart contracts make the blockchain stronger. Blockchain allows patients to control their data and provides a secure and robust platform from malicious attack. In this paper, the authors review the system based on security, privacy, and efficiency. The implementation of blockchain in the healthcare domain is a pervasive social network (PSN)-based health system, record management system, data-sharing system, medical data and privacy preserving platform, and mobile application architecture. The paper discusses the advantages and limitations in these fields.

4.5 MAJOR COMPANIES ASSOCIATED WITH BLOCKCHAIN IN HEALTH CARE

With its potential in reducing spending, protecting patient information, and improving the overall healthcare experience, blockchain appears to be a valuable tool in the healthcare industry. Blockchain technology is now doing a lot, from securely encrypting patient's information to managing harmful diseases. Estonia is well setup in terms of its capability of blockchain healthcare, as it initiated the use of blockchain technology in 2012 for securing healthcare information and processing transactions. Currently, the whole of its healthcare billing is carried out through blockchain and 99% of prescription data is digital, whereas to and 95% of health data 'in other regions' is based on ledger. The mishandling of patient data and records in healthcare comes with heavy costs, but blockchain handles it easily. Supply chain management plays an important role in healthcare. Blockchain can help in tracing of medicine and will be reach to right person within stipulated time. Blockchain technology is also helpful in genomic studies of various diseases, so that medical practitioner can correlate their study and will find out solution for complex problems (see Table 4.2).

Security is a major concern in the healthcare industry. More than 176 million patients' information was prone to data breaches between 2009 and 2017, resulting in stolen banking and credit card information as well as genomic and health testing records. The technology's potential at keeping decentralized, transparent, and incorruptible logs of patient information tends to make it common for security applications. In addition, blockchain is private and transparent, hiding an individual's identity with secured and complex codes that keeps information confidential. Its decentralization feature permits doctors, patients, and others involved in the process to share information safely and quickly. Miscommunication among health experts costs the healthcare industry $11 billion a year. Accessing patient records is a time-consuming process that delays patient care and drains staff resources. Medical records based on blockchain technology provide a cure to this problem. The decentralization feature of the technology creates a system of patient information that can be efficiently and quickly referenced by hospitals, doctors, and others involved in treatment. Thus, blockchain can enable faster personalized care and diagnostic strategies.

What amount of knowledge do we truly have about medicine? Are we certain it has not been meddled with? Is there a genuine supplier behind it? Such questions are key worries of the connection between business and the laboratory. Blockchain technology offers smart ideas for the management of supply chain of pharmaceutical companies; its decentralization almost warrants complete transparency in the distribution procedure. Upon the creation of a ledger for a drug, it marks the lab (i.e., a point of origin) and then continues recording the data along with details of every step of the process, including where it was and who managed it until it reaches the buyer. The procedure

TABLE 4.2

Blockchain Functionality and Its Application in Healthcare

Company	Place	Industry	Functions	Applicability of Blockchain	Effect on Real Life
BURSTIQ	Colorado Springs, Colorado	Big Data, Cybersecurity, Software	This platform assists healthcare companies in managing huge amounts of their data securely and safely. It uses blockchain technology to provide the safekeeping, sharing or licensing and trade of information, preserving strict adherence to HIPAA rules.	Blockchain technology is used to improve the way in which medical information is used and shared.	This platform includes comprehensive and updated data on patients and their healthcare issues, hence it assists in rooting out the misuse of opioids or other related drugs.
FACTOM	Austin, Texas	IT, Enterprise Software	This company develops products that benefit the health industry in storing data securely on some platform that is reachable by only healthcare administrators and hospitals. Physical papers holding patient data equip special security chips that open only to approved individuals.	This company uses blockchain technology for storing digital medical records in a secured manner.	United States Department of Homeland Security granted 200,000 USD for beta-testing a platform in June 2018 to integrate safe data from Border Patrol sensors and cameras for better understanding the effects of technology in the real world.
MEDICAL CHAIN	London, England	Electronic Health Record, Medical	It helps in maintaining integrity of medical records. Only laboratories, medical practitioners, and hospitals can request patient data, thus securing the data from unknown users.	This platform tends to maintain information of origin and, thus, safeguards patient confidentiality.	Medical chain launched MyClinic.com in May 2018. MyClinic is a telemedicine platform and assists patients in consulting their doctors via video and encourages payment with MedTokens.

(Continued)

TABLE 4.2 (Continued)
Blockchain Functionality and Its Application in Healthcare

Company	Place	Industry	Functions	Applicability of Blockchain	Effect on Real Life
GUARDTIME	Irvine, California	Cybersecurity, Blockchain	This platform helps governments and healthcare companies implement blockchain into cybersecurity methods. The company made important contributions toward Estonia's healthcare systems and has recently locked an arrangement with a private United Arab Emireate healthcare provider for applying blockchain to its security schemes.	It uses blockchain for cybersecurity functions involving the healthcare field.	It recently collaborated with Verizon Enterprise Solutions in deploying various platform services that are built on its KSI (Keyless Signature Infrastructure) blockchain.
SIMPLYVITAL HEALTH	Watertown, Massachusetts	AI, Blockchain, Enterprise Software, Personal Health	The company confers decentralized technology to the healthcare industry. Its platform, namely Nexus Health, is a open-source database that allows healthcare workers to access appropriate information. Open access helps the healthcare professionals in coordinating medical efforts faster than conventional methods.	It uses blockchain in creating open-source databases through which healthcare providers can help coordinate care and access patient data.	The company recently teamed with precision medicine and genomics company Shivom in forming a Global Healthcare Blockchain Alliance that utilizes blockchain for protecting DNA sequencing data.
CORAL HEALTHRESEARCH AND DISCOVERY	Vancouver, Canada	Healthcare, IT	Coral Health utilizes technology for enhancing care procedures, automating administrative procedures, and improving health results. It introduces patient information into a distributed ledger technology and brings together scientists, lab expert, doctors and community health officials seven times faster. It employs smart contract between healthcare professionals and patients for ensuring that data as well as treatments are correct.	This technology provides a more rapid care system, computerized secretarial organization, and it forms an elegant concord among doctors as well as patients	The company is exploring the opportunity by means of a blockchain as well as a smart fast healthcare interoperability resources (FHIR) protocol that confirms patients have all rights to track their medical records.

(Continued)

TABLE 4.2 (*Continued*)
Blockchain Functionality and Its Application in Healthcare

Company	Place	Industry	Functions	Applicability of Blockchain	Effect on Real Life
ROBOMED	Moscow, Russia	Blockchain, Medicine	It combines artificial intelligence and blockchain to offering one area of care to the patients, and applies wearable diagnostic tools, chatbots, and telemedicine sessions for gathering patient data and sharing it with their health officials. It also provides smart contracts to clients that describes benefit as well as shows ways to improve health.	This company uses blockchain forgathering patient data and sharing it securely with healthcare administrators.	Blockchain technology was recently employed by the Taipei Medical University Hospital, comprising Robomed's network, for storing and sharing patient records more securely.
PATIENTORY	Atlanta, Georgia	Blockchain, Cybersecurity, Healthcare, IT	It is ensured that client data is shared securely as well as effectively through end-to-end encryption, provided by Patientory. The platform enables patients and healthcare administrators to store, access, and transfer all significant information with blockchain technology and thus facilitate the healthcare workers to work more efficiently by holding all client data in single place.	It uses blockchain technology for providing secured storage and transferring significant medical data.	In a healthcare summit that assembled numerous healthcare professionals for discussing and learning healthcare applications based on blockchain, this company also hosted its first North American blockchain.

(Continued)

TABLE 4.2 (Continued)
Blockchain Functionality and Its Application in Healthcare

Company	Place	Industry	Functions	Applicability of Blockchain	Effect on Real Life
CHRONICLED	San Francisco, California	Blockchain, Supply Chain Management	The company establishes blockchain networks for demonstrating chain-of-custody, which helps pharmaceutical companies make sure that medicines are distributed proficiently and enable law-enforcement to check any questionable or illegal activity. Chronicled formed the MediLedger Project in 2017, which is a ledger system devoted to the privacy, security, and proficiency of medical supply chains.	This company ensures that the onset of a drug is to be secure. Also reassess of shipment of drugs.	Results from the company's recent MediLedger Project verify that its system is based on blockchain, can act as the interoperable system for the pharmaceutical supply chain, and can fulfil the data confidentiality needs of the pharmaceutical industry.
BLOCKPHARMA	Paris, France	Blockchain, Pharma-ceuticals, Supply Chain	Blockpharma offers the ability to trace a drug and, most importantly, those drugs that are counterfeit. The company's app can track counterfeit medicines and notify a patient quickly and easily. The company claims that their program can identify 15% of the world's counterfeit drugs with their SCM system, which is fully functioned by the blockchain.	Patients can be made aware of counterfeit drugs by using the company's app, purely based on blockchain techniques.	
TIERION	Mountain View, California	Saas, Blockchain	This company audits records, documents, and medicines for keeping clear history of ownership by using credentials and timestamps to keep proof of possession within a medical supply chain.	To keep a proper ownership history throughout medical supply chains, the company uses blockchain technology.	The company recently suggested a 'multinetwork coin' for making BTC more applicable and versatile.

(Continued)

TABLE 4.2 (*Continued*)
Blockchain Functionality and Its Application in Healthcare

Company	Place	Industry	Functions	Applicability of Blockchain	Effect on Real Life
Centers for Disease Control and Prevention (CDC)	Atlanta, Georgia	Government Agency, Healthcare, Security	The CDC uses blockchain for monitoring diseases in a supply-chain like way. According to the US government agency, blockchain's timestamps, data processing abilities, and peer-to-peer health reporting help account for real-time disease outbreak. Origins of disease and means to conquer disease can be found by analysing the track of reported outbreaks. For tracking opioids, the company might employ blockchain as well.	The CDC uses blockchain for monitoring diseases and reports outbreaks in real time.	The CDC works with IBM to develop a surveillance system based on blockchain so that public health agencies can collect medical information.
NEBULA GENOMICS	Boston, Massachusetts	Biotechnology, Genetics	Nebula Genomics uses distributed ledger technology for eliminating redundant expenditure and traders in the genetic study procedures. The companies related to pharmacy and biotechnology pay a huge sum for obtaining genetic information from others. Hence, the company helps building a huge genetic database by removing costly middle men and equipping users for securely selling genetic information that is encrypted.	Nebula Genomics applies blockchain for lowering the costs and streamlining the study of genetics.	

(*Continued*)

TABLE 4.2 (*Continued*)
Blockchain Functionality and Its Application in Healthcare

Company	Place	Industry	Functions	Applicability of Blockchain	Effect on Real Life
ENCRYPGEN	Coral Springs, Florida	Blockchain, Data-Sharing	The EncrypGen gene-chain simplifies the sharing process of genetic data as a blockchain-backed platform. The company provides security to the users as it allows additional members to buy genetic data only by means of safe and observable DNA tokens. Genetic data can be utilized by member companies for building their own genetic knowledge as well as for progress in the industry.	The blockchain platform backing this company simplifies sharing, searching, storage, and trading in genetic data.	EncrypGen plans to enlarge the user base to include behavioral and medical information. As per CEO and cofounder, Dr. David Koepsell, the company is also planning to integrate blockchain payment and auditing platforms. Additionally, it plans to collaborate with companies engaged in testing as well as analytics software developers.
DOC.AI	Palo Alto, California	AI, Blockchain, Medical, Software	DOC.AI uses machine intelligence, like AI, for decentralizing medical data on the blockchain. Its users can choose their platform for sharing genomic and medical data with scientists, who further uses it for predictive modelling. The company does not keep patient information. The information is encrypted, after uploading, on a blockchain, is then utilized in trial, and data is removed for ensuring security and privacy.	The company employs machine intelligence for decentralizing patient information on blockchain technology.	DOC.AI recently collaborated with Anthem, a health insurer, in studying the usage of AI for forecasting incidence of allergic responses.

can even supervise labour costs and inefficient use of resources. The dream of using genomics to enhance the future of human health has transformed into a financial and scientific reality. It cost 1 billion USD in 2001 to process the human genome. However, it costs just around 1,000 USD today. Corporations such as Ancestry and 23 and Me are devising DNA tests that reveal hints regarding health. Blockchain is good fit for genomics research data as it has the potential to securely cover enormous genetic data-points. Individuals can send in encrypted genetic information to help create a broader database, which scientists can access more quickly. The following companies use blockchain to enhance healthcare security, maintain health records, manage the supply chain in the medical sector, and record futuristic aspects of the human race.

4.6 ANALYSIS OF CASE STUDY

It has been found that various authors have introduced case studies in their research articles. The data for the proposed case study has been taken from Abu-elezz (2020) and Hasselgren et al. (2020). Abu-elezz et al. (2020) has considered the data regarding blockchain techniques in healthcare sector from 2017 through March 2020. These researchers have selected some known journal to show that how much work has been done in blockchain technology in different sub-sectors of healthcare. But also their concerns is to show the popularity of blockchain. Information was collected on the bases of publication, country of publication, and type of publication. They have not used statistical analysis in their study. As far as the research regarding the study in year 2020, the relevance of blockchain in health care has increased many-fold as shown in Figure 4.3. Figure 4.4 represents the number of countries in which the study on blockchain in health care has been published. Figure 4.5 shows type of commutation of the manuscript in different types of publications. Now, Hasselgren et al. (2020)

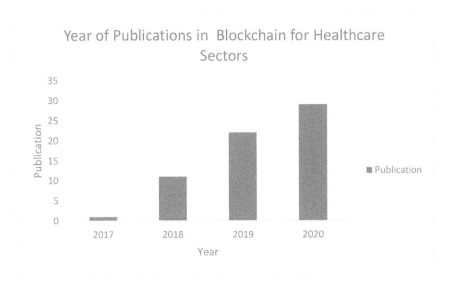

FIGURE 4.3 Increase in the publication of health care using blockchain.

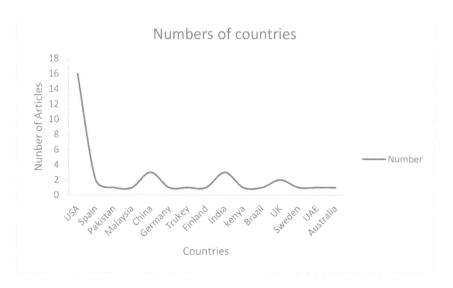

FIGURE 4.4 Number of countries work in blockchain.

has revealed that EHRs are gaining in popularity among personal health records, clinical trial support systems, etc. as depicted in Figure 4.6.

The researchers analysed the scoping survey for the blockchain concept in the healthcare sector. They have shown that there is no limit for this concept. Data was collected from 2016 to 2018 for their study. Data contained in Hasselgren et al. (2020) revealed and some more information is used. A high correlation has been seen between the blockchain type and the platform used in blockchain, r = 0.95. Figure 4.6 depicts the

FIGURE 4.5 Articles published in journals, conferences, and book chapters.

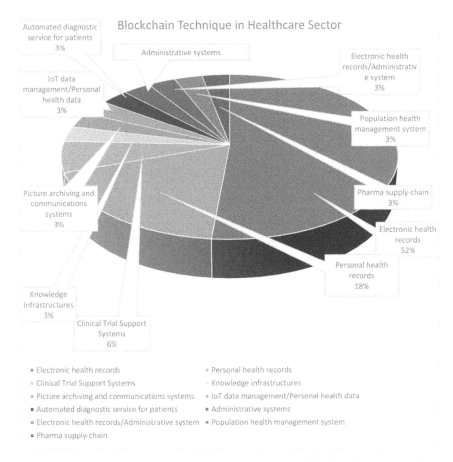

FIGURE 4.6 Pie diagram showing percentage-wise work of blockchain in the healthcare sector.

involvement of blockchain in different fields of health care. The hypothesis H_0: Type_Blockchain and Blockchain_Platform have no correlation. In the alternative hypothesis H_1: There is correlation between Type_Blockchain and Blockchain_Platform. Descriptive statistics are shown in Table 4.3. In Table 4.4 it is suggested that coefficient of correlation is very high, i.e. 0.968. A test of significance also confirms that there is a highly positive correlation between Type_Blockchain and Blockchain_Platform.

TABLE 4.3
Descriptive Statistics Between Type of Blockchain and Blockchain Platform

	Descriptive Statistics		
	Mean	Standard Deviation	N
Type_Blockchain	7.8000	4.91935	5
Blockchain_Platform	8.7500	4.85627	4

TABLE 4.4

Significance between Type of Blockchain and Blockchain Platform

Correlations			
		Type_Blockchain	Blockchain_Platform
Type_Blockchain	Pearson Correlation	1	.968[a]
	Sig. (2-tailed)		.032
	N	5	4
Blockchain_Platform	Pearson Correlation	.968[a]	1
	Sig. (2-tailed)	.032	
	N	4	4

[a] Correlation is significant at the 0.05 level (2-tailed).

4.7 CONCLUSION

Blockchain technology is a pioneering technology that can resolve various issues related to real-life problems. Amongst these problems, the health sector is one of the major concerns because it contains various issues that have not been addressed until now. An attempt has been made in this chapter to show how blockchain can be introduced to enhance the medical sector. Different subsectors of health care have been shown diagrammatically where blockchain empowered this sector. A statistical analysis has been done in this regard. Future prospects will require a lot of research to reach to an optimal decision.

REFERENCES

Abu-elezz, I., Hassan, A., Nazeemudeen, A., Househ, M. and Abd-alrazaq, A. (2019). The benefits and threats of blockchain technology in healthcare: A scoping review. International Journal of Medical Informatics, 142, 1–9.

Ahram, T., Sargolzaei, A., Sargolzaei, S., Daniels, J. and Amaba, B. (2017). Blockchain Technology Innovations. 2017 IEEE Technology & Engineering Management Conference (TEMSCON).

Alkhushyni, S. M., Alzaleq, D. M. and Kengne, N. L. D. (2019). Blockchain Technology applied to Electronic Health Records. EPiC Series in Computing, 63, 34–42.

Badr, S., Gomaa, I and Abd-Elrahman, E. (2018). Multi-tier Blockchain Framework for IoT-EHRs Systems. The 9th International Conference on Emerging Ubiquitous Systems and Pervasive Networks (EUSPN 2018). Procedia Computer Science, 141, 159–166.

Casino, F., Dasaklis, and Patsakis, C. (2019). A systematic literature review of blockchain-based applications: Current status, classification and open issues. Telematics and Informatics, 36, 55–81. https://doi.org/10.1016/j.tele.2018.11.006.

Chen, H. S., Jarrell, J, T., Carpenter, K. A., Cohen, D. S. and Huang, X. (2019). Blockchain in Healthcare: A Patient-Centered Model. Biomed J Sci Tech Res., 20(3), 15017–15022.

Cost of Data Breach Study (2018). Impact of Business Continuity Management. Available online: https://www.ibm.com/downloads/cas/AEJYBPWA (accessed on 15 March 2021)

Dagher, G. G., Mohler, J., Milojkovic, M. and Marella, P. M. (2018). Ancile: Privacy-preserving framework for access control and interoperability of electronic health records using blockchain technology. Sustainable Cities and Society, 39, 283–297.

Efanov, D. and Roschin, P. (2018). The All-Pervasiveness of the Blockchain Technology. 8th Annual International Conference on Biologically Inspired Cognitive Architectures, BICA 2017. Procedia Computer Science, 123, 116–121.

Ekblaw, A., Azaria, A., Halamka, J. D. and Lippman, A. (2016). A Case Study for Blockchain in Healthcare: 'MedRec' Prototype for Electronic Health Records and Medical Research Data. [Online]. Available: https://www.healthit.gov/sites/default/files/5-56-onc_blockchainchallenge_mitwhitepaper.pdf

Hasselgren, A., Kralevska, K., Gligoroski, D., Pedersen, S. A. and Faxvaag, A. (2020). Blockchain in healthcare and health sciences—A scoping review. International Journal of Medical Informatics, 134, 1–10. https://doi.org/10.1016/j.ijmedinf.2019.104040.

Heston, T. F. (2017). A case study in blockchain healthcare innovative. International Journal of Current Research, 9 (11), 60587–60588.

Hussein, A. F., Kumar, N. K., Gonzalez, G. R., Abdulhay, E., Tavares, J. M. R. S. and Albuquerque, V. H. C. (2018). A medical records managing and securing blockchain based system supported by a Genetic Algorithm and Discrete Wavelet Transform. Cognitive Systems Research, 52, 1–11.

Koul, S. Machine learning and deep learning in agriculture in Patel et al. (Eds.), (2021). Agriculture: Emerging Pedagogies of Deep Learning, Machine Learning and Internet of Things, CRC Press, pp.1–19. https://www.taylorfrancis.com/chapters/edit/10.1201/b22627-1

Liu, X., Wang, Z., Jin, C., Li, F. and Li, G. (2019). A blockchain-based medical data sharing and protecting scheme. IEEE Access, 7, 1–11.

Maesa, D. D. F. and Mori, P. (2020). Blockchain 3.0 applications survey. Journal of Parallel Distributed Computing, 138, 99–114.

Mohsin, A.H., Zaidan, A.A., Zaidan, B.B., Albahri, O.S., Albahri, A.S., Alsalem, M.A. and Mohammed, K.I. (2019). Blockchain authentication of network applications: Taxonomy, classification, capabilities, open challenges, motivations, recommendations and future directions. Computer Standards & Interfaces, 64, 41–60.

Omar, A. A., Bhuiyan, M. Z. A., Basu, A., Kiyomoto, S. and Rahman, M. S. (2019). Privacy-friendly platform for healthcare data in cloud based on blockchain environment. Future Generation Computer Systems, 95, 511–521.

Viriyasitavat, W. and Hoonsopon, D. (2019). Blockchain characteristics and consensus in modern business processes. Journal of Industrial Information Integration, 13, 32–39. https://doi.org/10.1016/j.jii.2018.07.004.

Wood, G. (2014a). Ethereum: A secure decentralized transaction ledger. http://gavwood.com/paper.pdf.

Wood, G. (2014b). Ethereum: A secure decentralized generalised transaction ledger eip-150 revision

Yaga, D., Mell, P., Roby, N. and Scarfone, K. (2018) Blockchain technology overview. Nat. Inst. Standards Technol., Gaithersburg, MD, USA, Tech. Rep. 8202. https://doi.org/10.6028/NIST.IR.8202

Yang, L. (2019). The blockchain: State-of-the-art and research challenges. Journal of Industrial Information Integration, 15, 80–90.

Zheng, Z., Xie, S., Dai, H., Chen, X. and Wang, H. (2017) An Overview of Blockchain Technology: Architecture, Consensus, and Future Trends, 2017 IEEE International Congress on Big Data (BigData Congress), Honolulu, HI, 2017, pp. 557–564, doi: 10.1109/BigDataCongress.2017.85.

Zubaydi, H. D., Chong, Y. W., Ko, K., Hanshi, S. M. and Karuppayah, S. (2019). A Review on the Role of Blockchain Technology in the Healthcare Domain. Electronics, 8, 679–700.

5 Emerging IoT Applications
Smart Dialysis Monitoring System

N. Vedanjali, Pappula Rajasri, Mahima Rajesh, V.R. Anishma, and G. Kanimozhi

CONTENTS

5.1 INTRODUCTION

Chronic kidney disease is one of the key public health issues faced all over the world today. It is characterized by progressive loss of kidney function that delicately leads to end-stage renal disease (ESRD), requiring a kidney transplant or dialysis [1]. The main function of the kidneys is to remove excess urine and waste from the body. But at times, the kidneys fail to function normally due to other health problems that have resulted in permanent damage of kidneys over time. As damage to the kidneys continues to worsen, it can lead to chronic kidney disease, the last stage of which is described as kidney failure or ESRD [2]. Diabetes and high blood pressure (BP) are two of the foremost causes of kidney failure. Other causes include immune response diseases like lupus and immunoglobulin disorder, genetic diseases like polycystic kidney disease, and urinary tract issues [3].

Dialysis and kidney transplant are the major treatments for kidney failure. Dialysis is outlined as the removal of excess water, solutes, and contaminants from a patient's blood whose kidneys do not perform these functions on their own. It is also called renal replacement therapy. The three different types of dialysis are haemodialysis, peritoneal dialysis, and continuous renal replacement therapy (CRRT).

Haemodialysis is the process during which a dialysis machine and a special filter known as an artificial kidney, or a dialyzer, are employed to scrub the blood. Blood

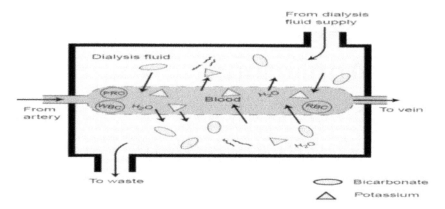

FIGURE 5.1   Schematic representation of a haemodialysis system.

from the body is transferred to the dialyzer through the blood vessels with the help of minor surgery, described later [4]. A pump within the haemodialysis machine slowly draws out blood and passes it through the dialyzer machine. This works like a kidney and filters out extra fluid, waste, and salt. The clean blood is then sent back to the body through a second needle within the arm, as depicted in Figure 5.1. Haemodialysis needs to be performed about three times a week, each for 4 hours duration.

The three ways of performing the surgery are as follows: (a) Graft: An artificial tube is implanted just under the skin and attached to an artery on one end and a vein on the other. Generally, this access needs a lot of maintenance and includes an increased risk of clotting. (b) Catheter (central venous catheter): Generally used for temporary access, this can be an extended, double-sided tube inserted into a vein through the skin [5]. (c) One of the veins has been rejoined to an associate artery, permitting bigger blood flow into the vein. As the vein is taken from the body of the patient, it usually lasts longer and might have fewer issues than the other two types.

A cellophane membrane separates the blood and dialysis solution compartments. With the exception of plasma proteins and blood cells, this membrane is porous enough to allow all contents to diffuse between the two compartments [5].

Diffusion, osmosis, and ultrafiltration are also used in peritoneal dialysis, similar to haemodialysis. The dialyzing membrane is the serous membrane of the peritoneal cavity. To gain entry, a Silastic catheter is inserted into the peritoneal cavity below the navel. The catheter is tunnelled into subcutaneous tissue, exiting on the abdomen's facet. The entire dialysis process involves the flow of a sterile dialyzing solution through the catheter for an amount of roughly 10 minutes. A schematic representation of peritoneal dialysis is shown in Figure 5.2.

The solution remains in the peritoneal cavity for a small period of time, allowing metabolic end products and extracellular fluid to diffuse into the dialysis solution. Once the appropriate time has elapsed, the dialysis fluid is pumped out of the cavity into a clean bag. Water is removed from the dialysis solution by glucose. The higher the dextrose concentration, the more osmosis takes place, resulting in more fluid being absorbed. Continuous ambulatory peritoneal dialysis (CAPD) is one of the most commonly used procedures, in which the patient controls the dialysis and the form of solution used at home [5].

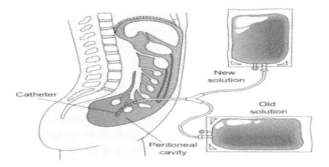

FIGURE 5.2   Schematic diagram of peritoneal dialysis [5].

CRRT is a continuous blood purification process that provides continuous removal of retained endogenous and exogenous contaminants, as well as maintains the acid-base, electrolyte, and volume homeostasis. Though CRRT is designed to work 24×7, it is often disrupted [6]. The primary emphasis of this research paper is on cost-effective health care.

5.2   HAEMODIALYSIS

ESRD, as depicted in Figure 5.3, is an overall general public health issue [7]. ESRD has become a worry in increasing the number of patients undergoing haemodialysis treatment proceeding to renal transplantation [8]. Time needed for a patient to undergo dialysis relies upon how well the kidneys work and on how much fluid weight the patient acquires between treatments. Normally haemodialysis treatment continues for about 4 hours, three times a week [8]. When dialysis was first introduced, most patients aged 80 and older used to undergo this treatment, but in this new era of longer life expectancy, people aged even up to 65 years or older can undergo this treatment [9]. In early dialysis treatment, the procedure needed to occur more than three times each week and last longer than 4.5 hours; however, nowadays traditional haemodialysis procedure uses low-versus high-flux dialyzer membranes [10].

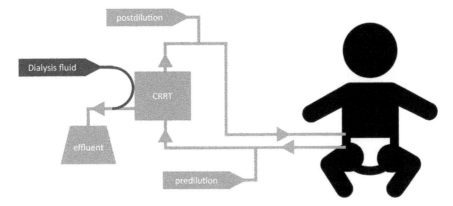

FIGURE 5.3   Schematic representation of continuous venovenous haemodiafiltration or continuous venovenous haemofiltration setup [11].

TABLE 5.1
Blood Pressure Targets as Stated by Clinical Practice Guidelines

Guidelines	Blood Pressure Target
Canadian Society of Nephrology 2006 guidelines	Predialysis BP <140/90 mm Hg
KDOQI 2005 Guidelines	Predialysis BP <140/90 mm Hg
	Postdialysis BP <130/80 mm Hg
Japanese Society for Dialysis Therapy 2012 guidelines	Predialysis BP <140/90 mm Hg

Body temperature, dialysate temperature, and room temperature play a major role in the dialysis room [12]. Bringing down the temperature of the treatment room from 37°C to 34–35.5°C has improved the cardiovascular stability of numerous haemodialysis patients undergoing the dialysis process [12].

According to the Kidney Disease Outcomes Quality Initiative guidelines from 2005, predialysis BP should be less than 140/90 mm Hg and postdialysis BP should be less than 130/80 mm Hg. According to Canadian Society of Nephrology guidelines from 2006, predialysis BP should be less than 140/90 mm Hg, while the Japanese Society for Dialysis Therapy guidelines 2012 recommend predialysis to be less than 140/90 mm Hg (Table 5.1) [13]. The most common health complications during haemodialysis is low blood pressure since significant amounts of fluid being eliminated from the blood during haemodialysis can cause BP to drop [14].

The heart rate of a healthy person should be between 60 and 100 beats per minute. The kidneys are responsible for maintaining a consistent amount of blood that remains in the body and also help remove excess fluid way of urination. If kidney function is weakened, blood volume increases and can result in increased stress on the heart, which stretched and furthermore trigger an abnormal heart rhythm [15].

In Table 5.2, the pre-HD systolic BP for men is 153.4 mm Hg as mentioned and the diastolic BP is 78.8 mm Hg. The pulse rate taken before the HD was 74.6 beats per minute [16].

Now, BP is compared to the pulse rate relatively as mentioned in Table 5.3. When a patient's pulse rate is between 40 and 69 beats per minute, their blood pressure is 151.3/75.8 mm Hg; when the pulse rate is between 70 and 129 beats per minute, the blood pressure is 154.5/80.2 mm Hg, which is measured before the dialysis process [16].

As shown in Figure 5.4, the block diagram shows the inputs of temperature, pulse rate, and BP. These readings are read by the temperature sensor, pulse rate sensor,

TABLE 5.2
Pre-HD Blood Pressure and Pulse Rate in Men

	For Men	For Women
Pre-HD systolic and diastolic BP, mm Hg	153.4/78.8	140/90
Pre-HD pulse rate, bpm	74.6	74

TABLE 5.3
Comparison of Blood Pressure and Pulse Rate Variations

	Pulse Rate 40–69 bpm	Pulse Rate 70–129 bpm
Pre-HD systolic and diastolic BP, mm Hg	151.3/75.8	154.5/80.2

and BP apparatus. This information is sent to an Arduino device, which shows the temperature and pulse rate readings on an LCD display and BP readings in the BP display. The Bluetooth module is also connected to the Arduino, which sends the information to the Mobile app [17] used by a doctor or nurse.

5.3 HARDWARE SETUP

The block diagram of the proposed model is presented in Figure 5.4. The following are the components (Table 5.4) used for hardware implementation:

Blood Pressure: An I2C EEPROM is connected to the ASIC of the BP monitoring device. The ASIC master transfers to the slave through the I2C
EEPROM bus. Further, the data is bypassed by 11 connecting the Arduino
Uno as a slave on the I2C bus. Hence, the Arduino is also able to read the
data when the data is sent from the ASIC to the I2C. The pin 14 VCC of
EEPROM is connected to 3.3 V. The pin 7 of I2C EEPROM is grounded.
Pin 9, 10 SCL, and SDC of EEPROM are connected to the A5 and A4 pins
in the Arduino Uno board. The valve of the BP machine is connected to the
digital pin 3 in the Arduino. A switch is also connected to the Arduino Uno,
which helps to start the blood pressure measurement.

Temperature Sensor: A temperature sensor is directly connected to the microcontroller and is used to determine the temperature of a patient. In the proposed model, the LM35 temperature sensor is used. The data is received in

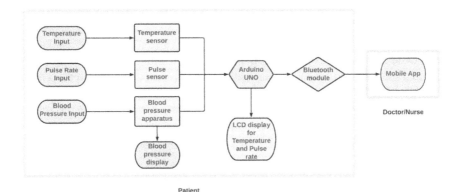

FIGURE 5.4 Block diagram of the proposed model.

TABLE 5.4
Hardware Components

Component Name	Specification
EEPROM	I2C
Blood Pressure Sensor	BPM180
Arduino Uno	R3 CH340G ATmega328p
Temperature Sensor	LM35
Pulse Sensor	SEN-11574
LCD Display	JHD 126A
Bluetooth Module	HC-05
Handcuffs, Breadboard, Jumper Wires	-

analogue form by the microcontroller, which transforms it to digital form before sending it to the radio frequency (RF) transmitter for transmission to the remote end. The data is received by the RF receiver, which is further transferred to the microcontroller for processing. The results are reflected on the LCD beside the heartbeat data. The LM35 sensor has a scaling factor of 0.01 V/°C. The patient's body temperature is determined by holding the LM35 with his or her finger, and the resulting shift in temperature is transformed into analog voltage, that is then fed to the microcontroller through the LM35's middle pin. The microcontroller contains an ADC, which performs additional processing before transmitting the calculated data to the remote end through an RF transmitter. The data is received by the RF receiver at the other end.

Pulse Sensor: The change in amount of absorbed infrared (IR) light with the flow of blood can be directly connected to the heart rate. Further, the signal is amplified, screened, and sent to the microcontroller for analysis. The heart rate sensor should be placed on the ring finger for best results. After filtering, the sensor produces a clean wave that can be used on an oscilloscope to validate that it accurately measured the patient's pulse. The analog signal is initially very small to be detected and proved to isolate the heart rhythm without amplification. Operational amplifiers were used to remove the heart rate signal as a result. The signal is transferred to the comparator after amplification. The signal is obtained in the form of pulses. A microcontroller's digital port is used to interface the pulsed signal with it for further processing.

Android app: This mobile application is connected with the Bluetooth HC-05 and the readings received via Bluetooth are displayed on the screen. The doctor/medical staff can easily connect the app with the Bluetooth module with just a click. Moreover, the patient's medical history can be stored in the app, which makes it easy for the doctor to review the patient's condition. In case of an emergency, a call is automatically made to the doctor through the app.

As shown in Figure 5.5, the patient ID is to be entered and then the saved history— name, age, gender, mobile number, type of dialysis and last visit of the patient to the doctor along with the on-going status of the patient—will be displayed on the screen.

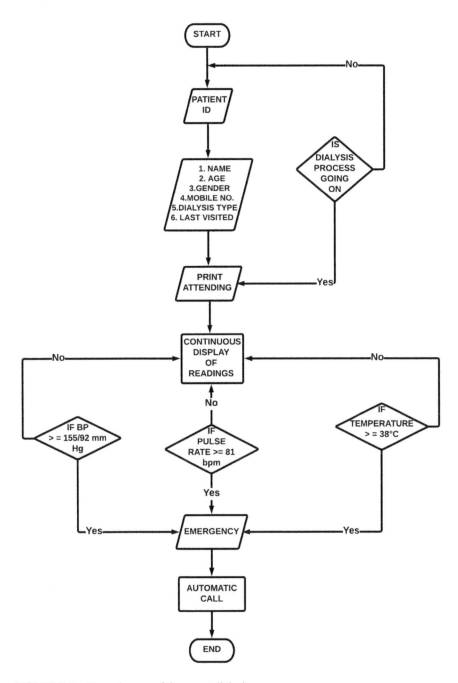

FIGURE 5.5 Flow diagram of the smart dialysis app.

The present status menu indicates whether the dialysis is being done or not. If the dialysis machine is on, the on-going status shows 'attending'. The doctor can click on the next button to observe the readings continuously. An alert message will be displayed on the mobile screen if the temperature is greater than or equal to 38°C, if BP is greater than or equal to 155/92 mm Hg, or if the pulse rate is greater than or equal to 81 beats per minute (bpm). During an emergency, a phone call will be made to the doctor immediately.

5.4   MOBILE APPLICATION

The mobile App is developed for monitoring parameters during the dialysis process. Figure 5.6a–c shows the details—via the mobile app—of the patient during a dialysis procedure. Figure 5.7a–d displays the notification of an abnormality to the doctor.

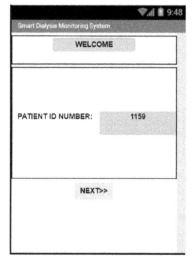
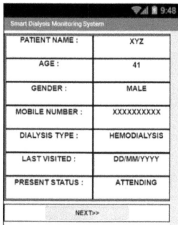

FIGURE 5.6   Case-1: (a) Welcome page, (b) patient details, and (c) readings during dialysis.

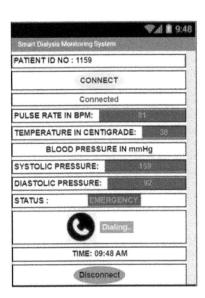

FIGURE 5.7 **Case-2:** (a) Welcome page, (b) patient details, (c) readings during dialysis, and (d) phone call to doctor/nurse.

As depicted in Figure 5.6a, the patient id number is to be entered in the welcome page of the mobile application and the saved patient details would be displayed on clicking on the 'next' button, as shown in Figure 5.6b. Upon selecting the 'next' button and by connecting to the Bluetooth device, a continuous monitoring of pulse rate, body temperature, blood pressure as well as time and status of the patient are displayed, as shown in Figure 5.6c.

If the readings are normal, as shown in Tables 5.2 and 5.3, the status of the person is specified as normal and the readings are displayed in Figure 5.6c. If any of the readings exceeds the normal range, then the readings are displayed in Figure 5.7c, and the patient is considered to be in a state of emergency. In the case of an emergency, the doctor or nurse receives a notification through a call or message alert immediately.

5.5   HARDWARE RESULTS

The pulse sensor, blood pressure sensor, temperature sensor, Arduino, and the Bluetooth module are connected, as shown in Figure 5.8a.

As the device gets successfully paired with the sensor of the Bluetooth module, the LED blinks at a slower rate than usual. After a successful connection, the 'connected' message will be displayed on the main screen of the mobile application. Then, the Android app will display the data received from the transmitter side as shown in Figure 5.8a. The temperature and pulse rate readings are displayed in LCD as shown in Figure 5.8b, and blood pressure readings are displayed in the BP apparatus display as shown in Figure 5.8c.

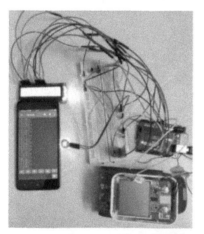

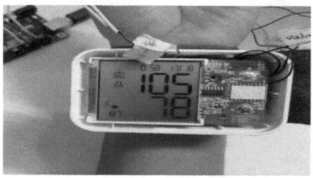

FIGURE 5.8   (a) Experimental setup, top view, (b) temperature and pulse rate readings on the LCD display, and (c) blood pressure readings on the LCD display.

5.6 CONCLUSION

A cost-effective healthcare monitoring system during haemodialysis has been developed successfully and a working device has also been verified. This healthcare monitoring system offers very good medical assistance with integrated Internet of Things (IoT) devices to improve the efficiency of the system. This not only saves time, but also improves quality of service as doctors would be notified in case of any medical emergency through the mobile app.

REFERENCES

[1] Mousa, I., Ataba, R., Al-Ali, K. et al. Dialysis-related factors affecting self-efficacy and quality of life in patients on haemodialysis: a cross-sectional study from Palestine. *Renal Replacement Therapy*. 2018;4:21. https://doi.org/10.1186/s41100-018-0162-y

[2] Bi, Z. et al., A practical electronic health record-based dry weight supervision model for hemodialysis patients. *IEEE Journal of Translational Engineering in Health and Medicine*. 2019;7:1–9, Art no. 4200109. https://ieeexplore.ieee.org/document/8882347

[3] Larson, K. M., Houglum, M., Axley, B., Dinwiddie, L., Smith, K., Twaddell, J. W. End Stage Renal Disease Briefing Book for State And Policymakers, *Health Policy Committee*, June 2009.

[4] John T. Daugirdas, J.T., Blake, I.P.G. "*Handbook of Dialysis*". Fifth Edition. Wolters Kluwer Health, 2015.

[5] Paul, A., Girish, C., Shilpa, T., Manogna, K., Susmitha, A. Renal vascularisation causing end-stage failures and outcomes: a pooled analysis of community based studies. *International Journal of Pharmaceutical Sciences and Drug Research*. 2017;9. 10.25004/IJPSDR.2017.090510.

[6] Rewa, O., Villeneuve, P.M., Eurich, D.T. et al. Quality indicators in continuous renal replacement therapy (CRRT) care in critically ill patients: protocol for a systematic review. *Systematic Reviews*. 2015;4:102. https://doi.org/10.1186/s13643-015-0088-1

[7] Mukakarangwa, M.C., Chironda, G., Bhengu, B., Katende, G. Adherence to hemodialysis and associated factors among end stage renal disease patients at selected nephrology units in Rwanda: a descriptive cross-sectional study. *Nursing Research and Practice*. 2018;2018, Article ID 4372716:8. https://doi.org/10.1155/2018/4372716.

[8] Dad, T., Tighiouart, H., Lacson, E. et al. Hemodialysis patient characteristics associated with better experience as measured by the In-Center Hemodialysis Consumer Assessment of Healthcare Providers and Systems (ICH CAHPS) survey. *BMC Nephrology*. 2018;19:340. https://doi.org/10.1186/s12882-018-1147-3.

[9] Piccoli, G.B., Sofronie, A.C., Coindre, J.P. The strange case of Mr. H. Starting dialysis at 90 years of age: clinical choices impact on ethical decisions. *BMC Medical Ethics*. 2017;18(1):61. Published 2017 Nov 9. doi:10.1186/s12910-017-0219-4.

[10] Slinin, Y., Greer, N., Ishani, A., MacDonald, R., Olson, C., Rutks, I., Wilt, T.J. Timing of dialysis initiation, duration and frequency of hemodialysis sessions, and membrane flux: a systematic review for a KDOQI clinical practice guideline. *American Journal of Kidney Diseases*. 2015 Nov;66(5):823–36. doi:10.1053/j.ajkd.2014.11.031. PMID: 26498415.

[11] Jonckheer, Joop, Vergaelen, Klaar, Spapen, Herbert, Malbrain, Manu, De Waele, Elisabeth. Modification of nutrition therapy during continuous renal replacement therapy in critically ill pediatric patients: a narrative review and recommendations. *Nutrition in Clinical Practice*. 2018;34. 10.1002/ncp.10231.

[12] Pérgola, P.E., Habiba, N.M., Johnson, J.M. Body temperature regulation during hemo-dialysis in long-term patients: is it time to change dialysate temperature prescription? *American Journal of Kidney Diseases.* 2004 Jul;44(1):155–65. doi:10.1053/j.ajkd.2004.03.036. PMID: 15211448.

[13] McCallum, W., Sarnak, M.J. Blood pressure target for the dialysis patient. *Seminars in Dialysis.* 2019;32(1):35–40. doi:10.1111/sdi.12754.

[14] Taniyama, Y. Management of hypertension for patients undergoing dialysis therapy. *Renal Replacement Therapy.* 2016;2:21. https://doi.org/10.1186/s41100-016-0034-2

[15] Lertdumrongluk, Paungpaga, Streja, Elani, Rhee, Connie M., Sim, John J., Gillen, Daniel, Kovesdy, Csaba P., Kalantar-Zadeh, Kamyar. Changes in pulse pressure during hemodialysis treatment and survival in maintenance dialysis patients. *Clinical Journal of the American Society of Nephrology.* Jul 2015;10(7):1179–1191. doi:10.2215/CJN.09000914.

[16] Iseki, Kunitoshi, Nakai, Shigeru, Yamagata, Kunihiro, Tsubakihara, Yoshiharu. Tachycardia as a predictor of poor survival in chronic haemodialysis patients. *Nephrology Dialysis Transplantation,* March 2011;26(3):963–969. https://doi.org/10.1093/ndt/gfq507

[17] Sethuraman, T.V., Rathore, Kartik Singh, Amritha, G., Kanimozhi, G. IoT based system for heart rate monitoring and heart attack detection. *International Journal of Engineering and Advanced Technology,* June 2019;8(5):1459–1464.

6 Role of Analytics in IoT
A Development of AAAS

*S. Manikandan, K. Gowrishankar,
and Jagadeesh Pasupuleti*

CONTENTS

6.1   INTRODUCTION

The body mass index (BMI) is a common vital indicator of health. BMI is calculated as the ratio of weight and height. It will define a person as underweight, normal, overweight, or obese. A high BMI indicates an increased risk of cardiovascular diseases such as high blood pressure, diabetes etc. People who are overweight or obese have a high risk of getting gall stones. Also, waist circumference has a significant impact on health risk when it is high, for example, more than 40 inches. This implies those people have high health-related risks. Improper nutrition in adults is common these days usually due to many complex issues surrounding food or inadequate diet. BMI acts as a good indicator of person's health.

The purpose of this chapter is to show BMI and waist-hip ratio (WHR) analyses using the common system, which will provide a more accurate analysis than BMI. In previous studies, BMI is used as the main method of measurement [1] and can be a main indicator of many diseases. For example [2, 3] show the effect of BMI on lung function and respiratory muscle strength. The determination of neonatal birth weight from the BMI of the pregnant women was studied in [4–6], which helps in preventing the risk of low birth weight (LBW) and macrosomia among lean and obese women. Kalyan Gaud et al. [7] studied the thyroid dysfunction related to BMI and TSH levels in the body. In [8, 9], researchers studied the association of BMI with diabetes mellitus and the high level of obesity in pre- and postmenopausal women, finding that postmenopausal women have a high risk of health issues due to high

DOI: 10.1201/9781003166511-6

BMI and WHR. In [10], researchers studied the improvement in BMI over the course of aerobic training.

For gaining more insight into health, this automated adult anthropometry station (AAAS) uses both the standard BMI and WHR measurements. BMI shows into which category a person falls and the WHR shows the risk of health issues arising. Both measurements are combined to ensure the proper prediction about a person's health. This will help healthcare professionals to gather health-related information over a community or large population.

6.2   RELATED WORK

Some studies are working on measuring BMI from body measurements and also even with two-dimensional (2D) images. Yuki Matsuda et al. [11] proposed a health support system as a belt that can measure waist circumference and it also provides the output in graphical form. Upady et al. [12] created a BMI-measuring device for the visually impaired, which measures the values and dictates them for both height and weight. Jochen and Timo [13] designed a measuring tape used to measure waist and hip circumference, which sends the data the smart device to be stored and monitors any changes in weight of the user.

Min Jiang et al. [14] analysed body weight from human body images, computing essential body features. This model can predict BMI based on the image of the user. Ankur Haritosh et al. [15] proposed a method to estimate the height and weight of the person using the face image. Similarly, Antitza Dantcheva et al. [16] studied the estimation of BMI from the single face image.

In contrast to the research mentioned, we proposed an approach to measure BMI and WHR of a person using a sensor arrangement. This method is more accurate when compared to the previously mentioned methods. Both BMI and WHR values used together in the single approach will increase the accuracy of the system and measurement in a negotiable time.

6.3   SYSTEM ARCHITECTURE

The main components of the system as shown in Figure 6.1 are sensors, microcontrollers and the computer system. This measuring system is connected to the stand that contains the sensors at the top, middle, and in the bottom. Measured values are fed to the computer system. This will provide instant feedback through the computer monitor. Apart from the three sensors, there is a microcontroller that helps to convert analog data from the sensors to digital form. The microcontroller also helps transfer the data to the computer through the USB. The computer system has custom software written in Python to perform BMI and WHR calculations by using the values sent from the microcontroller units. The Python version used to write the program is version 3.0. The computer will act a graphical user interface (GUI) for the user to both use the system and receive feedback from it. This software 'tells' the microcontrollers to measure the value based on the user trigger and also receives and assigns the values from the microcontroller to the system program that contains the formula for calculation. All the conversion, which is needed before the values are assigned to

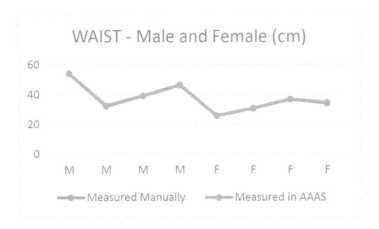

FIGURE 6.1   Hardware diagram of the system.

the formula, is done in the software program itself. It provides triggers to the micro-controller from the user to measure the value at the correct time.

This system provides the output in values such as height, weight, BMI, waist and hip circumference, and WHR. This will be shown to the user with labels that indi-cate the specific values, the ranges the user falls among, and the WHR. Users can view their various parameters and a description of the values on the output screen.

6.4   DESIGN AND IMPLEMENTATION

6.4.1   HARDWARE IMPLEMENTATION

The sensors used to measure the height, weight, and circumference of the waist and hips are placed in the system as shown in Figure 6.2. The height is measured by the ultrasonic sensor. The ultrasonic sensor used in the system is HC-SR04, which can measure distance up to 400 cm. It is placed at the top of the stand. It will mea-sure the time delay to reach the user's head by ultrasound and send that data to the

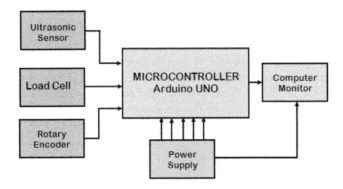

FIGURE 6.2   Sensor placement on the automated adult anthropometry station (AAAS).

microcontroller. In the microcontroller, the time delay is converted into the height of the user in centimeters.

The weight of the user is measured using a series of load cell which are connected in a Wheatstone bridge configuration to measure the change in the resistance in the load cell proportional to the weight the user. Each has the capacity up to 50 kg, measuring weight up to 200 kg total. The sensors are placed at the four corners under the glass platform and are connected to the amplifier circuit; the circuit used in the system is HX711. The circuit amplifies the voltage from the sensor, which is in millivolts (mv), and it also helps to reduce the noise from the analog signal. The data from the HX711 circuit are fed to the microcontroller. This weighing module is placed at the bottom of the stand and parallel to the ultrasonic sensor and measures weight in kilograms. The circumference of the waist and hips can be measured by the rotary encoder, which measures based on the number of revolutions the sensor shaft makes; that information is then fed to the microcontroller. This shows the circumference in centimetres. This is placed in the middle of the stand and operated by the user by rotating over their waist and hips.

The Arduino UNO was used as the microcontroller for this system; all the sensors are connected to the microcontrollers by serial port communication through a USB cable. The system creates a software interrupt, which tells the microcontroller when to measure the parameters based on the input of the user and returns the measured values.

6.4.2 SOFTWARE

The Arduino IDE is used to write the code in embedded C and feeds the code to the microcontroller. This program tells the microcontroller to capture the values from the sensors based on the signal provided by the computer system. This program measures the value, converts it into a definite value, and prepares those values to be sent to the computer system. Based on the request of the computer, the values are fed from the microcontroller to the computer via serial communication. In the computer, the software program was written in Python. The version used for the program is Python 3.0. The program contains a GUI that helps the user easily interact with the system and also get the appropriate feedback; a simple flowchart of the software program as shown in Figure 6.3.

All the calculations are done in the system itself so it will not be shared or stored outside of the system. The program will also have a registration and login system, which is also stored in the computer system itself. After the login, the system shows the user to the measuring window, where it will show the virtual button to start the measurement. Based on the first signal, the computer sends the signal to the microcontroller to send the data of the ultrasonic sensor and load cell module to calculate BMI. Similarly, the second method of calculation is WHR, which is done after the calculation of BMI by measuring each value of waist and hip circumference of hips by the signal from the computer. The system then calculates the range in which the user falls. After the output is shown, the user logs out, and the system will again show the login window, which indicates the measuring system is ready for the next user.

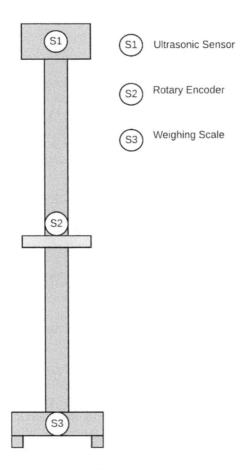

FIGURE 6.3   Simple flowchart of AAAS program.

6.5 METHODOLOGY

To classify the person into a category, the first step is to know the range of values, normal and abnormal, for both BMI and WHR. According to the World Health
Organization (WHO), the normal ranges for BMI are shown Table 6.1. The waist
circumference is the better indication of risk due to obesity when compared to BMI,
because it directly measures the visceral fat in the abdomen region, which could be a
better identification of risk of serious health conditions. The normal ranges of WHR
given by the WHO are shown in Tables 6.1 and 6.2.

The person stands on the system as shown in Figure 6.4. If he/she is a new user,
they will register, if not, they will login. After logging in to the software in the computer, the person will click the start button in the window. The program will send
the values to the microcontroller through the serial port. When the microcontroller
receives these values, it runs the appropriate function based on the value. First, it will
measure the sensor value.

TABLE 6.1
Body Mass Index

Category	BMI Range
Underweight	Less than 18.5
Normal	18.5–24.9
Overweight	25–29.9
Obese	30 and above

The sensor used to measure height will sense the time delay of the ultrasound pulse as it travels from the sensor transmitter at the head of the person and returns to the sensor receiver. Those values are converted into distance in centimeters by using the velocity and distance relation formula:

$$\text{Distance} = \frac{\text{time taken} \times \text{speed of sound}}{2} \tag{6.1}$$

$$\text{Speed} = 340\,\text{m/s} = 0.034\,\text{cm/}\mu\text{s} \tag{6.2}$$

The height of the person is measured by subtracting the distance after the person stands on the weighing module. The weight measured by the weighing module comprises a four-load cell and amplifier module and these values are sent to the microcontroller after the conversion from analog voltage to a discrete signal. The hip and waist circumference are measured by the rotary encoder, which is rotated over the hip and waist of the person. The values are then transferred to the computer from the microcontroller through a USB serial port. In the Python program, the unit conversion is done for the height parameter in the BMI calculation because the system needs the value in meters and the microcontroller initially records the data in centimeters. After that, data from both the hip and waist are fed to the formula normal BMI:

$$\text{BMI} = \frac{\text{weight}_{kg}}{\text{weight}_m^2} \tag{6.3}$$

TABLE 6.2
Waist-Hip Ratio

Men	Women	Health Risk
0.95 or Lower	0.80 or Lower	Low
0.96–1.0	0.81–0.85	Moderate
1.0 or Higher	0.86 or Higher	High

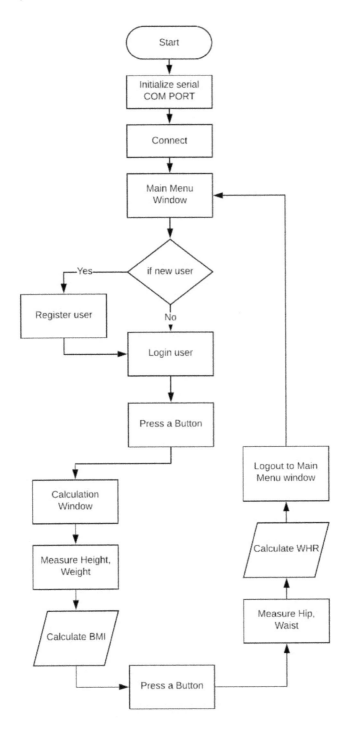

FIGURE 6.4   Designed prototype.

$$BMI = \frac{weight_{lb}}{weight_{in}^2} \times 703 \qquad (6.4)$$

The newly proposed formula had been used in calculation of BMI to reduce the distortion caused by the standard formula due to shorter and taller individuals. The formula is as given:

$$BMI_{new} = 1.3 \times \frac{mass_{kg}}{height_m^{2.5}} \qquad (6.5)$$

Similarly, the hip and waist measurements are also fed to separate formulas. The WHR is calculated by the formula as given:

$$WHR = \frac{waist\,circumference}{hip\,circumference} \qquad (6.6)$$

Finally, the output is shown as the weight, height, and waist and hip circumference and is also labeled as to which range the person fall into.

6.6 RESULTS

To evaluate the system, we performed a test with eight participants. The system provided the output correctly with low error when compared to the manual method for calculation of both the BMI and WHR values. The values measured for BMI by the manual method as shown in Table 6.3 and the values measured using the system are shown in Table 6.4. The comparison of height measured by the manual method and through the system for BMI showed only a small variation as shown in Figure 6.5.

TABLE 6.3
BMI Measured Using the Manual Method

		Measured Manually		
Gender	Height (cm)	Weight (kg)	BMI	Category
M	167	87.6	31.41	Obese
F	171	53.8	18.39	Underweight
F	178	58.6	18.49	Underweight
M	175	83.6	27.29	Overweight
F	165	63.6	23.36	Normal
M	177	57.9	18.48	Underweight
M	162	82.3	31.35	Obese
F	174	81.4	26.88	Overweight

TABLE 6.4
BMI Measured Using AAAS

		Measured in AAAS		
Gender	Height (cm)	Weight (Kg)	BMI	Category
M	168	88.2	31.25	Obese
F	173	54.2	18.10	Underweight
F	180	58.8	18.14	Underweight
M	177	84.0	26.81	Overweight
F	166	63.9	23.18	Normal
M	178	58.3	18.40	Underweight
M	164	82.6	30.71	Obese
F	175	81.9	26.74	Overweight

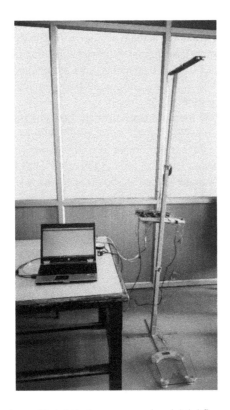

FIGURE 6.5   Comparison of height between manual and AAAS.

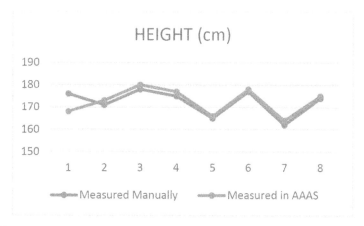

FIGURE 6.6 Comparison of weight between manual and AAAS.

Similarly, the comparison of weight shown in Figure 6.6 varied only slightly when compared to the height measurement. The final BMI measured by the system is also compared with the manual method, and shows less fluctuation in values. The system provided the accurate category for each user, the same as the manual method as shown in Figure 6.7.

In addition to BMI, the system also measured the hip and waist circumference and the values for both male and female as shown in Tables 6.5, 6.6, 6.7, and 6.8. Waist and hip circumference are compared between the manual method and with the system, with the measured values nearly the same as the manual method as shown in Figures 6.8 and 6.9. The WHR measurements between both methods are low and accurate as shown in Figure 6.10.

This system shows low measurement error for both the measurements taken for BMI and WHR as shown in Figures 6.11, 6.12, 6.13, and 6.14.

The system's output is accurate compared to the manual method and it is more efficient and reliable because it eliminates human error. The output for the measured value is shown in the computer screen as shown in Figure 6.15.

FIGURE 6.7 Comparison of BMI between manual and AAAS.

TABLE 6.5
WHR Measured Using AAAS (Male)

	Measured in AAAS			
Gender	Hip (cm)	Waist (cm)	WHR	Category
M	48.2	54.3	1.12	High
M	39.4	32.6	0.82	Low
M	42.5	39.2	0.92	Moderate
M	45.6	46.5	1.01	High

TABLE 6.6
WHR Measured Using Manual Method (Male)

	Measured Manually			
Gender	Hip (cm)	Waist (cm)	WHR	Category
M	48	54.0	1.12	High
M	39	32.0	0.82	Low
M	42	39.0	0.92	Moderate
M	45	46.0	1.02	High

TABLE 6.7
WHR Measured Using AAAS (Female)

	Measured in AAAS			
Gender	Hip (cm)	Waist (cm)	WHR	Category
F	38.6	25.8	0.66	Low
F	42.8	30.7	0.71	Low
F	44.2	36.8	0.83	Moderate
F	47.6	34.4	0.72	Low

TABLE 6.8
WHR Measured Using Manual Method (Female)

	Measured Manually			
Gender	Hip (cm)	Waist (cm)	WHR	Category
F	38	25.6	0.67	Low
F	42	30.5	0.72	Low
F	44	36.5	0.82	Moderate
F	47	34.0	0.72	Low

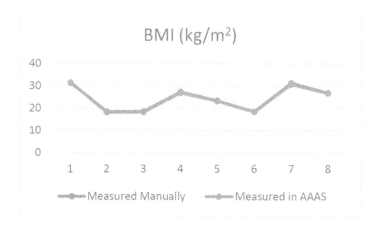

FIGURE 6.8   Comparison of hip circumference between manual and AAAS.

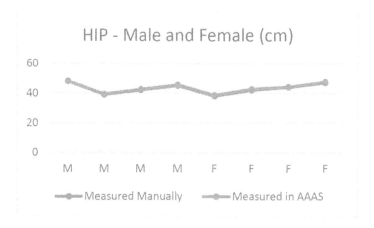

FIGURE 6.9   Comparison of waist circumference between manual and AAAS.

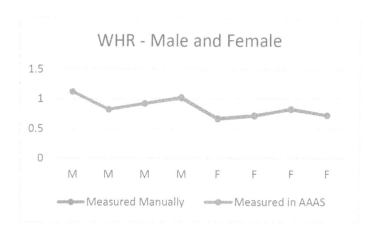

FIGURE 6.10   Comparison of WHR between manual and AAAS.

FIGURE 6.11 Comparison of height error between manual and AAAS.

FIGURE 6.12 Comparison of weight error between manual and AAAS.

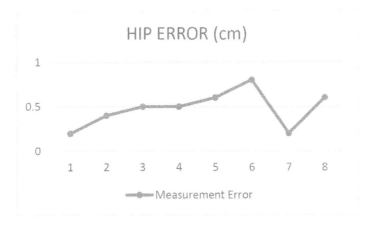

FIGURE 6.13 Comparison of hip error between manual and AAAS.

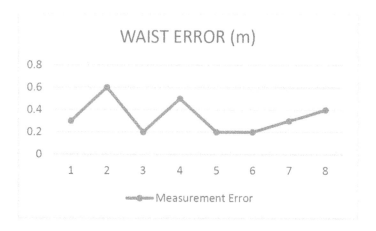

FIGURE 6.14 Comparison of waist error between manual and AAAS.

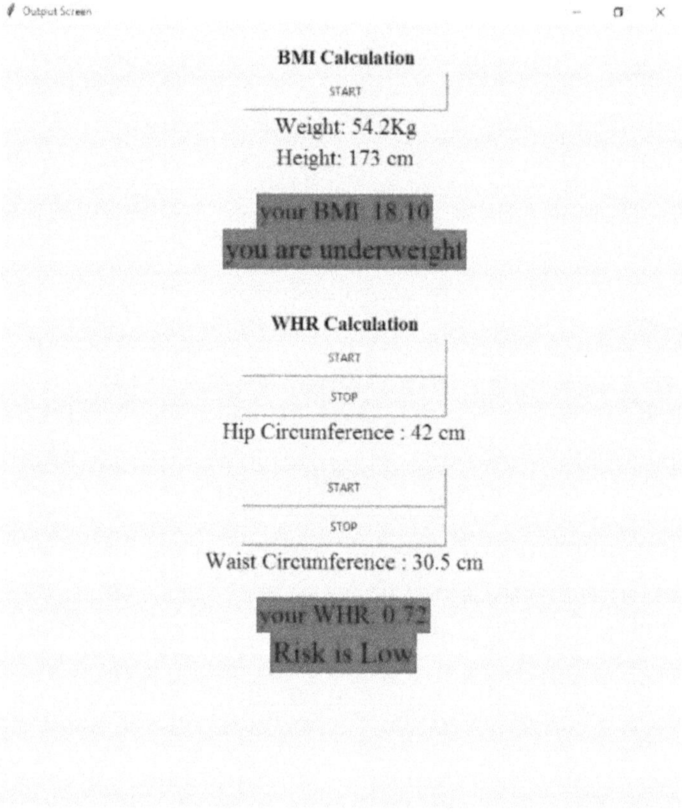

FIGURE 6.15 Output screen from AAAS.

6.7 CONCLUSION

In this chapter, we presented a system for measuring both BMI and WHR, which will increase efficiency and rectify the problem that exists in BMI calculations for taking into account tall and short people by adding the WHR measurement to the calculation. This will more accurately categorize users based on risk level. The system also provides a simple user interface, which helps the user easily operate the system and receive clear output. This system has low measurement and overall mean error, which will allow healthcare professionals to obtain more data from the community. Additional features can sync the system to the user's phone, which will show them full statistics of their health and also automatically update the system whenever they measure again using the system.

REFERENCES

[1] M. K. Malviya, "Body mass index (BMI): Mirror of health", Journal of Applied Research, vol. 4, no. 10, (2014), pp. 603–605.
[2] P. V. Shimpi, S. H. Mulkutkar, "Effect of body mass index on lung function parameters in young healthy adults", Journal of Applied Research, vol. 7, no. 12, (2017), pp. 89–91.
[3] Seemi Retharekar, Radhika N. Nivasarkar, "Correlation of waist circumference with respiratory muscle strength in healthy individuals with normal body mass index", Journal of Applied Research, vol. 8, no. 10, (2018), pp. 79–80.
[4] Madhulika Kumari, Gajanan R. Daiv, "Study of the association between early pregnancy BMI and gestational weight gain in relation to neonatal birth weight", Journal of Applied Research, vol. 6, no. 2, (2016), pp. 645–647.
[5] Deepika N. Nandanwar, Ratnendra R. Shinde, "Body mass index of pregnant women as an epidemiology determinant of birth weight of a new born child – A longitudinal study in a tertiary care hospital", Journal of Applied Research, vol. 5, no. 11, (2015), pp. 629–631.
[6] Shilpa Joshi, Amruta Kulkarni, Girish Godbole, "Weight gain, correlation with obstetric outcome", Journal of Applied Research, vol. 3, no. 5, (2013), pp. 467–469.
[7] Kalyan Gaud, Shilpa Jaiswal, "Prevalence of subclinical thyroid dysfunction in general population: Focus on TSH co-relation with BMI", Journal of Applied Research, vol. 1, no. 11, (2012), pp. 114–115.
[8] Rani. N. Parvatha, N. Neelambikai, "Effect of body mass index waist hip ratio on cognitive performance I pre- and post-menopausal women", Journal of Applied Research, vol. 8, no. 4, (2018), pp. 30–32.
[9] Kirti Vinayak Kinge, Amit Chandrakant Supe, "Association between body mass index and diabetes mellitus in premenopausal woman in an urban slum India", Journal of Applied Research, vol. 6, no. 1, (2016), pp. 49–50.
[10] Jince Kappan, "Effect of aerobic training in BMI on sendentary obese women", Journal of Applied Research, vol. 2, no. 2, (2012), pp. 134.
[11] Yuki Matsuda, Takashi Hasegawa, Ismail Arai, Yutaka Arakawa, Keiichi Yasumoto, "Waiston Belt – 2 A belt- type wearable device for monitoring abdominal circumference, Posture and Activity", IEEE, International Conference on Mobile Computing and ubiquitous Networking (ICMU), Kaiserslautern, Kaiserslautern, Germany, (2016) October 4–6.
[12] Upady Hatthasin, Thanakorn Khongdeach, Patchararudee Kuntahong, Arnuparb Artharnsri, Nol Premashthira, "Assessment on a Talking device of weight and height for the visually impaired students", IEEE WIECON – ECE, Chonburi, Thailand, (2018) December 14–16.

[13] Jochen Meyer, Timo Schoormann, Daniel Wegmann, Ahmad Albuhasi, "A smart health device to measure waist circumference", IEEE, International Conference on Pervasive Computing Technologies for Healthcare (PervasiveHealth), Istanbul, Turkey, (2015) May 20–23.

[14] Min Jiang, Guodong Guo, "Body weight analysis from human body images", IEEE Transactions of Information Forensics and Security, vol. 14, no. 10, (2019), pp. 2676–2688.

[15] Ankur Haritosh, Ayush Gupta, Ekam Singh Chahal, Ashwin Misra, Satish Chandra, "A novel method to estimate Height, Weight and Body Mass Index from face images", 12th International Conference on Contemporary Computing (IC3), Noida, Delhi, (2019) August 8–10.

[16] Anitza Dantcheva, Francois Bremond, Piotr Bilinski, "Show me your face and I will tell you your height, weight and body mass index", IEEE, International Conference on Pattern Recognition (ICPR), Beijing, China, (2018) August 20–24.

7 IoT in M-Health Care

Himanshu Singh, Ahmad Faraz,
Justice Ohene-Akoto, and D.V. Sneha

CONTENTS

7.1 INTRODUCTION

Due to increase in the population over the years, there have been a lot of challenges in many public service sectors. Health service is one of the major sectors that has been affected due to the sudden growth of population. The challenges need to be addressed with a prompt solution based on the available resources. IoT, mobile, and network connectivity offers the best solution due to their less cost, reliable network and handy features. To understand the solutions, it becomes necessary to know about Mobile health (m-health) and Internet of Things (IoT).

Mobile health (m-health) refers to the use of mobile devices, digital sensors and meters in collecting health data of the patients in the real-time, and storing it on the network servers which are connected to the Internet. This stored data can be used by different groups and organizations depending on the requirement (e.g., hospitals,

DOI: 10.1201/9781003166511-7

health-insurance companies, etc.). The m-health data can be used by doctors to monitor, diagnose and quickly treat patients. The advancement in the technologies has led to development of wearable devices and body sensors which promote mobile health. The m-health devices in integration with the patient's environment help in early detection of health anomalies in real time. The development taking place in the micro and nanotechnologies lead to efficient information processing and wireless communication which provides secure infrastructure for mobile health systems.

The Internet of Things (IoT) refers to the network of physical objects that are embedded with sensors, software, and other technologies for the purpose of connecting and exchanging data with other devices and systems over the internet. These devices range from ordinary household objects to sophisticated industrial tools like RFID tags, medical devices, mobile phones, etc. [1].

Figure 7.1 shows the amalgamation of IoT and m-health provides opportunities to several medical applications such as mobile and remote health monitoring. The health is monitored by using different sensors and wearable devices which record the patient's data. This generated data is then securely transmitted to the designated servers. These medical sensing devices provide information about the real time condition of the patients which leads to early diagnosis, treatment or in case of emergency hospitalization. Other than this, IoT infrastructure in integration with smart health monitoring, and wireless communication leads to enormous possibilities of improvement in the quality of health care systems. The idea of m-health with regards to the Internet of Things (m-IoT) guarantees a better framework for health management by the efficient allocation of restricted assets for better use and administration of more patients. The IoT-based m-health system will aid individuals by setting aside their time and cash of visiting emergency clinics except if there is a genuine requirement for it. The basics of m-health and IoT are clinical devices equipped with sensors

FIGURE 7.1 IoT in M-health.

and specialized communication devices. These clinical devices are in fact shrewd sensors that can be utilized to screen different parameters, for example, sugar-level, blood pressure, pulse, and so forth. Insight calculations examine the m-health information continuously to recognize certain examples and raise diverse alarm levels, for example, ordinary, wary, crisis, and so forth, contingent on the state of the noticed patients. The volume of information at IoT servers is enormous as it is gathered from millions of individual clients or patients. This clinical information can be accessed by different associations such as medical coverage insurance organizations, medical clinics, government, etc. A diverse degree of security control instrument is applied to rely on who accesses the information and what is admissible? Nationwide health records of patients are maintained with the help of a centralized medical server and database which enables access to data anytime and anywhere [2].

7.2 IoT ARCHITECTURE FOR HEALTHCARE SYSTEMS

The architecture of an IoT-based health monitoring system which can be used in smart hospitals or homes is shown in Figure 7.2. In such frameworks, patient health related data is recorded by wearable or embedded sensors, with which the patient is prepared for individual checking of different parameters. This health-related information can be likewise enhanced with other information (e.g., date, time, area, temperature). Context-awareness enables one to recognize bizarre examples and make more exact deductions about the circumstance. Different sensors and actuators (e.g., clinical hardware) can be likewise associated with the frameworks to send information to clinical staff, for example, high-resolution images (e.g., CAT filter, magnetic reverberation imaging). The system architecture includes the following main components [3].

7.2.1 MEDICAL SENSOR NETWORK

Enabled by the pervasive identification, detecting, and communication limit, biomedical and setting signals are caught from the body/room utilized for treatment and diagnosis of clinical states. The response is then communicated to the gateway with

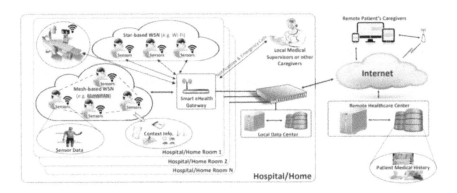

FIGURE 7.2 IoT-based health monitoring architecture.

the help of wireless communication or wired communication protocols such as SPI, Wireless Fidelity (Wi-Fi), Bluetooth, Serial, or IEEE 802.15.4.2.

7.2.2 SMART e-HEALTH GATEWAY

The gateway, which upholds distinctive communication conventions, acts as the contacting point between a sensor network and the nearby switch/Internet. It gets information from various sub-networks, performs convention change, and offers other more elevated level types of assistance, for example, information accumulation, filtering, and dimensionality decrease.

7.2.3 BACK-END SYSTEM

The back-end of the framework comprises two segments, a local switch and a cloud computing platform that incorporates broadcasting, information stockroom, and Big Data servers, lastly Web customers as a graphical UI for conclusive visualization and apprehension. The gathered health-related information contributes to the Big Data for the statistical and epidemiological medical research (e.g., detecting approaching epidemic disease).

There are several types of architecture followed in the m-health system. Some examples of the currently used architecture are mentioned below:

- 6LoWPAN-based healthcare system
- Constrained application protocol-based architecture
- IEEE 11073 health standard-based architecture

The healthcare system demands certain standards that have to be maintained everywhere. This is the reason for development of different architectural parameters and standards. These standards differ from each other depending on the requirement of the particular m-health system. They are developed following certain standards and incorporating the additional changes for the system. 6LoWPAN based healthcare system is widely accepted. Table 7.1 shows the protocols used in health care sector.

For any communication system to be successful there is a dire need of a fast, active network. IP based networks are present everywhere. Thus, it makes a compelling

TABLE 7.1
Protocol Stack for Sensor Augmented Health Care Systems

Healthcare IoT Sensor

UDP	ICMP
IPv6	
6LoWPAN	
IEEE 802.15.4 MAC	
IEEE 802.15.4 PHY	

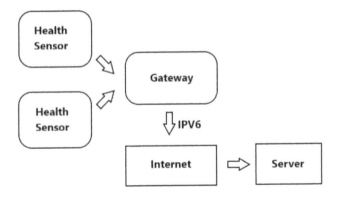

FIGURE 7.3   End-to-end architecture for 6LoWPAN based healthcare system.

case to use IP networks to transfer healthcare related data. There are certain requirements and limitations of this network as well. IPV6 protocol needs huge processing
power and bandwidth. It also requires "always-on" behavior. This behavior is not
favorable for IoT devices as they have to power efficient. Therefore, 6LoWPAN has
emerged as the preferred approach for such networks. A protocol stack for sensor
augmented health care systems using 6LoWPAN protocol [4].

As discussed in the characteristics, end-to-end networks are one of the benefits of
IoT in the m-health sector. In Figure 7.3, end-to-end architecture for 6LoWPAN based
healthcare systems is shown. The sensor data is enclosed within a 6LoWPAN datagram
and transmitted in IEEE 802.15.4 frame to the edge router or gateway. The gateway
serves a special purpose of converting the packets received to IPV6 packets and transmit it over the traditional IPV6 network to the server for processing of data.

7.3   CHARACTERISTICS M-HEALTH DEVICES

The Big Data related to mobile health (m-health) is generated as a result of several
compact and easy to use m-health devices. These m-heath devices are in continuous
communication with the IoT servers and can store, receive, and transmit data.

In this section, we identify and describe the following main characteristics of
m-health devices:

7.3.1   COMPACT AND EASY-TO-WEAR

One of the main things about m-health devices is for it to be compact and comfort-
able. These small sensors are in constant touch with the body of the patient or client.
The size and mobility also make the device attractive. There are several devices
available in the market that are small in size, easy-to-wear and have great specifica-
tions, some of them are listed below:

- *TICKR* is a heart rate monitor by Wahoo Fitness. This device can simply be
  strapped across the chest to take the heart rate measurements.

- *FitBit Surge* is a convenient smartwatch with abilities to get notifications from smartphones. It can track heart rate, sleep patterns, and number of calories burned during a workout. The FitBit Surge supports Bluetooth wireless connectivity and is compatible with iOS and Android operating systems.
- *OPTA SB-092 Fitness Smart Watch* is a fitness tracker which has an OLED display through which you can monitor your blood pressure and heart rate. And, this fitness tracker band supports automatic heart rate and BP oxygen monitoring as well. In addition to monitoring your health status, the smartwatch also lets you make calls anytime, anywhere and have quick access to your phone book.
- *Forerunner 920XT:* It monitors the heart, a record of calorie calculation, step counter, swimming stroke counter, and tracking elevation
- *iBGSta:* It measures the sugar and glucose level in blood, and its compatibility is good with iPhone and iPod [1]

7.3.2 IP ENABLED AND WIRELESS CONNECTIVITY

The devices used in m-health have a unique IP address, which enables the device to communicate over the network. The infrastructure of IoT m-health devices is designed in such a way that it provides continuous connectivity in different network environments. M-health devices receive and transmit data using wireless technology. These devices are in communication with each other over the network and streamline the process of treatment, monitoring, diagnosis, billing, admission, etc. According to the requirement, there are different standards for wireless connectivity which depends on factors such as low initial cost, compactness, efficiency and simplicity. Table 7.2 discusses various standards for wireless connectivity:

- *The Infrared Data Association (IrDA):* It is a ultra-high speed network variant, yielding output of 1 Gbps. Be that as it may, it just works over a distance of under 10 cm.
- *Nike+:* It is a restrictive wireless innovation created by Apple and Nike fundamentally to screen the activity levels of clients while working out.

TABLE 7.2
Various Standards for Wireless Connectivity

Wireless Technology	Peak Power Consumption	Throughput ≈	Range ≈
IrDA	10 mA	1 Gbps	5 cm
Nike+	12.3 mA	272 bps	10 m
BLE	12–16 mA	305 kbps	50 m
ANT	17 mA	20 kbps	10 m
ZigBee	30–40 mA	100–250 kbps	100–300 m
NFC	30–40 mA	424 kbps	10 cm to 1 m
Wi-Fi	116 mA	6 Mbps	150–500 ft

- *Bluetooth Low Energy (BLE):* The principal point of this wireless innovation is to empower power sensitive gadgets to be forever associated with the network for extensive stretches of time. BLE sensor gadgets may work for a long time without need to supplant the battery.
- *ANT:* It is a low-power restrictive wireless innovation which works in the 2.4 GHz bandwidth spectrum. Its essential objective is to permit clinical and sports sensors to communicate with a showcase unit, for instance, a watch or cycle computer. It regularly works from a coin cell.
- *ZigBee:* It is a power efficient wireless specification based on IEEE Standard 802.15.4-2003. It was a joint project by a group of 16 companies which was established in 2002. It introduces mesh networking to the low-power wireless space.
- *Near field communication (NFC):* It is comparatively unique from other power efficient technologies as it consumes more power and it is bound to operate between a range of 1–5 cm.
- *Wi-Fi:* It is an efficient technology which is optimized for large data transfer with the help of high-speed communication. It is the most suited for large medical data as it is most power efficient technology. [1, 5]

7.3.3 Low-Power Consumption

M-Health devices are designed with a view to offer more active time. For this design to work, certain parameters are considered like power consumption and thermal efficiency. The components of m-health devices such as sensors, circuits and processors are optimally designed to perform a specific task using less power offering longer battery life. M-health devices are the result of the perfect integration of software to the hardware. This enables the m-health devices to incorporate the benefits of power-saving hardware features and also to make intelligent power management decisions. Power amplifiers frame buffer compression (FBC) and content-adaptive backlight (CABL) are used to suppress the power-draining, less efficient components such as a display. A general mobile health and IoT architecture is based on IPv6 over Low power Wireless Personal Area Networks (6LoWPAN). [6]

7.3.4 Availability of Apps

From a medical services viewpoint, cell phone applications live inside progressively ground-breaking (versatile, hand-held) equipment programming conditions, permitting refined information obtaining, correspondence, and calculation concentrated cycles to be done locally, for example, different sorts of mathematical and non-mathematical estimations, information investigation, show designs, and video, alongside megabytes to gigabytes of neighborhood information stockpiling. For instance, the development of cell phone capacities can bring significant investigation to drive treatment choices in flare-ups in provincial or underserved populaces, for example, the utilization of a magnifying lens application that breaks down recordings of entire blood tests for microfilariae parasite L loa movement, evaluating thickness for assurance of treatment within 2 minutes. Comparative cell phone applications are in the plan, improvement, or creation for in vitro and ecological testing straightforwardly supporting nearby recognition of microbes, for example, sickness markers by means of nucleic corrosive segregation, gold nanoprobe Tuberculosis diagnostics, computer chip ELISA identification of ovarian malignant growth through HE4 biomarker and other disease cell diagnostics, fluorescent imaging cytometry, parallel stream immunochromatographic examines, circle intervened isothermal enhancement hereditary testing, and acoustic wave immunoassay to give some examples. Consequently, even in asset helpless conditions, cell phone applications in the possession of medical services providers can bring basically required purpose of care or purpose of need investigations already inaccessible to underserved populaces.

7.3.5 DATA ASSORTMENT AND ANALYSIS

The devices used in IoT and m-health systems are in constant communication over the network. These devices send and receive data continuously and in order to collect all the medical data, a cloud storage facility is required. If a cloud facility is not available, it becomes a slow and tedious task to manually analyze the data and process it. With IoT devices, the raw data is collected, reported, and analyzed in real-time as shown in Figure 7.4. All these things will take place on the cloud which means that the providers will only get access to the reports and graphs obtained at the final stage. Additionally, such solutions help the organizations to get important data-driven insights and healthcare analytics, which is less prone to errors as well as speeds up the decision-making process.

7.3.6 MONITORING AND REPORTING SIMULTANEOUSLY

In case of serious medical emergencies such as heart failure, asthma attacks, diabetes, etc. the IoT m-health plays an important role as the devices are connected with

FIGURE 7.4 Data assortment and analysis.

FIGURE 7.5   Monitoring and reporting.

each other over the network and are monitored in the real time which can be lifesaving. The real time monitoring can be easily achieved with the help of smart m-health devices and smartphone applications which are connected through the network as shown in Figure 7.5. These smartphone applications collect the medical as well as other health related data of the patient which is transmitted by the smart m-health devices.

With the advantage of real time monitoring of m-health devices, it was recorded that there was a reduction in the cases of readmission by 50% within a month, according to the study done by the Centre of Connected Health Policy on heart failure patients. The IoT m-health devices can be utilized to gather and move medical data like glucose levels, ECGs, blood pressure, weight, and so on. This data can be stored over the cloud and can be made accessible for admission to approved individuals like the doctors, physicians or insurance agency. The major advantage of storing data over the cloud is that it can be easily accessed from any device at any time or place [7].

7.4   APPLICATIONS IN M-HEALTH SECTOR

The Internet of Things is being widely applied in every sector. It has wide applications ranging from autonomous driving vehicles to home automations. IoT as a technology is still developing and it is evolving with the growing infrastructures. With the help of IoT, the collection, processing and evaluation has reduced not only man power but also the time required. It becomes very easy to collect the required data efficiently. No doubt the healthcare industry existed before but, it was limited to few doctor visits and communications in the form of text and calls. In such an arrangement there was no way possible for the hospital staff or the doctors itself to monitor the health of the patients continuously and make medical recommendations then.

The introduction of the Internet of Things has made it possible in the healthcare industry to remotely monitor the patients and make it a point that they stay healthy and safe. This way doctors will be empowered to offer healthcare service of superior quality. This way the interactions with the doctors have become more efficient and easier making it a satisfactory and engaging experience for the patients. Moreover, from the patient point of view, such kind of remote monitoring helps them have lesser visits to the hospital and even reduce the scenario of re-admissions. With IoT, it is also possible to improve the treatment while reducing healthcare costs very much. [1]

7.4.1 SINGLE CONDITION APPLICATIONS

Glucose Level Sensing: Diabetes is an illness of metabolic in which the remaining glucose level parts over the typical level for an extensive stretch of time. Blood glucose monitoring framework shown in Figure 7.6, identifies a unique type of blood glucose and assists with recommending daily meals, fitness workouts, and medicine times. For the measurement of non-invasive glucose level on an actual basis, an m-health IoT configuration technique is introduced. In this technique, IPv6 connectivity is used for the communication between the different sensors from patients and respective healthcare service providers. According to this, it enables a transmission device which sends and receives the medical data collected from glucose level in blood based on IoT networks. This device is a collection of different components such as blood glucose collector, computer or smartphone, and a processor.9

Blood Pressure Monitoring System: Blood pressure measures the force of the blood circulating around the body by the heart. For monitoring and controlling various medical constraints like hemoglobin (HB), blood pressure (BP), irregular

FIGURE 7.6 Glucose Level Sensor.

cellular development and sugar level in blood, an IoT-based method is introduced. An IoT-based healthcare service is also proposed to monitor the blood pressure, diabetes, and overweightness.

Body Temperature Monitoring: Checking and estimating temperature of the body level is a significant part of medical services applications. As indicated by m-IoT discernment, the homeostasis support changes as per the temperature of a body. The body monitoring sensors are fixed with the TelosBmote (a wireless sensor network which is used for effective transmission of body temperature, relative humidity and light), and it gives exact and viable outcomes in processing. The temperature of the body monitoring framework depends on the home gateway over the IoT system. It likewise aids infrared location and RFID module for the checking and estimating of body temperature.

Oxygen Saturation Monitoring System: A measuring instrument "Pulse oximeter" is utilized for constant monitoring of oxygen immersion in blood. The utilization of the IoT with pulse oximetry is helpful for innovation based medical healthcare applications. A study of the CoAP-based medical care framework examines the advantages of IoT-based pulse oximetry. A pulse oximeter Wrist OX2 gadget usefulness is shown in Figure 7.7. This gadget has the capacity of availability to Bluetooth and straightforwardly interfaces the sensor to the Monere platform. An IoT-based low-power and cost-efficient pulse oximeter device is proposed for monitoring remote patients. This device is capable of continuously monitoring the health of the patient with the help of an IoT network.**9**

ECG (Electrocardiogram) *Monitoring System:* It has the ability to show the ECG waves to the user or patient. This device produces a particular clinical report of a patient by gathering ECG bio-signals and transfers the information to the cloud network. It likewise gives a proper response to the user dependent on the gathered information. IOIO-OTG microcontroller changes ECG signals to digital numbers by utilizing the analog to digital converter, and then the binary file created is uploaded to the cloud network for further analysis and detection of irregular medical issues.

FIGURE 7.7   Nonin oximeter wrist band.

The primary favorable principle of this hardware is to lessen holding up time in clinics and emergency wards and to limit visits to the hospitals. [2]

7.4.2 Clustered Condition Applications

Wheelchair Management System: A fully computerized smart wheelchairs shown in Figure 7.8 are introduced by the researchers considering the health of the aged group and disabled people. In this, IoT plays a vital role for its execution and working. These smart wheelchairs are designed in such a way that they have various sensors which are used for the movement of the chair and also to detect and record the status of the patient.9

Rehabilitation System: IoT can build up the rehabilitation system as per the populace development related issues and absence of health expertise. It can improve the capabilities of the physically impaired individuals. To improve the rehabilitation system, Body Sensor Network is introduced. The implementation of an IoT in this field can be more efficient in providing actual information interactions, determined by an ontology-based automateding design. There are a number of IoT-based rehabilitation systems such as language training systems for childhood, smart city medical rehabilitation system, and integrated application system for prisons.

Healthcare Solutions Using Smartphones: In the present time, the cell phone has demonstrated to control electronic gadgets with sensors as shown in Figure 7.9. In the field of medical services, distinctive applications for cell phones are available

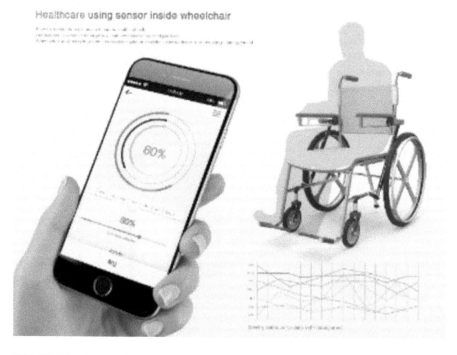

FIGURE 7.8   Smart Wheelchair.

FIGURE 7.9 Integration of smartphones with IoT.

to help patients, furnish medical education, and provide initial training. A few programming and equipment items are created which shows cell phones as a helpful device in medical care administrations. A rundown of the basic cell phone applications for general medical care is given in Table 7.3.

RQ-4: For quite a long time, various analysts and researchers are attempting to get to information all over the place, measure them on schedule, and remotely appropriate in medical care utilizing IoT innovation. As per ABI Research, around about 90 million wearable gadgets devices were utilized for medical services, sport applications, and fitness in 2014. This number is by all accounts expanded in the coming years. Analysts played out a lot of work in the field of medical care utilizing Internet IoTof Things, as in China, which is the most populated nation, a framework Current Market Scenario: The market of IoT wearable and other medical devices has substantially grown. The number of connected wearable devices worldwide has more than doubled in the space of three years, increasing from 325 million in 2016 to 722 million in 2019. The number of

TABLE 7.3
A Rundown of the Basic Cell Phone Applications for General Medical Care

Apps	Description
Health Assistant	Health Assistant keeps record of health parameters like weight, blood pressure, body temperature, and other physical activities.
Healthy Children	Helps in finding a nearby paediatrician and requests for quick response
Google Fit	Using sensors, it automatically tracks walking, running, and cycling activities.
Noom Walk	It is a health and fitness app that counts users' steps.
Heart Rate Monitor	This app allows a user to measure and monitor the heart rate in real-time and keep a record for later analysis.
Eye Care Plus	This app helps in naturally improving vision by testing eye health information.
Blood Pressure Watch	This is a wearable device that collects, monitors, and keeps record of blood pressure data.

devices is forecast to reach more than one billion by 2022. The underlying reason for this substantial increase is the awareness regarding health issues and their prevention. Ever since COVID-19 was declared a pandemic, people started showing interest in the blood oxygen meter or pulse oximeter. Fitness brands capitalized on the situation and innovated several wearable bands which include pulse oximeter [2].

7.5   SECURITY AND DATA PRIVACY

A few common techniques and standard protocols are used to help development a safe framework, including the common criteria evaluation methodology (CEM) and the Open-Source Security Testing Methodology Manual. The three primary network protection standards for security control—confidentiality, integrity, and availability—are known as the CIA standards. Confidentiality is where data isn't revealed to clients, cycles, or devices unless they have been approved to receive it. Integrity is the property whereby data has not been altered or exploited. Availability describes the property of data being able to be used. Every one of these three standards includes applicable insurance systems, which are depicted in Table 7.4, as they are derived from the the standards mentioned here and related research efforts [8].

The rules for secure IoT improvement, as also recommended by computer giants and programming merchants (e.g., Microsoft, IBM, Siemens, Gemalto), incorporate the accompanying three security territories:

- Device security: components and procedures for protecting the device itself, whenever it is deployed in the field.

TABLE 7.4
Security Aspects and Protection Mechanisms

Aspect	Protection Mechanism	Description
Confidentiality	Confidentiality	Guarantees that a processed asset is not known outside the interacting entities
	Authentication	Challenges credentials on the basis of identification and authorization
	Resilience	Maintains protection in case of failure
Integrity	Integrity	Guarantees that the interacting entities know when an asset has been changed
	Subjugation	Guarantees that transactions occur based on a defined process, removing freedom of choice and liability in the case of disclosure
	Nonrepudiation	Prevents the interacting entities from denying their role in an interaction
Availability	Continuity	Preserves interactivity in the case of failure
	Alarm	Informs that an interaction is happening or has happened
	Identification	Includes a contract between the asset owner and the interacting entity. It may also involve warnings as a precursor of legal action and public legislative protection

- Availability security: components and strategies for ensuring that the communicated information between the IoT devices and the IoT hub/gateway is private and carefully designed.
- Cloud security: Instruments and strategies for defending information while it is communicated to and put away in the cloud. Famous IoT stages, similar to the Microsoft Azure IoT Suite and the IBM Watson IoT Platform, tackle these issues and give the standard security arrangements [9].

In the subsequent text, we give a design of best-in-class IoT security assembled under the three primary zones recorded previously.

7.5.1 DEVICE SECURITY

Device security implements the different aspects of authenticating a device in an IoT application. Two fundamental segments are needed for this reason: A unique identity key or security token for every device. The device uses this key to confirm and communicate with the IoT smart gateway. An on-device X.509 certificate and private key verify the device to the IoT gateway. The confirmation system should ensure that this private key isn't known to external devices, hence accomplishing a more elevated level of security. In a typical device routine, the device token gives verification to every exchange that is made by the device to the IoT network. In this way, the symmetric key is related to every exchange. The X.509-based system empowers the validation of the device at the actual layer during the foundation of the transport layer security (TLS) association (availability security). The certificate contains information that is related to the devices, like its ID, and other organizational details. The security token can be additionally utilized alone without requiring the X.509 validation, however in a less-secure setting. The decision between the two techniques is dictated by the accessibility of satisfactory assets on the device end (for example secure storage of the private key) and the degree of verification security that is required by the application [10].

7.5.2 CONNECTIVITY SECURITY

Connecting IoT devices over the internet presents dangers for information classification and integrity. It is, consequently, imperative to guarantee that all the communicated information between the devices, IoT gateways, and the cloud is encrypted with help of key or tokens. The IoT passage uses security tokens to confirm devices and administrations. The cycle is overseen by the IoT platforms. The seamless communication is supported by relevant protocols, such as the Advanced Message Queuing Protocol (AMQP), MQTT, and HTTP, and is safeguarded by the security mechanisms that are implemented by each one of them. Nevertheless, these standard conventions measure the security tokens diversely and the right utilization should be assessed in each case. This is a specialized issue and concerns the correct planning of token-related data to every convention's information design. For instance, the MQTT association demand uses the device ID in the username and the security token in the password field, while HTTP incorporates the legitimate token in the approval demand header. Additionally, some application settings need the client to produce the security tokens and use them straightforwardly. Instances of these situations incorporate the immediate utilization of AMQP, MQTT, or HTTP surfaces.

The IoT door keeps a character library for the protected storage of device personalities and security keys. Distinct devices or groups of them can be added to an allow or block list, achieving complete control over device access.The advanced device features incorporate the accompanying advances: ability to associate an identifier at the actual device (i.e., the device character and additionally X.509 certificate and privacy key) at the assembling or charging stages, create a significant passage at the door's personality library, and securely store the X.509 declaration thumbprint in the vault (however, the device should likewise confirm the entryway). In the standard setting, a root declaration, which is remembered for the device programming advancement pack software development kit (SDK), is used for validating the passage's accreditations. In spite of the fact that the root declarations are seemingly perpetual, they can lapse or be rejected. Accordingly, a protected method should be predicted for refreshing the root declaration on the device end or the IoT devices might become unable to associate with the IoT entryway or the cloud administrations. Finally, the Internet connection between the devices and the gateway is generally protected by the SSL/TLS 1.2 standards. Old versions of each protocol may also be supported for backward compatibility (i.e., TLS1.1, TLS 1.0).

7.5.3 CLOUD SECURITY

Cloud computing suffers from a number of security issues that, if overlooked, may lead to catastrophic consequences. The main security vulnerabilities can be categorized as:

- Shared technologies: An attacker can exploit shared memory technologies to gain access to unauthorized content such as encryption keys.
- Data breach: Personal data containing sensitive information such as credit card information can be lost or worse can be leaked.
- Account/service hijacking: If login credentials are lost or leaked, hackers can gain access to critical areas of services and could potentially compromise confidentiality, integrity, and availability.
- Denial of Service (DoS): Cloud infrastructure mechanisms cope with DoS attacks by scaling up its resources. This first provides the attacker with more resources to achieve his malicious goals and, secondly, this type of attack can have monetary impacts.
- Malicious insiders: A company's employee can leverage his position to access sensitive information of the hosted services [12].

7.6 CONCLUSION

Health care is a very sensitive public sector that requires sophisticated technology and infrastructure. IoT has become that sophisticated technology, opening the gateway for the development of vast technologies in the healthcare system.

When IoT is seen in the light of mobile systems, it results in a strong network of several connected devices that perform various specialized tasks such as data collection, transmission, computing, and processing. IoT and mobile systems collectively address problems like patient management, emergency handling, and quick diagnosis. This fusion also comes with the benefits of remote applications, for example, a rural doctor can easily communicate with specialized doctors over the internet to tackle one of the emergencies. The remote system has also resulted in effective data collection with the help of various sensors. This collected data can further be used for better diagnosis and early detection of certain anomalies. All these features are very effective, but they come at their own cost. IoT and mobile systems are still developing and evolving as per the requirement. These systems are expensive to install and securely collecting data and transmitting it to the cloud or other devices pose a challenge. Every technology has its own set of pros and cons, and so is the case of IoT in mobile healthcare systems. It is a developing technology that is evolving within the health care system. With the ongoing development in infrastructure and technology, IoT will greatly benefit the mobile healthcare system.

REFERENCES

[1] S. H. Almotiri, M. A. Khan, and M. A. Alghamdi, "Mobile health (m-Health) system in the context of IoT," *Proc. - 2016 4th Int. Conf. Futur. Internet Things Cloud Work. W-FiCloud 2016*, no. January 2018, pp. 39–42, 2016, doi: 10.1109/W-FiCloud. 2016.24.

[2] S. Nazir, Y. Ali, N. Ullah, and I. García-Magariño, "Internet of Things for Healthcare Using Effects of Mobile Computing: A Systematic Literature Review," *Wirel. Commun. Mob. Comput.*, vol. 2019, 2019, doi: 10.1155/2019/5931315.

[3] A. M. Rahmani et al., "Smart e-Health Gateway: Bringing intelligence to Internet-of-Things based ubiquitous healthcare systems," *2015 12th Annu. IEEE Consum. Commun. Netw. Conf. CCNC 2015*, no. June, pp. 826–834, 2015, doi: 10.1109/ CCNC.2015.7158084.

[4] N. Kumar, "IoT architecture and system design for healthcare systems," *Proc. 2017 Int. Conf. Smart Technol. Smart Nation, SmartTechCon 2017*, pp. 1118–1123, 2018, doi: 10.1109/SmartTechCon.2017.8358543.

[5] A. J. Jara, L. Ladid, and A. Skarmeta, "The internet of everything through IPv6: An analysis of challenges, solutions and opportunities," *J. Wirel. Mob. Networks, Ubiquitous Comput. Dependable Appl.*, 2013.

[6] L. Wang, S. Hao, P. Yu, and Z. Huang, "Low-power Wireless Sensor Network protocol of Mobile Health based on IPv6," 2016, doi: 10.1109/ChiCC.2016.7554710.

[7] K. K. Patel, S. M. Patel, and P. G. Scholar, "Internet of Things-IoT: Definition, Characteristics, Architecture, Enabling Technologies, Application & Future Challenges," *Int. J. Eng. Sci. Comput.*, 2016, doi: 10.4010/2016.1482.

[8] G. Hatzivasilis, O. Soultatos, S. Ioannidis, C. Verikoukis, G. Demetriou, and C. Tsatsoulis, "Review of security and privacy for the internet of medical things (IoMT): Resolving the protection concerns for the novel circular economy bioinformatics," *Proc. - 15th Annu. Int. Conf. Distrib. Comput. Sens. Syst. DCOSS 2019*, pp. 457–464, 2019, doi: 10.1109/DCOSS.2019.00091.

[9] A. Chacko and T. Hayajneh, "Security and Privacy Issues with IoT in Healthcare," *EAI Endorsed Trans. Pervasive Heal. Technol.*, vol. 4, no. 14, pp. 1–7, 2018.

[10] F. A. Alaba, M. Othman, I. A. T. Hashem, and F. Alotaibi, "Internet of Things security: A survey," *Journal of Network and Computer Applications*. 2017, doi: 10.1016/j.jnca.2017.04.002.

[11] M. S. Virat, S. M. Bindu, B. Aishwarya, B. N. Dhanush, and M. R. Kounte, "Security and Privacy Challenges in Internet of Things," 2018, doi: 10.1109/ICOEI.2018.8553919.

[12] C. Stergiou, K. E. Psannis, B. G. Kim, and B. Gupta, "Secure integration of IoT and Cloud Computing," *Futur. Gener. Comput. Syst.*, 2018, doi: 10.1016/j.future.2016.11.031.

8 IoT-Based Anaesthesia Control and Monitoring System

Mangolik Kundu, Souvik Datta, and G. Kanimozhi

CONTENTS

8.1 INTRODUCTION

Anaesthesia is applied to induce unconsciousness during surgery. The medicine is either inhaled through a breathing respirator or tracheal tube or delivered through an intravenous (IV) line. The primary notion of a continuous-flow anaesthesia device was publicized by Henry Boyle in 1917. Primarily, anaesthesia is further subdivided into four categories based on their area of application: (a) local anaesthesia is defined as an agent given to momentarily reduce the sense of pain in a specific area of the body. A patient remains conscious once a local anaesthetic is administered. For minor operations, it can be used via injection into the site. (b) General anaesthesia induces unconsciousness throughout the surgery. The medicine is either inhaled through a breathing respirator or tube or given through an intravenous (IV) line. Drugs used in intravenous and inhaled administration of anaesthesia are presented in Table 8.1. A tracheal tube may be inserted into the windpipe to support proper breathing throughout the surgery. Once the surgery is completed, the anaesthesiologist stops the anaesthetic and the patient is taken to the recovery room for further monitoring [4]. (c) Regional anaesthesia is injected into a bundle of nerves to numb a large region of the body. (d) Neuraxial anaesthesia is placed near the spinal nerve column, making an even greater portion of the body numb compared to regional anaesthesia. Epidurals are usually given to ease the pain during childbirth [9]. Since the 1940s, the specialization of anaesthesia has contributed greatly to major advances in health care [10].

DOI: 10.1201/9781003166511-8

TABLE 8.1
Drugs Used During Intravenous and Inhaled
Administration of Anaesthesia

Intravenous Drugs	Inhaled Volatile Drugs
Propofol	Nitrous oxide
Midazolam	Isoflurane
Etomidate	Sevoflurane
Ketamine diazepam	Desflurane

Commonly used analgesic drugs originated from the opioid family (sufentanil, remifentanil, alfentanil, morphine, fentanyl, and hydromorphone). A patient can be connected to various electrodes to measure electroencephalography (EEG), electro-cardiography (ECG), and galvanic skin response (GSR) values. These signals while analysed using a microcontroller can set appropriate anaesthesia doses to maintain adequate hypnosis and analgesia as shown in Figure 8.1.

Anaesthesia Index (AI) is obtained from EEG and used to measure the depth of hypnosis. Depth of analgesia is determined by an Analgoscore (AS), derived from ECG and GSR Index (GI). An AI value ranging from 40 to 60 is considered as representing an adequate state of hypnosis. The AS is an index that ranges from −9 to +9 and a value between −3 and +3 represents adequate analgesia. The GSR also indicates the extent of pain or pain relief of the patient. The GI is a value from 0 to 5 where 0 represents extreme pain and 5 represents no pain.

The various inputs are given to the controller, which calculates the appropriate dosage of the anaesthetic drug to be given to the patient. The controller can range from a simple PID controller to a more complex fuzzy controller. The controller initiates the

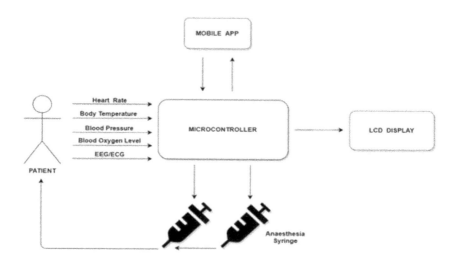

FIGURE 8.1   Diagram representing the workflow of the system.

actuator system, which will administer the required propofol dose based on the AI. The analgesic drug remifentanil is administered based on the AS and GI [5].

The regulation of a high or low dose of anaesthesia may cause lethal effects in the patient. To dismiss any irregularities, an anaesthetist supplies a few millilitres of anaesthesia at structured intervals. But this method gives rise to its share of problems; about one-quarter of anaesthesia-related failures were found to be related to human error [1]. A study between handwritten and computer-generated anaesthesia records was conducted and the result proved that readings errors affect manual anaesthetic records, may cause notable inaccuracy, and may be avoided by using automated information management systems [2]. Human error is a factor during anaesthesia-related fatalities and this frequency can be as high as 83% [7]. Certain mistakes in the dosage of anaesthesia still linger as the entire process is recurring and requires keen attention from the anaesthetist [6].

Seven percent of all cases of local anaesthesia fail during general practice. Some causes for this failure include infection, wrong selection of a local anaesthetic solution, and technical mistakes [12]. Although anaesthesia-related perioperative mortalities have fallen from 21.97/10,000 in 2006 to 16/10,000 as of 2016, which can be further reduced by appropriate management [8].

Precise documentation of an anaesthetic procedure is a key root of information for the assessment of dosage during surgery [3]. As the world adopts cloud storage services, the same is chosen for our digital documentation, making the data accessible from anywhere in the world. This allows the data to be secure and makes the overall system cost-efficient. So, there was a need to develop an automated anaesthesia control system to minimize errors. With this chapter, we wanted to analyse the frequency, type, and severity of equipment-related problems and come out with a solution to improve safety standards. The primary use of the proposed model is to design an improved automatic anaesthesia delivery system that overcomes the disadvantages of the manual methods.

8.1.1 PROPOSED BLOCK DIAGRAM

The block diagram shown in Figure 8.2 depicts the entire working model of our project. We take various body parameters as input parameters from the patient's body. Various sensors like the LM35 Temperature sensor are used to measure body temperature. The MAX30100 Heart Rate and Blood Oxygen Level sensors are used to measure the heart rate and the patient's blood oxygen level. The MPX5050DP Pressure Transducer is used to measure the blood pressure of the patient. These input parameters are passed on to the Arduino UNO microcontroller, which then processes the input parameters and displays them on an LCD screen and runs the motor or the pump to inject the desired amount of anaesthesia into the patient's body. It also sends the data to an IoT-enabled mobile application so that an anaesthetist or a doctor can remotely monitor the vitals while performing surgery on the patient. The mobile application will be able to detect any abnormal vital readings and declare an 'EMERGENCY' and alert/notify the doctors. The application will also have a separate 'EMERGENCY' button to explicitly invoke an emergency and alert the doctors if required.

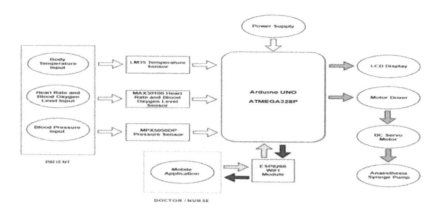

FIGURE 8.2   Block diagram depicting the operation of the system.

The block diagram in Figure 8.3 depicts how the mobile application works. The smart mobile application will help doctors/anaesthetists to remotely monitor the operation. The first page of the application will require the doctors/anaesthetists to login (see Figure 8.7a) into the application with their login credentials. Figure 8.7b will direct them to a list of categories of surgeries, once the doctor chooses an option from the list, he/she will next be directed to a page containing a list of types of surgeries under that category. Once the doctor chooses the type of surgery from the list, he/she will next be directed to the page containing the list of patients he/she has for that particular type of operation on that day. After selecting the patient from the list, he/she will next be directed to the patient login page and the doctor will be required to login into the patient's account with the Patient ID and the patient's phone number.

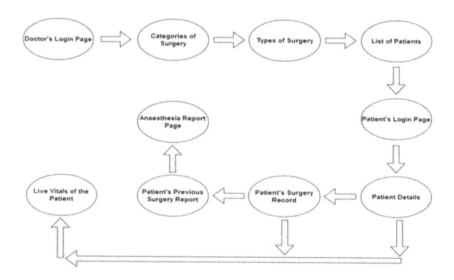

FIGURE 8.3   Working diagram of the mobile application.

After logging in, the doctor will be directed to the next page containing the patient's details, after verifying every patient detail, the doctor will be given the choice to move to the page showing the live vitals of the patient or to the page containing the list of surgeries that the patient has undergone previously.

Once the doctor chooses from the list of surgeries that the patient has undergone previously, he/she will be shown the report of the surgery, from there he/she may also move to another page showing the anaesthesia report of the patient for that particular surgery. The final page of the application will lead the doctor to the live vitals of the patient currently undergoing the surgery. The application will automatically detect any emergency in vital readings, highlight the critical body parameters, and alert/notify the doctors in the operation theatre. If the doctor using the application wishes to raise an emergency separately, he/she can click on the 'EMERGENCY' button provided to alert/notify the doctors in the operation theatre.

8.2 CIRCUIT DIAGRAM OF THE PROPOSED MODEL

In Figure 8.4, the circuit diagram of our Automated Anaesthesia System depicts the overall layout of our system. We have used the Arduino UNO (ATmega328p) for managing the overall system. The Arduino UNO will receive body vitals from the various sensors and show them on the 16×2 LCD display and on the display of IoT-enabled mobile application and run the servo motor accordingly to pump and inject anaesthesia into the patient. The MAX30100 Pulse Oximeter sensor has been used to measure the heart rate and blood oxygen level of the patient. An LM35 Temperature Sensor has been used to measure the body temperature of the patient and the MPX5050DP Pressure Transducer has been used to measure the blood pressure of the patient. In case the vitals become abnormal, the microcontroller will check it and show an 'EMERGENCY' message on the Mobile Application and notify the doctors.

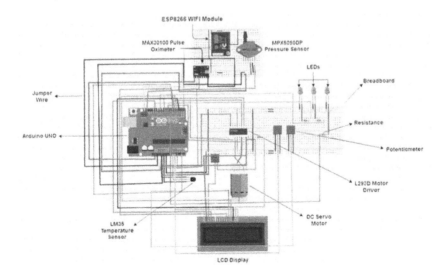

FIGURE 8.4 Circuit diagram made using Fritzing.

The ESP8266 Wi-Fi Module is required to communicate with the remote mobile application. All the components in the circuit diagram work on a 5V power supply except for the ESP8266 Wi-Fi Module, which works at 3.3.V, and the LEDs, which work at 3V. Three LEDs have been used to depict the various blood pressure levels and conditions. A red LED has been used to indicate a low BP (hypotensive) condition, a green LED has been used to indicate the normal (prehypertensive) condition, and a blue LED has been used to indicate the S1 hypertensive, S2 hypertensive and hypertensive crisis conditions.

8.3 FLOWCHART

The body temperature of the patient is captured by the LM35 Temperature Sensor, the blood pressure of the patient is captured by the MPX5050DP Pressure Sensor, the heart rate and the blood oxygen level of the patient is captured by the MAX30100 Pulse Oximeter Sensor. These inputs are given to the Arduino UNO microprocessor (Figure 8.5) and if all the input body parameters satisfy the medical conditions, then the Arduino UNO runs the Micro Servo Motor via the L293D Motor Driver. A syringe containing anaesthesia is connected to the Micro Servo Motor so that as soon as the motor runs, the syringe injects the anaesthesia into the patient's body. The Arduino UNO also displays the input body parameters (vitals) of the patient on a 16 × 2 LCD Display and Adafruit 0.96″ OLED display and the vitals are also sent in real-time to the IoT-enabled smart mobile application for remote monitoring of the patient. If, while remote monitoring of the patient, a critical or emergency condition arises, the mobile application will highlight the abnormal readings and raise an auto-generated emergency, thus alerting and notifying the doctor present in the operation theatre. If the anaesthetist or the doctor in charge remotely monitoring the operation wants to invoke an emergency separately and manually stop the anaesthesia administration system, he/she may click the 'EMERGENCY' button

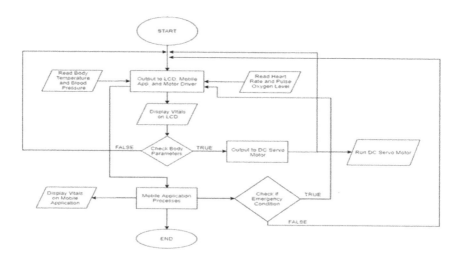

FIGURE 8.5   Flowchart of the system.

provided on the Mobile Application, which also alerts the doctors present in the operation theatre.

8.4 HARDWARE DEVELOPMENT

The components required for prototype design are shown in Table 8.2 and the hardware prototype is depicted in Figure 8.6a–d

- **Arduino UNO:** A microcontroller board based on the ATmega328P chip using Arduino programming language and running on Arduino IDE. The Arduino programming language is similar to C++. The board runs on 7.5V–12V. It comprises six analog inputs, 14 digital input and output pins, a USB connection for power and data transfer, and a reset button [12].
- **Heart Rate and Oximeter (MAX30100):** Comprises two LEDs transmitting waves in the infrared (IR) spectrum (950 nm) and the red spectrum (650 nm). This sensor can be placed anywhere the skin is thin enough for the light of both frequencies to steadily infiltrate the tissue. Once both light sources have passed through the skin, their absorption is measured using a photodiode. The ratio between the absorbed red light and IR light will vary depending on the amount of oxygen in the blood. Using this ratio, it is possible to calculate the oxygen level in haemoglobin [13].
- **L293D Motor Driver:** A dual H-bridge driver-integrated circuit that acts as a current amplifier. The amplified signal is used to drive the servo motors. Its electronic circuitry allows a voltage to be administered over a load in both directions [14]. This component allows the Arduino UNO to drive

TABLE 8.2
The Required Components

Components Used	Quantity
Arduino UNO	1
100K Potentiometer	1
10K Potentiometer	2
Resistors	4
Heart Rate and Oximeter Sensor—MAX30100	1
LCD Display—16 × 2	1
Adafruit 0.96″ OLED Display	1
L293D—Motor Driver	1
Micro Servo Motor	1
Temperature Sensor—LM35	1
LEDs	2
Jumper Wires	-
ESP8266	1
Pressure Transducer MPX5050DP	1

(a)

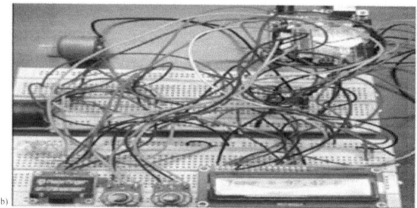

(b)

(c)

FIGURE 8.6a–d Images of the hardware depicting blood pressure, temperature, and vital parameters (a–c). Prototype with the sensors, microcontroller and a syringe respectively (d). (*Continued*)

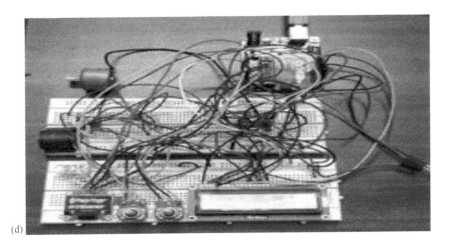

(d)

FIGURE 8.6 *(Continued)*

two servo motors simultaneously and in both anticlockwise and clockwise directions.

- **Temperature Sensor (LM35):** A precision integrated circuit (IC) temperature device from the LM35 series with an output voltage linearly proportional to the centigrade scale. These devices do not require any external calibration and can render average accuracy of ±¼°C at room temperature [15].
- **ESP8266:** A low-cost Wi-Fi Module integrated with a 32-bit Tensilica L-106
  Microcontroller that highlights extremely low power consumption [16]. This component allows the Arduino UNO to be IoT enabled.
- **MPX5050DP Pressure Transducer:** A highly precise sensor used to measure pressure and is widely used in the fields of medical instruments. It is a dual-port, differential integrated silicon pressure sensor in a six-pin system-in-package (SIP). It is a monolithic silicon pressure sensor used to provide an accurate and high-level analog output signal that is proportional to applied pressure.

8.5 IoT/MOBILE APPLICATION USER INTERFACE (UI)

The IoT-linked mobile application is a convenient way to keep the anaesthesiologists updated on live vitals as well as patient history, giving him/her complete insight about the patient and the respective operation. On entering into the application, the doctor is advised to login first to maintain privacy with patient details, as presented in Figure 8.7a. A doctor log in using a case-sensitive password and, upon successful authentication, is transferred to the page of Surgery Category as portrayed in Figure 8.7b. This page allows the doctor to select a type of surgery to administer. The purpose of adding this feature was to allow smooth accessibility to a particular

FIGURE 8.7   Doctor login page (a); surgery category page (b); and type of surgery page (c).

patient in a logical sequence instead of having to remember every surgery detail to get access to the patient. On selecting the type of surgery, the doctor is then introduced to a subcategory of the type of surgery the doctor had previously selected. The case of Cardiology with subcategories as coronary bypass surgery, angioplasty, and valvuloplasty are shown as examples in Figure 8.7c.

If coronary bypass surgery is selected, the doctor is introduced to his active patients as shown in Figure 8.8a. The doctor is then required to select his particular patient based on surgery type and asked to login using the patient unique ID or patient phone number as shown in Figure 8.8b. In case the patient isn't registered on the mobile application, a provision to create a new account has also been implemented. On successful login, the doctor can now get a comprehensive view of his/her patient as shown in Figure 8.8c. The following page also hosts the option to proceed to live vitals (see Figure 8.9a and Figure 8.9b) or patient surgery history. If the

FIGURE 8.8   Patient list page (a); patient login page (b); and patient details page (c).

FIGURE 8.9   Patient details page (a); patient details page (b); and patient surgery history page (c).

doctor wishes to get a brief on the patient's surgery history, he/she can simply select that option and is taken to the patient history page as shown in Figure 8.9c. Upon selecting a particular operation date and type, the doctor is presented with a detailed medical report as shown in Figure 8.10a and Figure 8.10b. The page also gives the doctor the option to view the anaesthesia report for that particular surgery as shown in Figure 8.10c. After careful examination of the patient's history, the doctor can visit the live vitals page as shown in Figure 8.11a.

The live vitals page shows the patients' heart rate, body temperature (°F), oxygen level (SpO$_2$) and systolic and diastolic pressure. The live vitals page exhibits a different user interface for normal and emergency conditions as shown in Figure 8.11b and 8.11c, respectively. During an autodetected emergency condition, the doctors in the operation theatre are alerted as shown in Figure 8.11c. A provision has been allocated for a manual emergency action with the help of a button as shown in Figure 8.11b.

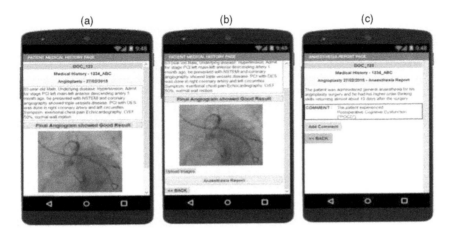

FIGURE 8.10   Patient medical history page (a); Patient medical history page (b); and anaesthesia report page (c).

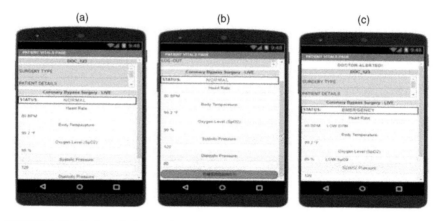

FIGURE 8.11   Patient vitals page (a); patient vitals page (b); and patient vitals page (c).

8.6   CONCLUSION

A device has been developed that automatically monitors the patient's vital signs and prescribes the necessary amount of anaesthesia. This system will not eliminate the need for an anaesthesiologist, but allows his/her job to be performed better and more safely. Automation of anaesthesia for monitoring vital functions is desirable as it will provide more time and flexibility for the anaesthesiologist to focus on critical issues. The system is extremely accurate and responsive (up to 98%). These parameters determine the overall condition of the patient. In case the vitals drop below the desired level, the anaesthesia dosage is controlled automatically with the help of the microcontroller and the motor actions. The syringe infusion pump is mechanically connected to the motor. The required level of anaesthesia is exactly calculated and administered so that future side effects due to variations in anaesthesia levels are eliminated. The data is reliable and can be effectively tracked with the aid of a robust record-keeping and IoT-enabled system.

REFERENCES

[1] Fasting, S., and S.E. Gisvold. "Equipment Problems during Anaesthesia—Are They a Quality Problem?" *British Journal of Anaesthesia* 89, no. 6 (2002): 825–31.

[2] Thrush, David N. "Are Automated Anesthesia Records Better?" *Journal of Clinical Anesthesia* 4, no. 5 (1992): 386–89.

[3] Heinrichs, W. "Automated Anaesthesia Record Systems, Observations on Future Trends of Development." *International Journal of Clinical Monitoring and Computing* 12, no. 1 (1995): 17–20.

[4] "Anesthesia." Johns Hopkins Medicine. Accessed May 12, 2021. http://www.hopkinsmedicine.org/health/treatment-tests-and-therapies/types-of-anesthesia-and-your-anesthesiologist.

[5] "Automated Anesthesia Delivery Pump - IOSR Journals." Accessed May 12, 2021. http://www.iosrjournals.org/iosr-jpbs/papers/Vol9-issue4/Version-2/L0942100106.pdf.

[6] Krishnakumar, S., J. Bethanney Janney, W. Antony Josephine Snowfy, S. Joshin Sharon, and S. Vinodh Kumar. "Automatic Anesthesia Regularization System (AARS) with Patient Monitoring Modules." *International Journal of Engineering & Technology* 7, no. 2.25 (2018): 48.

[7] Chandran, R. "Human Factors in Anaesthetic Crisis." *World Journal of Anesthesiology* 3, no. 3 (2014): 203.

[8] Pignaton, W., Braz, J., Kusano, P. S., Módolo, M. P., de Carvalho, L. R., Braz, M. G., & Braz, L. G. (2016). Perioperative and Anesthesia-Related Mortality: An 8-Year Observational Survey From a Tertiary Teaching Hospital. *Medicine, 95*(2), e2208. https://doi.org/10.1097/MD.0000000000002208

[9] "What You Should Know about Anesthesia." Harvard Health, June 17, 2020. https://www.health.harvard.edu/diseases-and-conditions/what-you-should-know-about-anesthesia.

[10] Manuel, P., and Miller, R. D. *Basics of Anesthesia E-Book*. Elsevier, 2017.

[11] Vinckier, F. (2000). What is the cause of failure of local anesthesia? *Revue belge de medecine dentaire, 55*(1), 41–50.

[12] Galadima, Ahmad Adamu. "Arduino as a Learning Tool." *2014 11th International Conference on Electronics, Computer and Computation (ICECCO)*, 2014. https://doi.org/10.1109/icecco.2014.6997577.

[13] Strogonovs, R. Implementing pulse oximeter using MAX30100. *Morf-Coding and Engineering* (2017).

[14] Bakibillah, S.M., A., Nazibur Rahman, and Md. Anis Uz Zaman. "Microcontroller Based Closed Loop Speed Control of DC Motor Using PWM Technique." *International Journal of Computer Applications* 108, no. 14 (2014): 15–18.

[15] "LM35 Temperature Sensor." Electronic Wings. Accessed May 12, 2021. https://www.electronicwings.com/components/lm35-temperature-sensor.

[16] Kodali, Ravi Kishore, and Kopulwar Shishir Mahesh. "Low Cost Ambient Monitoring Using ESP8266." *2016 2nd International Conference on Contemporary Computing and Informatics (IC3I)*, 2016. https://doi.org/10.1109/ic3i.2016.7918788.

9 Implantable Electronics
Real-Time Adaptive Image Security of Smart Visual Sensor Nod

R. Nithya Paranthaman and D. Dhanasekaran

CONTENTS

9.1 INTRODUCTION

The visual sensor node captures video information, which is more difficult to transmit over the cloud. Streaming video in real-time is converted into image frames or image screenshots and then transmitted. Before transmitting the image, it is encrypted in the sensor node itself to achieve image security. The system-on-chip (SoC) design for real-time image processing already exists and the basic image-processing blocks are available as an IP core for computation [1]. The custom component on demand can be synthesized using reconfigurable logic, which is available as a part of SoC design. The soft-core processor controls the overall operation of the SoC design so this process is a codesign approach to enforce real-time image security [2].

DOI: 10.1201/9781003166511-9

Image security can be achieved by several encryption algorithms. The encryption algorithms are classified into two types: symmetric and asymmetric encryption. The lightweight encryption is achieved earlier through elliptic curve cryptography (ECC). The advantage of ECC is a reduced key size with increased security [3]. Later, the image encryption can be done through the creation of chaotic sequences which act as logistic maps for increasing image security [4]. The encoding of the image using DNA rules also provides a very high confidential method. Differential attacks analysis shows clearly that DNA encryption provides maximum security [5]. Then the combination of several chaotic and cellular automata techniques is employed for increased image confidentiality [6]. Several hyperchaotic techniques are also utilized for achieving image security. The basic concept behind all the encryption techniques involves two mechanisms in common: They are diffusion and permutation. Image security also depends on the number of iterations involved in it.

9.2   RELATED WORKS

Selective image encryption plays a major role in the medical field. It converts the colour image into a grayscale image. The grayscale image, which is simply a two-dimensional binary matrix, is then split into two submatrices. One matrix is selected for encryption and the other is directly combined with the encrypted matrix to produce encrypted an image matrix [7]. Internet of Things (IoT)-friendly image encryption is proposed for the increased security through lightweight cryptographic techniques [8]. Even though security is increased, there is no parallelism in encryption, which, in turn, increases power consumption. If the computation of encryption is made parallel, then the performance of the entire security system is improved. Such a behaviour can be obtained by splitting the RGB colour image into three independent channels that are encrypted individually. This method increases the speed of computation [9]. The RGB colour image encryption can be fully synthesized in hardware using reconfigurable logic [10, 11]. The dedicated hardware for encryption provides an increased security level compared to a software-only technique. The maximum delay involved in the implementation of the logic circuitry is 6.37 ns. The method of achieving dynamic security in sensor nodes is possible by using reconfigurable ECC hardware coprocessors that in turn increase power consumption and resource utilization [12]. Security acceleration can be implemented on the visual sensor node by a codesign approach. It combines both hardware and software methodology to ensure the increasing security level in reduced time and power [13].

9.3   PROPOSED METHOD

The proposed method for image encryption is based on the SoC design to modify the IoT-enabled visual sensor node into a smart sensor node by adapting the security level based on the available power budget. The image encryption module utilizes the three dimensional (3D) chaotic encryption technique.

9.3.1 3D CHAOTIC IMAGE ENCRYPTION

The 3D chaotic image encryption uses three nonlinear chaotic sequences that were otherwise termed as 3D logistic maps [14, 15]. The chaotic sequence is simply given by the function

$$X(i+1) = \lambda x(i)(1-x(i)) \tag{9.1}$$

This is the logistic mapping equation in one dimension. If the dimension increases, the coupling between the elements increases, which in turn increases the security of the system.

The chaotic behaviour for three dimensions is given by

$$A(i+1) = \alpha A(i)(1-A(i)) + \beta B(i)^2 A(i) + \lambda C(i)^2 \tag{9.2}$$

$$B(i+1) = \alpha B(i)(1-B(i) + \beta C(i)^2 B(i) + \lambda A(i)^2 \tag{9.3}$$

$$C(i+1) = \alpha C(i)(1-C(i)) + \beta A(i)^2 C(i) + \lambda B(i)^2 \tag{9.4}$$

Steps involved in 3-D chaotic image encryption are as follows:

- The initial condition is setup for the parameters α, β, λ.
- Three chaotic sequences for key derivation is generated.
- Permutation of the column can be done through first chaotic sequence.
- Row permutation using the second chaotic sequence by considering the condition.
  If the chaotic sequence is odd, then the pixels of that row are shifted to the left
    If not, then the pixels of that row are shifted to the right.
- Finally, the Xor operation is performed on the pixels of the image through column-by-column computation based on the third chaotic sequence.

The histogram of the three chaotic sequences undergoes histogram equalization to obtain uniform distribution of pixels in the key image.

The histogram-equalized logistic maps are seen in Figure 9.1.

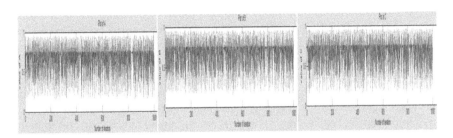

FIGURE 9.1 Plot of histogram-equalized logistic maps of the A, B, and C chaotic sequences.

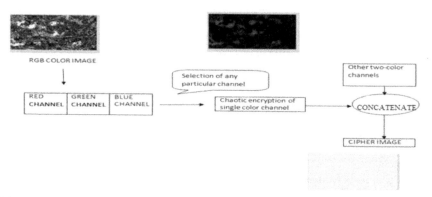

FIGURE 9.2   Selective channel encryption.

9.3.2   Need for Selective Colour Channel Encryption

The proposed model of selective colour channel encryption refers to partial encryption of the RGB image by encrypting one of the colour channels while the other two channels are concatenated to the encrypted single-channel component. Sometimes, two channels are selected for encryption in parallel and it is concatenated with the other channel. In some cases, all the three colour channels are encrypted as a single RGB colour image, which, in turn, leads to high-level data security. The need of single-channel encryption is:

- To reduce cryptosystem complexity.
- To achieve different levels of security.
- To reduce resource utilization and computation time.

The recovery of the original image now becomes a challenging task for the intruders. The attacker has to identify correctly the encryption technique implemented, generate the accurate chaotic sequence for key derivation, and then identify the particular encrypted channel to be identified. It is also more convenient than the existing three-channel encryption scheme because it results in speedy computation. The selective channel encryption is represented schematically in Figure 9.2.

9.4   SECURITY ANALYSIS OF IMAGE ENCRYPTION

For experimental verification of the proposed method, the entire RGB image is encrypted first using 3-D chaotic image encryption. Then, using the same encryption technique, only one colour channel of the RGB image is encrypted and other two are simply concatenated to the encrypted colour channel to generate the cipher image. The image used for demonstration is an RGB colour image of size $500 \times 300 \times 3$ pixels. If only one colour channel is encrypted, the input to the chaotic encryption is $500 \times 300 \times 1$ pixels. The decryption is the reverse process, which is difficult for hackers because the channel that is encrypted to be found correctly for further process. The original image, cipher image, and the reconstructed image for two different images is shown in Table 9.1.

TABLE 9.1
Encrypted and Decrypted Sample Images

S. No	Imagee	Original Image	Encrypted Image	Decrypted Image	Reconstructed Image
1.	greens.jpg	Single-colour channel	Encrypted channel	Decrypted Channel	Reconstructed Image
2.	babygirl.jpg	Single-colour channel	Encrypted channel	Decrypted channel	Reconstructed Image

From Table 9.1, it is clearly understood that the reconstruction of the original RGB image with full accuracy is possible only in conventional encryption techniques but by using single-channel encryption, it can be possible to retrieve almost the entire image informationwith lesser complex computation since it reduces the logic circuitry. This method seems to be more advantageous where the hardware implementation of image encryption is necessary. This method provides the initiative for achieving the adaptive security. The number of channels to be encrypted can be selected at run-time, which is directly proportional to the strength of the image encryption.

Security analysis is performed for both the techniques by two different attack mechanisms: statistical attack and differential attack.

9.4.1 STATISTICAL ATTACK

In statistical attack, the hackers concentrate on the distribution of the gray levels in the encrypted image for guessing the original image information. Histogram analysis, correlation coefficient analysis, and the entropy analysis are performed for the statistical attack verification.

9.4.1.1 Histogram Analysis

Histograms shows the distribution of pixels in an image. Figure 9.3 clearly reveals that, in both techniques, the histogram of the original and the encrypted image is highly uncorrelated. This ensures the confidentiality of the encryption mechanism.

9.4.1.2 Correlation Coefficient Analysis

The correlation coefficient measures the closeness of a pixel to the neighbouring pixel. The correlation coefficient value is 1 for highly correlated pixels. If the correlation coefficient is positive, it denotes the values of the adjoining pixels moves in the same direction. If the correlation coefficient is negative, the adjoining pixels are moving in the opposite direction. The zero coefficient value indicates that the two

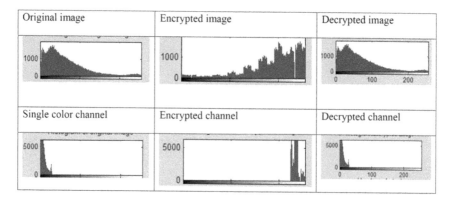

FIGURE 9.3   Histogram analysis.

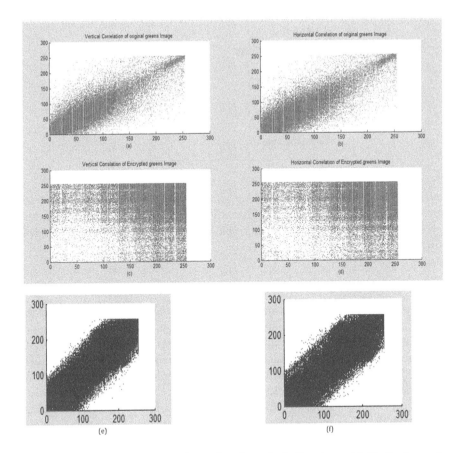

FIGURE 9.4 Correlation in horizontal and vertical directions. (a) Vertical correlation of original image. (b) Horizontal correlation of original image. (c) Vertical correlation of RGB encrypted image. (d) Horizontal correlation of RGB encrypted image. (e) Vertical correlation of one-channel encrypted. (f) Horizontal correlation of one channel encrypted.

adjacent pixels are uncorrelated. The correlation coefficients can be obtained for both the original and encrypted images in horizontal and vertical directions, which is shown in Figure 9.4.

From Figure 9.4, it is clear that the horizontal and vertical correlation of the encrypted RGB has uniform distribution of pixels, providing higher-level security compared to the single-colour channel encryption, which provides lower-level security.

9.4.1.3 Entropy Analysis

The randomness in the image content is measured using entropy. The probability of 256 likely outcomes of the image pixel values is determined using the entropy equation. If the entropy value becomes closer to the ideal value of 8, then the

TABLE 9.2
Entropy Analysis

Observed Image	Entropy
Original_image	7.3500
Encrypted_image	7.4099
Single_channel	3.1324
Encrypted_channel	3.4474

security of the encryption over entropy attack is maximum. Encryption of the entire RGB image is founds to be significantly better in entropy analysis, providing higher-level security compared to the single-colour channel encryption, which is shown in Table 9.2.

9.4.2 DIFFERENTIAL ATTACK

Differential attack refers to the sensitivity of the encryption algorithm to even the slightest changes in the key. It can be estimated through metrics such as number of pixel changing rate (NPCR) and unified average changing intensity (UACI). Both techniques provide similar resistance against differential attack, which is clearly shown in Figure 9.5. The NPCR and UACI of both techniques are closer to 99% and 33% respectively shown in Table 9.3.

From the overall analysis of various attacks using a Matlab tool, it is clear that the entire RGB image encryption provides a higher security level, whereas single-channel encryption provides the lesser security strength.

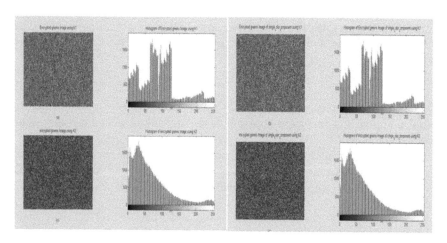

(a) Key sensitivity of encrypted image   (b) key sensitivity of encrypted Channel

FIGURE 9.5   Key sensitivity analysis.

TABLE 9.3
NPCR and UACI

Experimental Observation	NPCR (%)	UACI (%)
Encrypted_image	99.8358	32.8879
Encrypted_channel	99.9393	33.7075

9.5 SoC-BASED IMAGE ENCRYPTION FOR ADAPTIVE SECURITY

9.5.1 SINGLE-CHANNEL ENCRYPTION MODULE

The concept of adaptive security can be implemented in an IoT-enabled vision sensor node using SoC design [16, 17]. The SoC design consists of some predefined IP cores and also the reconfigurable logic available for the design of custom building blocks [18]. The register-transfer level (RTL) view of the image encryption module, which is made as a custom building block capable of encrypting a single channel, is shown in Figure 9.6.

The look-up tables (LUTs) utilized for synthesizing the single encryption module is 480 LUTs. Each of the pixel input is represented by an 8-bit integer value. The size of the single channel is 500×300 pixels, which is provided as the input to the image encryption module.

The module is created as an instance and can be utilized as needed. The number of modules to be activated can be controlled by the soft-core processor. If the entire RGB image has to be encrypted, then the soft-core processor activates the three image-encryption modules, each one able to perform the encryption of a single

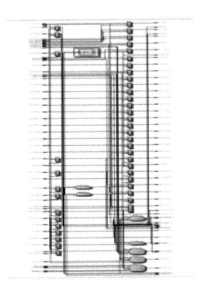

FIGURE 9.6 RTL view of single channel encryption module.

channel. Parallelism can be achieved since all the three modules perform encryption at the same time. The speed of the computation is also increased.

9.5.2 SoC Design for Encryption in IoT-Enabled Smart Vision Sensor

The complementary metal oxide semiconductor (CMOS) image sensor node captures streaming video in real-time, which is given as the input to the chroma resampler, which samples streaming video into image frames or image screenshots. Then, the real-time YCbCr input frames are converted into parallel sequences using a colour plane sequencer [19]. Then the parallel sequences of the YCbCr image is converted into parallel sequences of the RGB image by a colour space converter. The three channels of the RGB image can now be encrypted based on the security strength needed or based on the available power budget. The output of the channel encryption module is the encrypted channel module. If all the three modules are activated, then it provides higher-level security. The SoC design of image encryption is shown in Figure 9.7. It is designed in Quartus-SOPC builder tool and the system design generated is shown in Figure 9.8.

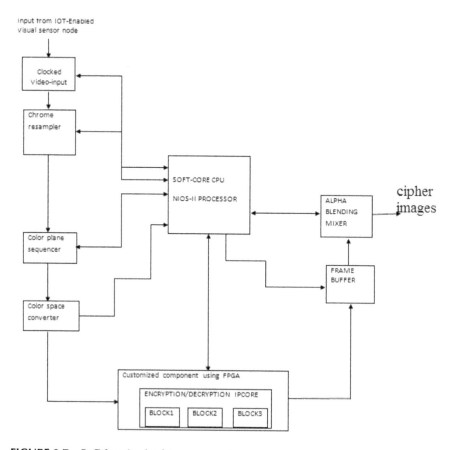

FIGURE 9.7 SoC for adaptive image encryption.

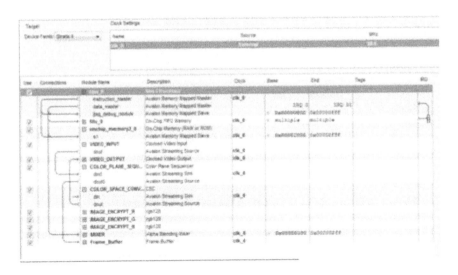

FIGURE 9.8   Generated SoC design for adaptive security.

9.5.3   CODESIGN APPROACH USING A SOFT-CORE PROCESSOR

The soft-core processor is a processor fully designed and synthesized in reconfigurable logic [20]. The soft-core processor controls the amount of hardware resources to be utilized to perform image encryption. The dynamic power manager of every IoT-enabled sensor node adapts its own behaviour to adjust dynamically to the critical power situations by switching to different power modes. The soft-core processor always checks the status of the power manager before performing image encryption. Based on the power mode of the power manager, the SoC adapts image encryption by selecting the number of channels to be encrypted. The flowchart of the above mechanism is shown in Figure 9.9.

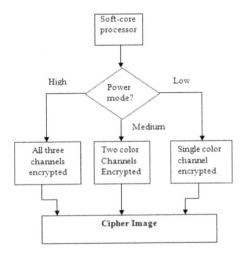

FIGURE 9.9   Flowchart for adaptive security.

TABLE 9.4

Evaluation Results of Image Encryption

Encryption	Resources Utilized (LUTs)	Power Consumption (mW)	Actual Computation Time (ns)
Single-channel	480	302.99	3.983
Two-channel	960	607.32	3.983
Three-channel	1440	909.47	3.983

9.6 EVALUATION RESULTS OF ADAPTIVE SECURITY

Comparison between the single-channel, two-channel, and three-channel encryption techniques were made based on metrics such as computation time, resources utilized, and power consumption. Experimental analysis was done on the Altera SoC with a NIOS-II soft-core processor. If the soft-core processor identified the low power mode, then it selects single-channel encryption to ensure minimal security even in critical power situations with the computation time of 3.983 ns. The medium power mode results in two-channel encryption, but the computation time remains the same because two encryption modules conduct the computation in parallel time.

In high power mode, all the three channels were encrypted independently by three separate encryption modules. This uses more power because of increased resource utilization. Table 9.4 gives the evaluation results of encryption and charts were plotted to show the performance in Figure 9.10. Ref. [12] provide an FPGA-based solution for image encryption implementation that achieves the computation time of 6.37 ns. The proposed method of adaptive security using SoC provides lesser computation time of 3.983 ns irrespective of the strength of the security provided and available power budget.

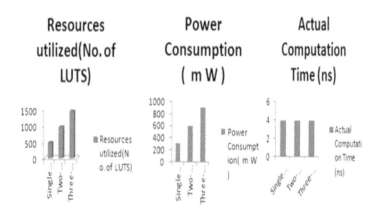

FIGURE 9.10 Comparison charts.

9.7 CONCLUSION

This paper provides an adaptive security approach for the image screenshots acquired from an image sensor using SoC design. A soft-core processor controls the overall operation, hence no external processors/coprocessors are needed. It is evident that the SoC design of adaptive security provides better performance compared to the hardware-only/software-only approach. Since the soft-core processor is highly synchronized with the dynamic power manager, the security of the images obtained from the visual sensor node is made to be dynamically adjusted to the changes in power modes. This real-time adaptive security introduces massive parallelism, which leads to less computation time. The major trade-off between security and power consumption in Iot-enabled visual sensor nodes can be treated by adaptive security using a codesign approach. Thus, a smart way to adapt a minimum security level even in low power mode is possible by a selective channel encryption technique through SoC design.

REFERENCES

[1] Elena S. Yanakova, Andrey A. Belyaev, Georgij Macharadza, 'Efficient software and hardware platform ≪multicore≫ for cloud video Analytics', ElconRUS, (2020).

[2] Vilabha S. Patil, Shraddha S. Deshpande and Yashwant B. Mane, 'FPGA based acceleration of security algorithm using co-design approach for WSN applications', Springer, ICICCS, PP 592–603, (2020).

[3] J. Portilla, A. Otero, E.de la Torre, T. Riesgo, 'Adaptable security in wireless sensor networks by using reconfigurable ECC coprocessor', International Journal of Distributed Sensor Networks, (2010).

[4] Chang-Hsiung Yang and Yu Sheng Chien, 'FPGA implementation and design of a hybrid chaos-AES color image encryption algorithm', www.mdpi.com/journal/symmetry, (2020).

[5] Fazal Noorbasha, K. Suresh, 'FPGA implementation of RGB image encryption and decryption using DNA cryptography', International Journal of Engineering and Technology, pp. 397–403, (2018).

[6] Satyabrata Roy, Umashankar Rawat, 'IECA: an efficient IoT Friendly Image encryption technique using programmable cellular automata', Journal of Ambient Intelligence and Humanized Computing, Springer, (2020).

[7] Prema T., AK. Kasaligar, Sumangala Biradar, 'Selective medical image encryption using DNA crptography', Information Security Journal: A Global Perspective, ISSN: 1939-3555, (2020).

[8] A. Biswas, A. Majumdar, S. Nath, 'LRBC: A lightweight block cipher design for resource constrained IoT devices', Journal of Ambient Intelligence and Humanized Computing, (2020).

[9] Sui Liansheng, Gaobo, 'Single channel color image encryption based on iterative fractional fourier transform', 4th International Symposium on Information Science and Engineering, IEEE, (2013).

[10] Emy Setyaningsih, Retantyo Wardayo, Anny kartika Sari, 'Securing color image transmission using compression-encryption model with dynamic key generator and efficient key distribution', Elsevier, (2015).

[11] Lahieb Mohammed Jawad, Ghxalisulong, 'A review of color image encryption techniques' International Journal of Computer Science Issues, ISSN: 1694-0814 (2013).

[12] Abdelmoughni Toubal, Billel Bengherbia 'FPGA implementation of a wireless sensor node with built-in security coprocessor for secured key exchange & data transfer', Measurement, Volume 153, Elsevier, (2020).

[13] R. Nithya Paranthaman, D. Dhanasekaran 'Nodal level Adaptive security for IoT-enable sensors through dynamic reconfigurable encryption', International Journal of Engineering & Advanced Technology (IJEAT), ISSN: 2249-8958 (2019).

[14] Bikash Bawah, Monjal Saikia, 'An FPGA Implementation of chaos based image encryption & its performance analysis' International Journal of Computer Science & Network, (2016).

[15] Ahmad Shokouh Saljoughi, Hamid Mirraziri, 'A new method for image encryption by 3D chaotic map', Springer, (2018).

[16] Sneha V. Jrivedi, M.A. Hasamnis 'Development of platform using NIOSII soft core processor for Image Encryption & Description using AES algorithm, IEEE ICCSP, (2015).

[17] R. Nithya, K.R. Sarath Chandran, V. Premanand Chandramani, 'Run-time Reconfiguration of Processing Elements through Soft-core processor' ICCSP, IEEE (2014).

[18] Sincy Abraham and Sijlmol AS 'Survey on Sensor Data Encryption using Cipher chip core', IJSTE, ISSN (Online): 2349-784X, (2016).

[19] 'NIOS-II Processor reference handbook', ALTERA Corporation, (2011).

[20] J.G. Tong, I.D.L. Andason and M.A.S. Khalid, 'Soft-core processors for Embedded systems', International Conference on Microelectronics, PP 170–173 (2006).

10 Security Concerns with IoT-Based Health and Fitness Systems

Pushpendu Rakshit, Pramod Kumar Srivastava, and Omkar Chavan

CONTENTS

10.1 INTRODUCTION TO IoT

Over the past few years, the industry has evolved through various phases and, presently, all sectors square measure within the fourth phase of evolution that comprises advanced technologies commonly known as smart devices [1]. This advanced technology is extensively used in all sectors of industry at each level. A smart device interacts with another device with the help of artificial intelligence (AI) and the data collected by this device is managed and stored in the cloud. The process of data allocation and storage is encrypted and secured with the help of sensors. Smart home automation, smart cities, smart industries, advanced surveillance network systems, and other daily-use smart devices such as activity trackers, mobile phones, etc. are a part of the Internet of Things (IoT).

Whether it is a vending machine or an advanced mechanism in production, both share a common goal of increasing the efficiency, productivity, and accuracy. Since

DOI: 10.1201/9781003166511-10

smart devices are widely used, they generate a huge amount of data each day [2]. The process of data management is done with the help of data analytical tools, data sensors, and cloud data management. This data is further used for product development or decision making. Also, these devices, with the help of AI and use of analytical tools, can draw conclusions on behalf of humans and convey them to other devices over a wireless network. Acceptance and use of IoT is growing day-by-day, making it crucial to safely store and uphold the 'CIA' parameters of confidentiality, integrity, availability. We discuss the safekeeping aspects of IoT in this chapter related to the healthcare system, then analyze and discuss contemporary IoT and traditional IT amenities [3].

10.2 REVIEW OF LITERATURE

An article on "security checklist for IoT sensors" gives a detailed explanation of IoT sensors and their functions of security [embeddedcomputing.com]. The sensors available in smart devices help to protect from cyber attackers and cybercrimes. An article entitled "10 IoT security concerns to keep in mind before developing apps" gives a detailed scenario about what needs to be considered while developing an IoT security network [magnetoitsolutions.com]. A research paper by Teng Xu 'Security of IoT systems: Design challenges and opportunities' discusses the design challenges that need to be focused upon and opportunities in the security of an IoT system [15]. A research paper by Mahmoud Ammar, 'Internet of Things: A survey on the security of IoT Framework', highlights security architectures of various frameworks and gives detailed information about model designs and approaches for the security framework of smart devices [16].

10.3 OBJECTIVES

1. To study the security concerns and challenges of IoT healthcare devices.
2. To explore preventive measures related to IoT healthcare security issues.

10.4 ADVANTAGES OF IoT

1. IoT devices help minimize technical errors. With the help of AI and advanced technology, these devices can carry out operations smoothly, resulting in increased efficiency.
2. IoT devices track real-time data and can forecast demand and supply of goods and services, which helps optimize resources.
3. IoT devices allow individuals to control them from any part of this world. With automation, we can now depend on technology and can invest more time in research and development, resulting in higher profits.
4. As machines can interact with other devices, this offers more transparency in the process, less inefficiency, and great quality.

10.5 SECURITY CONCERNS FOR IoT-BASED HEALTHCARE DEVICES

In the league of advanced devices and smart technologies, wearable fitness devices are one of the fastest growing segments as many individuals are now focusing on fitness and health [4]. This fitness equipment technology market is growing rapidly with the increasing use of these smart devices. Many known brands like Apple, Mi, OnePlus, and Samsung are introducing these fitness bands or similar smart technologies. Each device is connected to the internet and can be synchronized with other devices like a phone or computer [5]. Consequently, a large amount of data is generated in the form of cookies, cache files, etc. that contain personal user data, which can be easily hacked due to the devices being connected allowing a simultaneous attack. Other problems that can create serious trouble for users include data leakage and access control, both of which could lead to a hacker breaching and taking possession of consumer data [6]. Tech oriented devices have its own vulnerabilities that create a security threat. For instance, in 2015, hackers compromised a medical device with the help of malware to gain control of a hospital network system. It is difficult to manage high data security with a small processor and little connectivity, both of which can be exploited to allow cybercrimes.

Apart from cyber security problems, devices can also face malfunctioning that can create bodily injuries. Figure 10.2 shows the steps of security pathway. For example, the excessive use of a fitness band heated up the band's battery, resulting in technical issues of hardware. Another risk of a smart device is an error in technology. A false result due to an error in the technology can result in problems for users—especially in the medical field. Recently, it was recorded that medical assistance is based on the results of smart devices. Therefore, even a small error in technology can result in a major problem. We can conclude that smart devices can have various security loopholes that create distortion in digital space and can allow attackers to hack and gain information. Despite these various risks, the consumer wearables industry continues to grow. The devices are still in the development phase and research and development has come up with various solutions like cloud computing, upgraded software, and improved hardware that minimize the risk of data loss also improves the efficiency and quality of the product. Figure 10.1 explains the Security concerns for IoT-based health and fitness devices.

Although some IoT devices should be able to operate autonomously without any intervention from a user, they need to be physically secured from outside threats. These devices can be located in remote locations for long stretches of time, and they could be physically tampered with, for example, using a USB flash drive with malware. Physical safekeeping of an AI and IoT-based device begins from its manufacturer [7]. But building secure sensors and transmitters in the already low-cost devices is a challenge for manufacturers nonetheless. A single IoT device infected with malware does not pose any real threat; a collection of them, however, can bring down any system. To perform a botnet attack, a hacker creates an army of bots by infecting them with malware and directs them to send thousands of requests per second to bring down the target. Spying and intruding through IoT devices is a real problem, as sensitive data may be compromised and used against its owner. Thus, confidentiality is an additional prominent IoT safekeeping concern. The cases of IoT

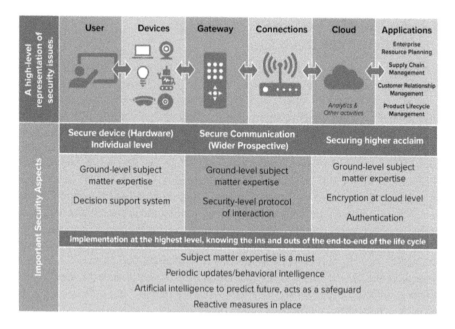

FIGURE 10.1 Security concerns for IoT-based health and fitness devices. (Source: complaincecosmos.com).

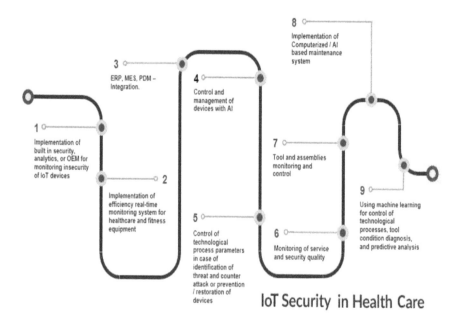

FIGURE 10.2 IoT security pathway.

devices being infected with ransomware are rare, but the concept is quickly becoming a trend in the black hat hacker world. Still, wearables, healthcare devices, smart homes, and other smart devices and ecosystems might be at risk in the future [8].

10.6   CHALLENGES OF SECURITY TOWARDS IoT DEVICES

10.6.1   Updates and Framework

With growing use and demand for smart devices, companies began building various versions of these devices, resulting in lack of security of data [9]. Many device versions, after some point in time, don't receive updates that helps the device to stay current with network settings and precautions. Most manufactures release their updated framework for the latest version so that they can discontinue the old version of their product. As a result, these devices don't receive proper timely updates for testing and to protect against attackers.

10.6.2   Malware and Ransomware Threats

With the rise in the use of smart devices comes a rise in malware and ransomware attacks. Malware and ransomware attackers disable the device functionality and steal user data available on the device. For example, if a device is attacked with ransomware, there is a high chance of data leakage from system such as locations, important documents, passwords, etc.

10.6.3   Artificial Intelligence (AI) Tools and Automation

Smart devices make use of AI with the help of an integrated system to communicate with other devices. The more these devices are used, the more data is generated [10]. Today, millions of users are using smart devices—and use of these devices in power, transportation, and healthcare industries ends up producing a massive volume of data. AI tools and automation helps to manage this data networking. These tools enforce data-specific rules and also detect anomalous data and patterns. The tools help to create an autonomous system that can make decisions based on data analysis. Such decisions can affect multiple functions across large infrastructures in various industries. A single error in an algorithm or in code can affect the functioning of the entire unit or industry. As a result, it can be a big risk, threat, and challenge for an industry.

10.7   PREVENTIVE MEASURES

1. Conduct a risk assessment of devices in development before releasing them for customer or for health care organizations. This evaluation of risk help developers to understand the loop holes in the security system of the device.
2. End-to-end encryption of data can help safeguard electronic networks against attackers who would try to manipulate data by any method of hacking.

3. System administrators can install various tools such as a deny list, which blocks harmful sites that include malware and ransomware viruses. This tool helps to restrict access to devices and reports malicious activity at the network system gateway, ensuring data stays protected.
4. The analytical tools of IoT allow devices to monitor network traffic and allow or filter data that is necessary for analysis. Network administrators can also approve or deny connection to protect from attackers.
5. The data can be transferred to the cloud database with the help of encryption and standards like transport layer security (TLS). It ensures that the data transferred to the cloud is completely secure and confidential.
6. A multilayered data management tool can help reduce the risk of a security breach. This can be done with a web-based application that abides with compliance and privacy rules.
7. Regular updates can help software strengthen the security of devices. Developers can launch a centralized software update across all devices and variants.

10.8   SENSORS AVAILABLE FOR IoT SECURITY AND BENEFITS

Security of IoT devices is critical. IoT sensors play a vital role in data collection, transfer, storage, and solutions. Built-in security codes in software allow sensors to function smoothly and secure the data in critical stages [11]. IoT sensors make use of secure boot to ensure that the device only executes codes produced by the original equipment manufacturer (OEM) or trusted party. An assigned public key helps to prevent malicious attacks from a third party and only allows OEM devices to execute software codes [12]. The firmware updates of devices help in server authentication before downloading or uploading and thereby add a layer of protection. For instance, an antivirus software on a desktop computer helps to protect the data on its hard drive. When we try to download an external file from through a web browser, the software first scans the file in boot scanner for any malicious threat. It then only downloads the file in encrypted form and decrypts it onto our hard drive. This end-to-end function is processed with the help of analytical sensors and detections available in software. Datagram transport layer security (DTLS) or transport layer security (TLS) helps to encrypt and transfer data in secured connection with the help of wireless protocols. Sensors secure the gateway while performing data collection or data analysis. For instance, the banking network contains data related to their clients and banking financial information.

Every time a change or a trade takes place in a client account, the banking network tools access files from the cloud database for analysis or operations, and again save it back to cloud storage with safety in encrypted form [13]. In healthcare systems, IoT devices are also used on a wide scale. Today, healthcare data is saved digitally on a cloud drive. IoT devices not only keep data safe but also remind patients and doctors about their treatment. The smart devices run the entire network system of health care and help to track the real-time recovery of patients. These devices also keep track of healthcare equipment inventory and availability of space in hospitals with the help of enterprise resource planning (ERP) software on behalf of organizations. For example, the centralized software installed on desktop computers has various verticals [14]. So, if there are availability issues with medicines or beds for patients, the program sends a reminder on screen with all the details on availability of resources. Healthcare smart devices are very secure as the sensors available on the device create multilayer security of the entire process. The sensor automatically detects problems in transaction or system networks and eliminates the errors on its own, securing the data.

10.9   IMPLICATIONS

Pharmaceutical companies in India must look for strategies to adopt the latest trends in technology in safe manner, following best branding practices, such as targeting the audience, creating brand image, trust building, word of mouth, and usage of industry 4.0. Pharmaceutical branding is a vital way to generate awareness among potential aids of drugs and benefits. IoT technologies are in their initial phase of growth in the pharmaceutical and healthcare sectors, but their influence across the worldwide healthcare space is undisputable [15-16]. Designing of low-energy, low-cost IoT networks and solutions will take more time. This chapter sketched the role of IoT and smart sensors in the pharmaceutical manufacturing sector while discussing its smart use in future discoveries and clinical trials. The pharmaceutical industry's mounting attention in IoT is actually motivated by increasing demand and pioneering healthcare businesses generating a market demand to boost modern pharmaceutical and healthcare needs. Users are increasingly consuming smartphones, digitally allied cellular sensing systems, and digital wearable devices.

10.10   CONCLUSION

Security is necessary for all IoT devices whether small or large. With excessive use of these devices, there is a massive amount of data generated every day that needs to be monitored and regulated by a secure network. Various measures and precautions include data security and data management. There are various tools available and various methods that practice data security. In the healthcare sector, all data is important and needs to be secured, including patients' personal data, hospital central systems, and networks. Therefore, the data must be regulated using cloud data management techniques. Also, updated software, firmware, and regular security upgrades all help in increasing the efficiency of security and bridging the gaps, if required.

REFERENCES

[1] Ariane P. Industry 4.0 in the medical technology and pharmaceutical industry sectors. BIOPRO Baden Wurttemberg GmbH 2016.
[2] Adoption of Internet of Things in Pharma Manufacturing [Internet]. 2017. [cited 12 May 2019].
[3] Automation, IoT and the future of smarter research environments [Internet]. Pharma IQ News 2018. [cited 26 May 2019].

[4] Burmeister, C., Lüttgens, D., Piller, F.T. Business model innovation for Industrie 4.0: Why the "Industrial Internet" mandates a new perspective on innovation. *Die Unternehmung* 2016, *70*: 124–152

[5] Dimiter, V. Medical Internet of Things and Big Data in Healthcare. *Healthc Inform Res*. 2016 Jul; 22(3): 156–163.

[6] Improving Efficiency in Pharma Manufacturing Through IoT Technologies [Internet]. SpendEdge 2018. [cited 15 April 2019]

[7] Internet of Things in Clinical Trials [Internet] JLI Social Media 2018. [cited 24 May 2019]. Lee, J.; Kao, H.-A.; Yang, S. Service innovation and smart analytics for industry 4.0 and big data environment. *Procedia CIRP* 2014, *16*: 3–8.

[8] Markarian, J. The Internet of Things for Pharmaceutical Manufacturing. Pharmaceutical Technology 2016, 40(9): 54–58.

[9] Pharmaceutical Manufacturing is Labeled a Success with Newly Integrated Plant Operations [Internet]. decisyon 2019. [cited 18 May 2019].

[10] Rayes, A., Salam, S. Internet of Things From Hype to Reality. Springer International Publishing 2017

[11] Sridhar, A., Varia, H. IoT Could Make a Difference in Pharmaceutical Manufacturing and Supply Chains [Internet]. aranca 2017. [cited 5 June 2019].

[12] Staines R. Healthcare AI market worth $10bn plus by 2024 – report [Internet]. pharmaphorum 2018. [cited 26 April 2019].

[13] Steven, M.N., Gail, F.D. Animal Research, the 3Rs, and the "Internet of Things": Opportunities and Oversight in International Pharmaceutical Development. ILAR Journal 2017. 57(2): 246–253.

[14] Wolf, C.; Floyd, S.W. Strategic Planning Research: Toward a Theory-Driven Agenda. *J. Manag.* 2017, *43*: 1754–1788.

[15] Teng Xu; James B. Wendt; Miodrag Potkonjak Security of IoT systems: Design challenges and opportunities 2014 IEEE/ACM International Conference on Computer-Aided Design (ICCAD).

[16] Mahmoud Ammar, Internet of Things: A survey on the security of IoT frameworks, February 2018, Journal of Information Security and Applications 38:8–27, DOI:10.1016/j.jisa.2017.11.002

11 Emerging eHealth IoT Applications
A Review on Kiosk-Based Systems

Sushant, Akarsh Saxena, Mokhtar Shouran, and D.V. Deepikaa

CONTENTS

DOI: 10.1201/9781003166511-11

11.1   INTRODUCTION

Healthcare monitoring is a difficult and tedious task for large and densely populated countries, particularly those with comparatively low per capita income and large spans of land area with significant portions of the population living in remote areas. It is found that in such cases, the data available to the healthcare monitoring authorities or the government is limited and unorganized. Such unorganized, unreported, or underreported data is useless for proper health monitoring purposes and doesn't lead to significant conclusions or solutions to these problems. Before further discussions on this, let us understand first what does monitoring and evaluation mean as defined by the World Health Organization (WHO).

11.2   IMPORTANCE OF MONITORING AND EVALUATION

Monitoring and evaluation give:

- Data on the purpose and goal of a mediation and how well it is performing toward its goals.
- Direction on future intercession exercises.
- A significant piece of responsibility to financing offices and partners.

Plans for monitoring and evaluation should be made at the beginning of an intervention development process.

11.2.1 MONITORING

Monitoring involves checking the assortment of data generated by practically all tasks and exercises. Monitoring reveals whether things have worked as planned and helps project directors notice and take care of issues rapidly. Monitoring involves keeping track of project data sources and yields, for example:

- Activities
- Reporting and documentation
- Finances and financial plans
- Supplies and hardware

Monitoring is a constant activity that should be a part of routine work duties.

11.2.2 EVALUATION

Evaluation helps discover if a venture is accomplishing what it set out to do and whether it is having an adverse effect. The process of evaluation tries to see how and why a mediation has functioned admirably. If a task is ineffective, questions are raised with regard to what could be improved or done differently. Evaluation accordingly monitors key results and effects identified with the diverse task parts, surveying whether the destinations, points, and objectives are being accomplished.

Evaluations happen at specific points during mediations. It is entirely expected to begin with standard exploration close to the start of mediation in order to acquire data with which future changes can narrow the scope. Further assessments are typically made at time intervals of two and three years.

11.2.3 WHO SHOULD MONITOR AND EVALUATE?

Monitoring is regularly completed by project staff, project accomplices and friend teachers as they monitor their work.

Evaluations can be performed by outside offices or by project staff, coworkers and partners, or by a mix of these groups and outside offices. Outer contribution offers specialized ability and objectivity to evaluations. The utilization of venture staff and companion networks an evaluation fabricates their ability and gives a feeling of responsibility for results.

Improved worldwide health monitoring requires new innovations and strategies, strong public limit, standards and norms, and best quality level worldwide revealing.

11.2.4 WORLDWIDE HEALTH SECURITY INDEX

The Worldwide Health Security (WHS) index is a primary far-reaching evaluation of worldwide health security capabilities in 195 nations. The GHS index score is 40.2 out of an expected 100. While significant high-income countries report an ordinary score of 51.9, the index shows that aggregately, worldwide preparation for plagues and pandemics is weak [9].

FIGURE 11.1 GHS index map [9].

11.2.5 FINDINGS AND RECOMMENDATIONS

1. Public health safety is essentially frail throughout the world. No nation is completely ready for plagues or pandemics, and each nation has significant gaps to address.
2. Nations are not ready for a universally cataclysmic biological event.
3. There is little proof that most nations have tried significant health safety precautions or shown that they would be useful in an emergency.
4. Most nations have not apportioned subsidizing from public financial plans to fill recognized readiness gaps.
5. The majority of countries face major political and security risks that could sabotage public ability to counter natural threats.
6. Most nations need fundamental health framework limits that are imperative for disease and pandemic reaction.
7. Coordination and preparation are insufficient among veterinary, natural life, and general health experts and policymakers.
8. Improving health framework of a country, consistence with global health and security standards, is fundamental.

Approximately, 75% of nations get low scores on universally disastrous biological danger-related markers, the major vulnerable point being oversight of double-use research.

Albeit 86% of nations use local funds or donations in health security, barely any country pays for health security and action plans out of national budgets.

Kiosk-based healthcare systems can be the solution to many of these problems in the healthcare sector.

11.3   SELF-SERVICE KIOSKS IN THE HEALTHCARE SYSTEM

The health sector is an indispensable part of every individual's life, making them highly dependent on hospitals and medical healthcare centers across the country. This need is often leveraged by healthcare providers who in turn charge exorbitant and unreasonable prices to vulnerable patients and their families.

The gaining control of political representatives and influential people in the country has created a system of referrals, which overlooks the validation and morality of streamlined practices in healthcare centers. Therefore, a self-service approach to healthcare is crucial for the system to be more available and efficient, eliminating the problem of recommendations and referrals.

Automated kiosks in the healthcare industry help in computerized check-ins and registration, patient status, online filling of forms and questionnaires, insurance confirmation, automated patient queuing, payment of bills, and reports of outstanding payments. Human intervention is reduced with the kiosk system, thereby increasing the role of technology in all spheres.

11.3.1   GAINS OF SELF-SERVICE KIOSKS

Kiosks reduce the waiting time for patients. Conventionally, the managerial healthcare staff manually fill out forms and update patient information and related figures. But with introduction of kiosks, the manual work has been eliminated, making the system quicker, simpler, and free from any kind of ambiguity caused by human error. Also, their use saves time in emergency situations and reduces the hassle of paper and its waste.

11.3.2   ELIMINATION OF ERRORS

The involvement of humans results in mistakes and errors. However, self-service kiosks can reduce the errors made by humans, as their role is minimized. Patients fill their details own their own, which is highly likely for the patients to give accurate data.

11.3.3   COST EFFICIENCY

Self-service kiosks in healthcare centers reduce costs as the self-check-ins at hospitals has removed the use of paper and human intervention. Moreover, nurses and staff spend less time doing paperwork; the reduced administrative responsibilities of the hospital allows staff to concentrate more on providing proper care to patients.

11.3.4   IMPROVED PAYMENT MECHANISM

The kiosks usually have all the updated and related information about the doctors and the patients, which helps in settling bills and payments. Patients pay their medical expenses through electronic platforms via credit and debit cards, and upon payment, can even see outstanding balances, if any.

11.3.5 CONFUSION AND WORRIES

The introduction of healthcare kiosks can reduce confusion and stress for patients and their families, as it provides them with clear information. This easy-to-understand healthcare information is usually presented in a precise and detailed manner. It also personalizes content and bases the delivery of the information on a user's language, education level, and other profile characteristics.

11.3.6 MISPERCEPTIONS

With the advancement and revolution of technology come concerns in the form of myths, threats, and ambiguities associated with it.

Difficult for the older patients to cope with evolving technologies: It is often thought that older patients find it tough and problematic to use the self-service technology, but with rising awareness amongst the advancing technologies, the scenario has changed. Older patients have started to become well-versed with newer trends and technologies. In cases where someone is not familiar with the technology, they could request help of younger family members accompanying them or center staff.

Self-service technology is difficult and takes a lot of time: The inventive changes in today's technology has surpassed the days when technology was slow and unsupported by legacy systems that were cumbersome and time consuming. Today's software has been designed, backed, and powered with research and implementation that is faster, streamlined, and accessible. The conveniences in approachability of tools and mechanisms have reduced the need of manpower.

Expanded openness to security threats: Regardless of the availability, comfort, and number of safety assurances offered, a few patients will be inclined to the customary technique for registration, payment, and appointment making. There are a few groups in India who believe that innovation is unstable and unprotected. However, there are various security measures worked in the self-administration systems that aren't accessible with standard pen and paper. If patients are reluctant to utilize a self-administration stand in light of protection concerns, associations can ease delay by adjusting devices and administrations that take into account potential misgivings.

The effective self-service solutions provide accurate and secure engagement of patients by protecting their data and making the appropriate use of the data exposed for a constructive and progressive experience.

11.3.7 PATIENT PRIVACY IN KIOSKS

The main aim and idea behind the introduction of kiosks in health care is the welfare of patients and their families and the system to be more organized and efficient. Along with this, their personal information is also a growing concern.

Self-administration of information comes with the expectation that patients will confirm their identity with a security question during registration. The registration doesn't store patient data and has a camouflage screen that shields data from others' view when the patient stands before the booth. It has certain encryptions that recognize the patient and produces data, when scrambled. In secure self-administration, all data entered streams safely to back-end frameworks and agrees with the installment card industry information security standard (PCIDSS).

11.3.8 HOW TO CHOOSE THE RIGHT KIOSKS

It is important to choose the right kiosk, which depends on the following factors:

11.3.8.1 Types of Kiosks

There are several types of kiosks like tablet, pedestal, freestanding, and desktop. Depending upon the layout, floor mapping, foot-traffic pattern, and the usage, one should decide which type of kiosks would be best used in each particular healthcare center.

11.3.8.2 Arrangement or Mapping

The surrounding environment matters while setting up a kiosk. Also, the need of the kiosk at a particular place should be evaluated, keeping in mind the layout of the space. In places with less space, freestanding kiosks must be avoided and tablets must be used. Figure 11.2 shows kiosk-based healthcare systems [10].

FIGURE 11.2   Kiosk-based healthcare systems [10].

11.4   HEALTH MANAGEMENT SYSTEMS BASED ON IoT

The medical system in India should be upgraded based on the current situation, which means systems should be more reliable and user-friendly so that treatment can be offered in better, faster ways. Also, patients should seek treatment as quickly as possible at the initial stage of disease.

New IoT systems—called self-reliant medical treatment system (SMRTS)—should be introduced. With these, the treatment of the patient is done automatically without the presence of doctor or any assistant at very low initial fee. These computerized patient check-in kiosk platforms increase support, permitting patients to self-recognize upon arriving at the office; see and affirm health record data, electronically sign assent reports, and ensure all information entered by the patient is seamlessly integrated into the healthcare organization's back-end system. This helps to reduce costs and overhead. Figure 11.3 shows a block diagram of the method of treatment.

When using a self-reliant medical treatment system, input is defined as the patient data given to the system, such as:

- Patient name
- Age
- Blood group
- Permanent address
- Contact details

Next, the system asks the patient to choose which symptoms he/she is experiencing—these are pre-programmed in the system.

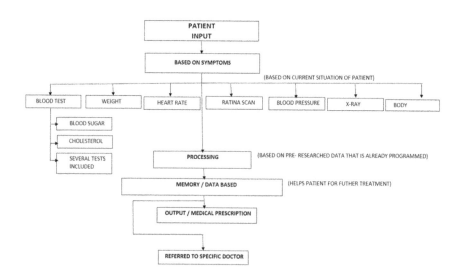

FIGURE 11.3   Block diagram shows the method of treatment for a patient.

On the basis of the selection of the symptoms, the system requires more data from the patient, including:

- Heart rate
- Retina scan
- Weight
- Blood pressure
- Cholesterol levels
- X-rays
- Electrocardiogram (ECG)
- Blood tests:
  - Random blood sugar (RBS)
  - Complete blood count (CBC)
  - Other tests based on requirement

Now these readings are taken into the system for analysis and further processing is done. Based on the results, medical prescriptions could be issued as an output of system and the final data is saved for the future.

If the treatment is beyond system understanding and treatment capabilities, the system has an emergency option to call an ambulance and to assign a specific doctor available nearby for expertise. Alternatively, if a patient is not satisfied with the treatment through SMRTS, they can request an appointment with the best recommended doctor for his/her case.

11.5   CYBERSECURITY RISK

The National Institute of Standards and Technology (NIST) itemized three contrasts between clinical IoT and customary IoT.

How healthcare IoT devices deal with the current world: NIST laid out that IoT medical care devices change actual frameworks and affect them in unexpected ways. Thus, their activities, application requirements, dependability, versatility, and security may not line up with conventional online protections for customary IoT devices.

How clinical IoT devices are overseen: Since these devices can require manual tasks, staff may not have the basic data and technology for monitoring the new risks. In addition, makers and outcasts having remote access or control can incite new risks.

Network safety and security: Network safety and security protections are important for monitoring accessibility, productivity, and adequacy. In light of the various manners by which clinical IoT devices interface with the actual world and the data they store, communicate, and measure, it is plausible that extra controls should be carried out to ensure security. However, these controls are not always accessible.

11.6   HIGH-LEVEL CYBERSECURITY RISK

Albeit like the Health Insurance Portability and Accountability Act (HIPAA) hazards, the dangers of the clinical use of IoT faces new battles.

Gadget security: Distributed denial of service (DDoS) and eavesdropping attacks can compromise device accessibility, availability, and secrecy, prompting a lack of information security.

Information security: Ensuring the confidentiality, integrity, and availability of personally identifiable information (PII) with which the devices store, communicate, gather, or interact can prompt information leaks. Compromised PII has a direct effect on a person's life.

11.6.1 Hazard Moderation Systems for Ensuring Device Security

To ensure device security, NIST proposes four danger mitigation methodologies.

1. **Asset management:** Medical services suppliers keep current, precise inventories of all IoT devices through their entire life cycle.
2. **Vulnerability management**: To secure the devices, medical services suppliers need to survey programming and firmware for known weaknesses.
3. **Access management**: To prevent unapproved or ill-advised physical and coherent admittance to, utilization of, or organization of IoT gadgets, medical care suppliers need to guarantee suitable access the board procedure.
4. **Device security episode discovery:** Clinical health providers need to continually evaluate IoT devices for potential security events.

What are the danger mitigation procedures for ensuring data security? NIST records two systems to prevent data security events:

Information security: Information very still or on the way should be shielded from exposure or bargaining the honesty of delicate data.
Data security incident detection: Medical care suppliers must constantly screen IoT device movement for potential data breaches.

11.6.2 Hazard Moderation Techniques For Securing Patient Data

NIST records five methodologies for securing patient protection.

1. **Management of information flow:** Medical services suppliers must make mappings that show PII lifecycles, consolidated information by activity type, PII components prepared, parties handling PII, and other relevant variables that compromise security.
2. **Management of PII process permission:** Consents overseeing PII handling need to prevent unpermitted preparing.
3. **Informed decision making:** Patient clients need to comprehend the potential data breaches that could occur from utilizing the devices, including how to determine if there is a problem.

4. **Disassociated data management:** With more clients and areas that store data, medical care suppliers may not have the capacity to oversee verifications.
5. **Privacy breach detection:** Medical service experts need to consistently screen device actions for indications of a data breach.

11.6.3 NETWORK PROTECTION HAZARDS IN MEDICAL CARE

Dealing with these new online protection dangers may prove overwhelming for a large number of professionals. Best practices as set out by NIST involve participating in new advances to keep up security control adequacy. Planning ahead, professionals may have to consider:

1. Maintaining various asset the board systems
2. Performing resource the board errands physically
3. Implications of dangers emerging from outer programming and administrations
4. Current danger the executives program viability
5. Permissions on devices for remote administration
6. Ability to maintain weakness the executives programs
7. Inability to administer or eliminate known shortcomings
8. Need for various weakness the board frameworks
9. Need to genuinely present security invigorates
10. Inability to utilize mechanization for constant monitoring
11. Inability to monitor customers and regulate character

While the utilization of IoT in medical care can prompt better quiet consideration results, it creates the chance that an expert will be unable to moderate. The money saving advantage examination may expect suppliers to pick between understanding actual health or patient information health.

11.7 THE FUTURE FOR HEALTHCARE SOLUTIONS

With the current progress in innovation, the eventual fate of medical care technology will give a general current and enabling experience for patients. Future registration systems will include:

- All-in-one designs that robotize the start-to-finish clinical registration measure
- Mobile registration from any device
- Data that streams with the patient—across specialists, insurance agencies, etc.
- A registration experience that is quick and intuitive, saving patients from dreary structures and long queues

Practices need to adjust to these changing patterns to give their patients the advanced insight, comfort, and protection that they need. By doing this, researchers can separate themselves when contrasted with their rivals, lower costs, increase income, and gather more precise data to additionally develop their business. Patient fulfilment is an objective that can be achieved through modernized and advanced insight and will assist training with getting the acknowledgement it merits from clients.

Uses of IoT in clinical and medical care are bountiful and include a wide scope of innovations, from modern robots to machine-learning-based information examination and prescient designs.

A portion of the supporters of clinical technology advancement from the principal long periods of isolate, for example, was the developing development of unmanned aerial vehicles (UAVs), popularity for telemedicine, versatile instruments and remote monitoring advances, and the expanding part of IoT in medical services perceived by governments and financial backers. UAV innovations in the clinical production network are now becoming ubiquitous. Robots are being utilized to convey medicines to patients for home treatment. In Rwanda, for instance, drones are even used to move donor blood.

There are many demonstrated advantages of radio-frequency identification (RFID) in the medical field. This is the reason the development of IoT medical care design occurs almost simultaneously with the developing combination of RFID advancements in this specialty. This innovation matched with other IoT solutions for medical services is now utilized in various territories, incorporating stock administration in clinical establishments consistent monitoring and in-clinic following of it.

Other cutting-edge opportunities are:

- **Telemedicine.** Clinical IoT matched with versatile applications presents a totally different model of availability and correspondence among patients and specialists.
- **RFID for patient observing.** RFID labels and markers have expansive compatibility from individuals following disinfection control.
- **Wearable devices that send information straight to doctors.** Watches, armbands, and different trackers can gather significant data about the patient condition (pulse, circulatory strain, beat, glucose, and so forth) and send it to emergency clinics or straight to specialists for investigation and treatment remedy.
- **Diagnosis and preventive medication.** Patient records, test results, treatment progress, and other information that can be gathered utilizing IoT are critical to improve symptomatic exactness and drive the advancement of preventive medication.

11.8 INNOVATION CAN BENEFIT IoT IN HEALTH CARE

Medical care is perhaps the main venture, however because of the intricacy, functionality level, and strict guidelines, developments need to make some amazing progress before they can be completely received in this space. The changes and needs in healthcare during the COVID-19 pandemic have shown the weaknesses and failures in the current system. IoT could be the innovation that will help tackle these and different issues in medical care.

11.8.1 Utilization of IoT Moves Slowly

The utilization IoT in medical services has tremendous freedoms—better and more open telemedicine, remote condition and treatment monitoring, power over drug adherence, and so on. However, IoT execution in medical care moves slowly.

What is IoT in medical care and what does it mean for business? Internationally, more than 60% of clinical associations overall now carry out or investigate IoT arrangements in medical care. In the coming years, the quantity of patients and experts in medical care utilizing IoT-associated devices for health monitoring is predicted to develop fundamentally.

11.8.2 Advantages of IoT in Health Care

The 'all-consuming' relationship of health devices and data centralization brings various benefits to the table, for instance:

- All-around creative update. Conveying clinical facility visits trivial, inactively totaling and significantly separating critical prosperity data, etc. we've adequately viewed as every one of these undeniable level tech limits in abundance enough. The IoT offers space to marvelous long stretch turns of events.
- Cost savings. Presumably, the best advantage of IoT in clinical benefits is that capable free systems will cost less to manage and 'use' as time goes on. Things are far better with respects than patient cost hold reserves due to less crisis center voyages similarly as accelerated diagnostics and treatment.
- Accessibility. Experts can see all the key data on the request and check consistent patient conditions without leaving their office.

11.9 DISADVANTAGES OF IoT IN HEALTH CARE

On the other hand, a few disadvantages join the massive use of IoT in the clinical field, including:

- Privacy can be possibly sabotaged. Systems can be hacked. Abundant thought and research ought to be fixated on data security, which requires enormous additional spending.
- Unauthorized access. Malicious intruders may access compatible systems and see some fierce objectives.
- Global clinical benefits rules. Overall prosperity associations are as of now setting guidelines that ought to be strictly followed by managerial clinical establishments utilizing IoT in their work cycle. These may restrict potential capacities fairly.

11.10   MARKET ANALYSIS

The overall value of IoT in the clinical market was regarded at $147.1 billion USD in 2018 and is required to notice a compound annual growth rate of 19.9% over the guess period. The rising use of wearable technology, hypotheses for executing progressed propels in clinical consideration associations, and the improvements of related consideration are the key components boosting industry advancement. Mechanical movements and creating geriatric people joined with the rising inescapability of persevering conditions are decidedly influencing market growth. Figure 11.4 gives the market analysis [11].

According to explore drove by an association provider association in Aruba, practically 87% of the medical care groups across the globe will accept IoT organizations by 2019. Researchers outlined about 3,100 IT scenarios, including clinical benefits and business pioneers across 20 countries. This assessment concluded that medical care groups have introduced IoT for improving patient monitoring, developing progressions, and reducing costs.

Related advancement is one of the fundamental employments of IoT in clinical care. Such devices are essentially used for patient monitoring, taking readings, seeing plans, and supporting patients if problems arise. This development is also used consistently when seeing sick patients, making tough decisions, and avoiding emergency room visits.

Abatement in holding up events at emergency rooms has moreover accelerated its gathering in clinical organization. Key associations are making inventive programming activities to address various issues in clinical benefits. For instance, to address am issue of the emergency office remain by times, GE Healthcare developed AutoBed, which helps reduce keep things under control events for half of the patients that important an inpatient bed.

Wide use of related advancements in clinical care settings for regulating operational work measures as clinical tasks is one of the biggest improvement drivers. It has engaged groups to develop a phase that guides in educating future individual time regarding the structures by giving the modified caution. Philips, collectively with Open Market, has developed a remote sensor advancement with adaptable learning called e-Alert, which monitors MRI systems and their outputs. This development won the Most Innovative IoT Solution award in 2017 at the World Communication Awards in London.

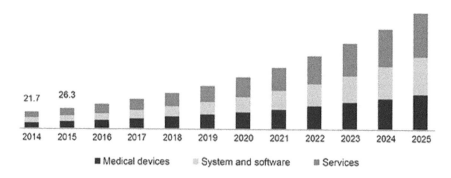

FIGURE 11.4   Market analysis [11].

11.10.1   IoT in Healthcare Market Report Scope [11]

Report Attribute	Details
Market size value in 2020	USD 219.5 billion
Revenue forecast in 2025	USD 534.3 billion
Growth Rate	CAGR of 19.9% from 2019 to 2025
Base year for estimation	2018
Historical data	2014 – 2018
Forecast period	2017 – 2025
Quantitative units	Revenue in USD million and CAGR from 2019 to 2025
Report coverage	Revenue forecast, company ranking, competitive landscape, growth factors, and trends
Segments covered	Component, connectivity technology, end-use, application, region
Regional scope	North America; Europe; Asia Pacific; Latin America; Middle East & Africa
Country scope	U.S.; Canada; Germany; U.K.; France; Russia; Italy; Spain; Netherlands; Sweden; Japan; China; India; Australia; Singapore; South Korea; Brazil; Mexico; Argentina; South Africa; Saudi Arabia; UAE
Key companies profiled	Microsoft Corp., Koninklijke Philips N.V.; Cisco Systems, Inc., IBM Corp.; Cerner Corp.
Customization scope	Free report customization (equivalent up to 8 analysts working days) with purchase. Addition or alteration to country, regional & segment scope.
Pricing and purchase options	Avail customized purchase options to meet your exact research needs

11.10.2   Architecture of Kiosk Systems

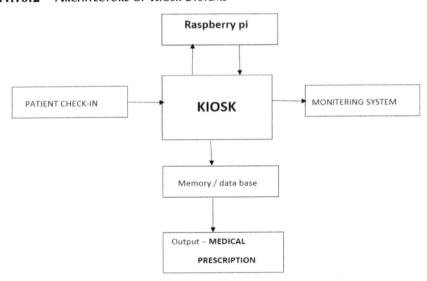

11.10.3   Challenges of Using Kiosks

Despite the benefits of using kiosks, there are challenges and concerns on the development of this technology. The security of data at the device, quality of information and services, calculation of service prices, advertising protocols, privacy, and most importantly the inability of technology to convey emotion, hope, and comfort to patients are some factors that need to be considered and appropriate solutions should be provided for them. Research studies have emphasized that if managers' attention and support decline over time, the acceptance and ultimately the effectiveness of this tool will weaken. For example, the Indian National Project (2008) provided 100 kiosks to rural areas (Sari) for their sustainable access; but, about 30 percent were disabled over time due to infrastructure problems such as the internet access and lack of financial support.

Due to cost-effectiveness constraints, on the other hand, the decision to deploy kiosks requires careful economic evaluation in all countries. Obviously, the opinions of all stakeholders, such as insurance agencies, medical equipment importers, electricity companies, telecommunications, and people need to be taken into consideration. For example, if the tariff is not consistent with the income of people, it can completely reverse the process of equality in health and lower the benefits of these services to the lucrative services level.

11.10.4   Limitations

Most studies have been conducted in the United States or European high-income countries; therefore, the generalizability of the findings to other countries is limited. Also, the diversity of integrated kiosks and their heterogeneity makes it difficult to summarize the findings. There is also limited evidence on the financial role of kiosks in health.

11.10.5   Kiosk Use During the Coronavirus Pandemic

As the COVID-19 pandemic puts immense pressure on our clinical care systems, providers are taking a closer look at telemedicine and how it can help providers better respond to the needs of those with the virus or any person who needs to converse with their doctor about their health.

As this health crisis increases, telemedicine is quickly obtaining affirmation as a fundamental device that could be used to limit the spread of COVID-19. Gains to the telehealth field include four fundamental parts.

11.10.5.1   Kiosks Used for Check-In

Self-service registration kiosks have become reasonably customary in clinical centers to grow patient security and speed up the enrollment process. These kiosks can also help keep an individual to a singular area, decreasing the threat of disease transmission among staff and patients. Transmission chances are much higher at typical clinical centers, since they often require patients to talk to front-desk staff and exchange paperwork and receipts. In centers with kiosks, patients tend to use that provided technology rather than talk with staff at the front counter.

11.10.5.2   Screening Remotely

Telehealth advances can be used to indirectly screen patients instead of having them visit a clinical center. The advancement can be used to help patients with cold or flu results and for inaccessible thought for those not requiring clinical mediation or the people who could get care at home. The goal of remote screening is to keep possibly infectious individuals out of centers and offices to cut down on the threat of transmission to other patients and clinical staff.

11.10.5.3 Routine Consideration for On-going Patients

Telehealth advances can be utilized to remotely screen patients as opposed to having them visit a clinic. The innovation can be utilized in emergency patients with cold or influenza side effects and for remote consideration for those not needing clinical intervention or for individuals who can receive care at home. The goal, again, is to keep conceivably infectious people out of clinics and facilities to bring down the danger of transmission to others.

11.10.5.4 Expand Handiness of Isolated Suppliers

Clinical benefits providers and their staff are not protected from illness. Surely, they are at extended threat for contracting COVID-19 because of their exposure to infected patients. With a telehealth setup, providers have the choice to continue seeing patients through remote monitoring. Amidst a crisis, this capacity can expand organizations when they might be required most.

11.11 ADVANTAGES OF TELEMEDICINE

Telemedicine offers an immense number of benefits, quantitative and abstract, for both the patients and clinical care providers.

11.11.1 What Patients Appreciate

- Increased admittance to medical services
- Less time away from work/family
- No travel expenses or time
- Increased security assurance
- Less threat of transmission to staff and various patients

11.11.2 Medical Services Suppliers Experience

- Improved office efficiency
- Opportunity to compete with retail health centers and online-only suppliers
- Improved patient follow-through and health outcomes
- Reduction in missed appointments and cancellations
- Elimination of the hazard of transmission from infected patients

REFERENCES

[1] A. Sagan, D. McDaid, S. Rajan, J. Farrington, and M. McKee. Screening: When is it appropriate and how can we get it right?. European Observatory on Health Systems and Policies, Copenhagen (Denmark), 2020.

[2] David DeVault, Ron Artstein, Grace Benn, Teresa Dey, Ed Fast, Alesia Gainer, Kallirroi Georgila, Jon Gratch, Arno Hartholt, Margaux Lhommet, Gale Lucas, Stacy Marsella, Fabrizio Morbini, Angela Nazarian, Stefan Scherer, GIOTa Stratou, Apar Suri, David Traum, Rachel Wood, Yuyu Xu, Albert Rizzo, and Louis-Philippe Morency. (2014). SimSensei kiosk: A virtual human interviewer for healthcare decision

support. In Proceedings of the 2014 international conference on Autonomous agents and multi-agent systems (AAMAS '14). International Foundation for Autonomous Agents and Multiagent Systems, Richland, SC, 1061–1068.

[3] R. K. Kodali, G. Swamy, and B. Lakshmi, "An implementation of IOT for healthcare," 2015 IEEE Recent Advances in Intelligent Computational Systems (RAICS), 2015, pp. 411–416. doi: 10.1109/RAICS.2015.7488451.

[4] B. Babu, K. Srikanth, T. Ramanjaneyulu, and I. Narayana. (2016). IOT for Healthcare.

[5] Anjali S. Yeole, and D. R. Kalbande. (2016). Use of Internet of Things (IOT) in health-care: A survey. In Proceedings of the ACM Symposium on Women in Research 2016 (WIR '16). Association for Computing Machinery, New York, NY, USA, 71–76. doi: https://doi.org/10.1145/2909067.2909079

[6] A. J. Jara, L. Ladid, and A. Skarmeta, "The internet of everything through IPv6: An analysis of challenges, solutions and opportunities," J. Wirel. Mob. Networks, Ubiquitous Comput. Dependable Appl., 2013.

[7] K. Venkatachalam, A. Devipriya, J. Maniraj, M. Sivaram, A. Ambikapathy, Iraj S. Amiri, "A novel method of motor imagery classification using EEG signal" Elsiever, Artif. Intell. Med. 103, 01787. https://doi.org/10.1016/j.artmed.2019.101787F

[8] Achyut Shankar, Nithya Rekha Sivakumar, M Sivaram, A Ambikapathy, Truong Khang Nguyen, and Vigneswaran Dhasarathan, "Increasing fault tolerance ability and network lifetime with clustered pollination in wireless sensor networks", J. Ambient Intell. Humaniz. Comput., Springer Berlin Heidelberg, ISSN 1868-5137, 9 July 2020. doi: 10.1007/s12652-020-02325-z

[9] https://www.ghsindex.org/

[10] https://kiosk.com/market-solutions/healthcare-kiosks/

[11] https://www.grandviewresearch.com/industry-analysis/internet-of-things-IOT-healthcare-market

12 Early Identification of Medical Image Analysis for Normal and Abnormal Fetal Heart Rate
A Predictive Optimization Design

N. Nalini, D. Dhanasekaran,
and N. Prabhakaran

CONTENTS

12.1 INTRODUCTION

With the overall improvement in the expectations for everyday comforts of individuals today, the requests of individual health care are continually rising, particularly for a patient's future health. Pregnant patients need prenatal healthcare. Radiologists comprehend the physiological information of the fetus continuously during the advancement of the baby, for example, to help and distinguish conceivable danger in prior stage to coordinate the improvement of fetal well-being, for example, fetal pulse and constriction pressure [1]. Various medical readings taken from a patient can differ in the clinic if the patient feels nervous or stressed by medical setting [2].

DOI: 10.1201/9781003166511-12

The utilization of fetal monitoring systems has allowed pregnant women to gauge significant edges and boundary, for example, circulatory strain, oxygen, and electrocardiography. The pregnant women feel more relaxed, which is helpful for continuous monitoring of the state of the foetus. Thus, pregnant women utilizing fetal monitoring systems at home will expand the nature of treatment.

The reason for this research is to utilize improvement calculations to monitor fetal pulse and acknowledge ongoing fetal well-being. The characterization of fetal heart rate (FHR) information utilizes a complex and continuous data-monitoring framework [3]. As a general rule, the time has come devouring and arduous to assess these FHR attributes, and it is hard to acquire clinical ends continuously practice. The enhancement calculation utilize fetal pulse information straightforwardly as an information and consequently separate key qualities utilizing suitable calculations to get precise order and optimization arrangement in the spaces [4]. Hence, to investigate the technique for fetal heart monitoring, an improved data-prediction calculation is examined. Fetal pulse monitoring data feature issues, such as large volumes of information extraction and feature detection, that significantly affect the outcome. The issue is the way to premeasure the crude information received from the advancement calculation, which coordinates with the data from the clinical picture investigation. The optimization models choose the ideal FHR data-grouping model by contrasting and dissecting the exhibition of various FHR information order models, and, finally, use it in clinical practice. The image recognizes via feature extraction and measurement is for accurate delineation of edges and boundary through current research by Hybrid-KELM method, PCA and FLD for MI BCI classification of EEG data in image processing analysis [5]. To model these kinds of framework, fault recognition and revitalization approaches for handling diverse faulty levels have to be considered, i.e., communication and network modes among them are used.

12.2 FUZZY C-MEANS CLUSTERING ALGORITHM FOR MONITORING FETAL HEART DISEASE

In clinical practice, fetal heart rate monitoring by electrocardiography is an excellent way to monitor fetal health during pregnancy. However, for biomedical and signal processing techniques, the study of fetal ECG is considered the difficult problem. This is due to the poor signal-to-noise ratio of the fetal ECG and the problems with QRS wave [6]. The unsupervised classification of optimization algorithms for abdominal ECG signal detection of fetal QRS wave is tested with optimization algorithm. The modified c-means clustering algorithms used to classify the signal characteristics of noise, QRS wave, hierarchical, k-means, k-medoids, fuzzy c-means, and dominant sets were the algorithms chosen for this work (Figure 12.1). To apply the clustering algorithms automatically and view FHR monitoring, a MATLAB interface was created. Real abdominal ECG signals, which validate the proposed method and demonstrate high performance, were used for this analysis [13]. A point density function weighted fuzzy c-means (WFCM) clustering algorithm is proposed for carrying fuzzy algorithm based on the uncertainty and fuzziness of remote sensing

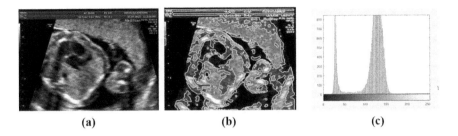

(a)   (b)   (c)

FIGURE 12.1 Normal image of fuzzy c-means clustering algorithm.

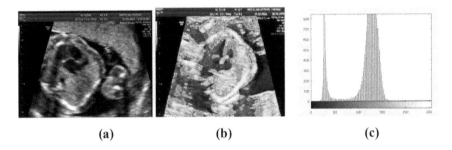

(a)   (b)   (c)

FIGURE 12.2 Abnormal fetal images of fuzzy c-means clustering algorithm.

images. The algorithm's clustering accuracy is influenced by its equal partition trend for datasets, which contributes to the optimal solution of the algorithm (Figure 12.2). The correct partition in the dataset may not be the correct one whose cluster sample numbers vary greatly [12]. In order to resolve this downside, this chapter proposes a WFCM algorithm for the dot density function. Table 12.1 shows the statistical parameters of normal fetal heart images. Table 12.2 shows the statistical parameters of abnormal fetal heart images.

TABLE 12.1
Statistical Parameters of Normal Fetal Heart Images

Parameter	Edges	Contrast	Texture	Precision	Entropy
Situs	0.3	0.72	1.1	0.21	0.12
Heart position	0.1	0.15	1.01	0.12	0.01
Cardiac size	0.02	0.25	1.02	0.14	0.11
Chamber identification	0.07	0.14	1.1	0.18	0.14
Septam appearance	0.05	0.25	1.0	0.32	0.12
Av value offset	0.12	0.32	1.0	0.11	0.15
Oval flap	*0.1*	*0.15*	*1.1*	*0.12*	*0.32*
Area behind the heart	0.32	0.1	1.2	0.10	0.11
Rate and rhythm	0.21	0.01	1.1	0.10	0.1

TABLE 12.2

Statistical Parameters of Abnormal Fetal Heart Images

Parameter	Edges	Contrast	Texture	Precision	Entropy
Situs	−0.1	1.1	1.1	1.2	0.1
Heart position	0.1	1.23	−0.7	0.78	0.1
Cardiac size	1.1	1.01	0.1	−0.1	−0.12
Chamber identification	0.7	0.12	1.2	−0.3	0.36
Septam appearance	0.7	0.14	1.1	0.2	0.1
Av value offset	0.3	1.14	0.2	1.1	0.17
Oval flap	*−0.1*	*−0.1*	*0.0*	*1.9*	*−0.8*
Area behind the heart	0.2	1.2	−0.8	−0.3	0.1
Rate and rhythm	1.2	−0.3	1.3	0.1	1.1

12.3 PARTICLE SWARM OPTIMIZATION FOR DIAGNOSING FETAL HEART DISEASES

Existing frameworks for diagnosing heart illnesses are tedious, costly, and prone to error. Focusing on instigating heart infections dependent on a particle swarm optimization support vector machine (PSO-SVM) upgraded by affiliation rules (ARs) was proposed [14]. Initially, AR was utilized to choose highlights from an illness informational index to enhance accuracy (Figure 12.3). At that point, PSO-SVM was utilized to order preparing and testing sets, and afterward, the elements prompting heart illnesses were analyzed. Finally, the adequacy and dependability of the proposed method was analyzed by investigates the UCI Cleveland informational collection with certainty as the list. The trial results showed that females have less danger of having a respiratory failure than males [7]. Independent of sex, when an individual experiences chest pains without manifestations and angina

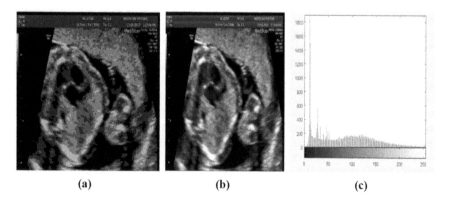

(a)   (b)   (c)

FIGURE 12.3   Normal images particle swarm optimization algorithm.

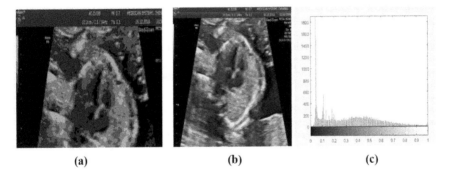

(a)   (b)   (c)

FIGURE 12.4   Abnormal image on particle swarm optimization algorithm.

brought about by working out, the individual is bound to experience the ill effects of coronary illness. The proposed calculation illustrates better grouping execution and certainty can be utilized as an amazing asset to assist specialists with diagnosing and treating heart disease. This examination proposed a location calculation for factors causing heart infections dependent on PSO-SVM and improved by ARs. Tests were then directed utilizing a dataset of heart disease, utilizing three diverse entire calculations to investigate the proposed outcomes [11]. It may be found from the well-being decide set that gender is one of the variables affecting heart health (Figure 12.4). That is, males are more prone to coronary illness, which concurs with existing clinical research. Here, the test results showed that the two males and females will likely experience the ill effects of coronary illness as indicated by variables, for example, asymptomatic chest pain and angina prompted by work out. Table 12.3 shows the statistical parameters of normal fetal heart images. Table 12.4 shows the abnormal image of the particle swarm optimization algorithm.

TABLE 12.3
Normal of particle Swarm Optimization Algorithm

Parameter	Edges	Contrast	Texture	Precision	Entropy
Situs	0.3	0.72	1.1	0.21	0.12
Heart position	0.1	0.15	1.01	0.12	0.01
Cardiac size	0.02	0.25	1.02	0.14	0.11
Chamber identification	0.07	0.14	1.1	0.18	0.14
Septam appearance	0.05	0.25	1.0	0.32	0.12
Av value offset	0.12	0.32	1.0	0.11	0.15
Oval flap	*0.1*	*0.15*	*1.1*	*0.12*	*0.32*
Area behind the heart	0.32	0.1	1.2	0.10	0.11
Rate and rhythm	0.21	0.01	1.1	0.10	0.1

TABLE 12.4
Abnormal Image of Particle Swarm Optimization Algorithm

Parameter	Edges	Contrast	Texture	Precision	Entropy
Situs	−0.1	1.1	1.1	1.2	0.1
Heart position	0.1	1.23	−0.7	0.78	0.1
Cardiac size	1.1	1.01	0.1	−0.1	−0.12
Chamber identification	0.7	0.12	1.2	−0.3	0.36
Septam appearance	0.7	0.14	1.1	0.2	0.1
Av value offset	0.3	1.14	0.2	1.1	0.17
Oval flap	*−0.1*	*−0.1*	*0.0*	*1.9*	*−0.8*
Area behind the heart	0.2	1.2	−0.8	−0.3	0.1
Rate and rhythm	1.2	−0.3	1.3	0.1	1.1

12.4 GENETIC ALGORITHM FOR EARLY DIAGNOSING OF FETAL HEART IMAGES

Hereditary calculations are propelled by the relating advancement of a populace of chromosomes under the use of hereditary administrators of get over and change (Figure 12.5). Here, a hereditary calculation for picture division is proposed on the basis that it permits us to investigate the arrangement by a methodology that isn't one-sided, as in every pixel is gathered with regard to both nearby and worldwide previously imaged segmentation for classification [8]. Quite possibly, the main advance of a genetic algorithm (GA) is the coding of information and its proficiency [15]. For our situation, data are addressed by a two-fold string. Another central issue is the decision of the capacity that relies upon the mid pixel issue to be addressed. For our situation, it is identified with the inward fluctuation of each picture fragment. As previously mentioned, the arrangement of a division issue isn't unique and it is identified with both the component space and the reason for the division. The pixel force and spatial position are utilized and distance work dependent on them characterizes the likeness between pixels (Figure 12.6) The development of the GA will be driven by the comparability that will be characterized between components of X. Table 12.5 shows the normal image of genetic algorithm. Table 12.6 shows the abnormal image of genetic algorithm.

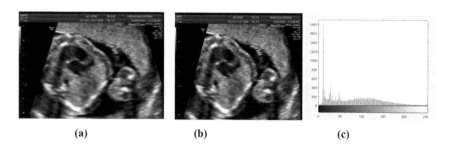

(a)   (b)   (c)

FIGURE 12.5   Normal images on genetic algorithm.

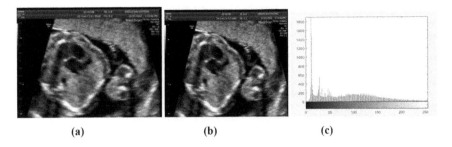

$$\text{(a)} \qquad\qquad \text{(b)} \qquad\qquad \text{(c)}$$

FIGURE 12.6 Abnormal images on genetic algorithm.

TABLE 12.5
Normal Image of Genetic Algorithm

Parameter	Edges	Contrast	Texture	Precision	Entropy
Situs	0.3	0.72	1.1	0.21	0.12
Heart position	0.1	0.15	1.01	0.12	0.01
Cardiac size	0.02	0.25	1.02	0.14	0.11
Chamber identification	0.07	0.14	1.1	0.18	0.14
Septam appearance	0.05	0.25	1.0	0.32	0.12
Av value offset	0.12	0.32	1.0	0.11	0.15
Oval flap	*0.1*	*0.15*	*1.1*	*0.12*	*0.32*
Area behind the heart	0.32	0.1	1.2	0.10	0.11
Rate and rhythm	0.21	0.01	1.1	0.10	0.1

TABLE 12.6
Abnormal Image of Genetic Algorithm

Parameter	Edges	Contrast	Texture	Precision	Entropy
Situs	0.3	0.72	1.1	0.21	0.12
Heart position	0.1	0.15	1.01	0.12	0.01
Cardiac size	0.02	0.25	1.02	0.14	0.11
Chamber identification	0.07	0.14	1.1	0.18	0.14
Septam appearance	0.05	0.25	1.0	0.32	0.12
Av value offset	0.12	0.32	1.0	0.11	0.15
Oval flap	*0.1*	*0.15*	*1.1*	*0.12*	*0.32*
Area behind the heart	0.32	0.1	1.2	0.10	0.11
Rate and rhythm	1.2	−0.3	1.3	0.1	1.1

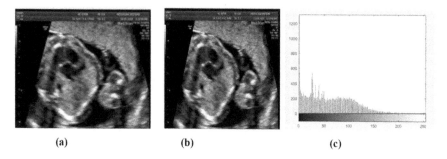

(a)   (b)   (c)

FIGURE 12.7 Normal images of firefly optimization algorithm.

12.5 FIREFLY OPTIMIZATION ALGORITHM FOR EARLIER DETECTION OF MEDICAL IMAGE ANALYSIS

Firefly calculation is another nature-motivated methodology for streamlining, which emulates the bioluminescent conduct of fireflies (Figure 12.7). In firefly calculation, there are three romanticized rules: all fireflies are unisex so one firefly is attracted to different fireflies with no regard to their sex; engaging quality corresponds to their brightness—fireflies that shine more dimly move toward the brighter ones [9]. If there is no brighter firefly to follow, it will move arbitrarily (Figure 12.8). Last, the brightness of a firefly is influenced or controlled by its surrounding pixel [10].

Table 12.7 shows the normal image of firefly optimization algorithm. Table 12.8 shows the abnormal image of firefly optimization algorithm.

12.6 CONCLUSION

Optimization algorithms work to extract enhanced image analysis of fetal heart rate for early detection and diagnosis of the medical image. The fuzzy c-means algorithm extracts about 65% of the growth in the input image within statistical parameter. The particle swarm optimization extracts the solution space with about 62%. The genetic algorithm extracts the image with 60% for future enhancement. Lastly, the firefly algorithm extracts the image with 68% of the original enhanced images. From Table 12.1–12.8 the statistical parameter defines the solution space with accurate analysis of the input image.

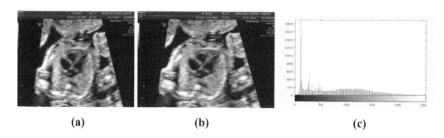

(a)   (b)   (c)

FIGURE 12.8 Abnormal images of firefly optimization algorithm.

TABLE 12.7
Normal Image of Firefly Optimization Algorithm

Parameter	Edges	Contrast	Texture	Precision	Entropy
Situs	0.1	0.70	0.003	1.02	2.1
Heart position	0.12	0.23	0.123	1.02	2.1
Cardiac size	0.12	0.56	0.021	1.01	2.2
Chamber identification	0.3	0.32	0.122	1.03	2.2
Septam appearance	1.02	0.32	0.12	1.08	2.1
Av value offset	0.07	0.56	0.114	1.02	1.98
Oval flap	*0.01*	*1.1*	*0.14*	*1.01*	*1.2*
Area behind the heart	0.32	0.12	0.12	1.02	1.2
Rate and rhythm	0.1	0.6	0.23	1.01	1.2

TABLE 12.8
Abnormal Image of Firefly Optimization Algorithm

Parameter	Edges	Contrast	Texture	Precision	Entropy
Situs	0.1	1.1	1.1	0.01	1.1
Heart position	0.1	1.2	1.02	−0.08	1.1
Cardiac size	−0.1	0.12	1.08	0.12	1.23
Chamber identification	−0.01	−0.36	1.21	0.32	1.1
Septam appearance	0.1	−0.25	0.21	0.35	1.2
Av value offset	1.1	0.25	−0.21	1.02	1.2
Oval flap	*0.2*	*0.25*	*1.21*	*0.23*	*1.1*
Area behind the heart	0.12	0.78	0.12	0.12	1.23
Rate and rhythm	0.12	0.12	1.12	1.23	1.1

REFERENCES

[1] M. A. Hasan, et al, "Detection and processing techniques of FECG signal for fetal monitoring", *Biol. Proced. Online*, vol. 11, pp. 263–295, Mar. 2009.
[2] H. D. Modanlou, and Y. Murata, "Sinusoidal heart rate pattern: Reappraisal of its definition and clinical significance", *J. Obstet. Res.*, vol. 30, pp. 169–180, Jun. 2004.
[3] M. Belfort, et al, "A randomized trial of intrapartum fetal ECG ST-segment analysis", *N. Engl. J. Med.*, vol. 373, pp. 632–641, Aug. 2015.
[4] M. Benmalek, and A. Charef, "Digital fractional order operators for R-wave detectionin electrocardiogram signal", *IET Sig. Proc.*, vol. 3, pp. 381–391, Sep. 2009.
[5] M. J. Lewis, "Review of electromagnetic source investigations of the fetal heart", *Med. Eng. Phys.*, vol. 25, pp. 801–810, Dec. 2003.
[6] L. D. Lathauwer, and P. V. Leeuwen, "Fetal electrocardiogram extraction by blind source subspace separation", *IEEE Trans. Biomed. Eng.*, vol. 47, no. 5, pp. 567–572, May 2000.

[7] H. M. Yeh, et al, "A new method to derive fetal heart rate from maternal abdominal electrocardiogram: monitoring fetal heart rate during cesarean section", *PLoS ONE*, vol. 10, no. e0117509, Feb. 2015.

[8] N. Motoki, et al, "Successful treatment of arrhythmia-induced cardiomyopathy in an infant with tuberous sclerosis complex", *BMC Pediatrics*, vol. 16, pp. 1–5, Jan. 2016.

[9] E. H. Hon, and S. T. Lee, "Noise reduction in fetal electrocardiography. II. Averaging Techniques", *Am. J. Obstet. Gynecol.*, vol. 87, pp. 1086–1096, Dec. 1963.

[10] P. V. Leeuwen, et al, "Aerobic exercise during pregnancy and presence of fetal-maternal heart rate synchronization", *PLoS ONE*, vol. 9, no. e106036, Aug. 2014.

[11] D. Hoyer, et al, "Fetal functional brain age assessed from universal developmental indices obtained from neuro-vegetative activity patterns", *PLoS ONE*, vol. 8, no. e74431, Sep. 2013.

[12] S. Abboud, et al, "Real-time abdominal fetal ECG recording using a hardware correlator", *Comput. Biol. Med.*, vol. 22, pp. 325–335, Sep. 1992.

[13] L. G. Tereshchenko, and M. E. Josephson, "Frequency content and characteristics of ventricular conduction", *J. Electrocardiol.*, vol. 48, pp. 933–937, Nov. 2016.

[14] K. Venkatachalam, A. Devipriya, J. Maniraj, M. Sivaramd, A. Ambikapathy, and Iraj S. Amiri "A novel method of motor imagery classification using EEG signal", *Elsiever, Artif. Intell. Med.*, vol. 103, pp. 01787. https://doi.org/10.1016/j.artmed.2019.101787

[15] Achyut Shankar, Nithya Rekha Sivakumar, M. Sivaram, A. Ambikapathy, Truong Khang Nguyen, and Vigneswaran Dhasarathan "Increasing fault tolerance ability and network lifetime with clustered pollination in wireless sensor networks", *J. Ambient Intell. Humaniz. Comput.*, Springer Berlin Heidelberg, ISSN 1868-5137, 9 July 2020, DOI 10.1007/s12652-020-02325-z

Index

Milton Keynes UK
Ingram Content Group UK Ltd.
UKHW031531071024
449327UK00005B/132